Intellectual Disabilities

Intellectual Disabilities

Genetics, Behaviour and Inclusion

Jean A. Rondal PhD(Psy), DLing
University of Liège, Belgium

Robert M. Hodapp PhD
Vanderbilt University, USA

Salvatore Soresi DPsy
University of Padua, Italy

Elisabeth M. Dykens PhD
Vanderbilt University, USA

Laura Nota PhD
University of Padua, Italy

W

Whurr Publishers Ltd
London and Philadelphia

© 2004 Whurr Publishers Ltd
First published 2004
by Whurr Publishers Ltd
19b Compton Terrace
London N1 2UN
England

British Library Cataloguing in Publication Data
A catalogue record for this book is available from the British Library.

ISBN 1 86156 350 7

Typeset by Adrian McLaughlin, a@microguides.net
Printed and bound in the UK by Athenæum Press Ltd, Gateshead

Contents

This book is dedicated to Dick Schiefelbusch, pioneer in the field.

Authors' affiliations

Jean A. Rondal, PhD(Psy), DLing., Professor of Psychology and Psycholinguistics, Department of Cognitive Sciences, University of Liège, Belgium.

Robert Hoddap, PhD, Professor of Psychology and Special Education, Department of Special Education, Kennedy Center, Vanderbilt University, Nashville, USA.

Salvatore Soresi, DPsy, Professor of Psychology of Disability, Department of Psychology, and Director of the Centro di Ateneo di Ricerca e Servizi sull' Handicap, Disabilità e Riabilitazione, University of Padua, Italy.

Elisabeth Dykens, PhD, Professor of Psychology and Special Education, Department of Special Education, Kennedy Center, Vanderbilt University, Nashville, USA.

Laura Nota, PhD, Assistant Professor of Inclusion Psychology, Department of Psychology, University of Padua, Italy.

Preface

Advances in biobehavioural science are bringing important changes in the field of intellectual disabilities (ID). With the success of the Human Genome Sequencing Project, new genetic causes for ID are being identified. Cytogenetic and molecular techniques for detecting ID syndromes are becoming more powerful almost every day. It is clear that, although many causes of ID still remain unspecified, increasingly accurate diagnoses of genetic ID will be made in the years and decades ahead. As a result of this 'genetic revolution' new treatments are on the horizon and in experimental use in animal models. Some time in the future, somatic gene therapy *in utero,* or soon after birth, may offer an effective means of correcting or alleviating some genetic defects (Warren, 2002). Animal experiments are already under way (Sohn, 2001). However, with all the potential inherent in the genetics revolution, one should not lose sight of possible caveats. There is plenty of evidence that inherited traits (even highly heritable ones) are often malleable and subject to environmental influences (Rutter, 2002). Genes do not directly determine behaviour – rather, they interact with environmental factors in ways that influence development over relatively long periods of time. The genetics revolution could lead to a golden age for the behavioural sciences (Warren, 2002).

This brings us one step closer to one of the central themes of this book: the existence of particular behavioural phenotypes in ID syndromes. This expression (Nyhan, 1972) concerns the distinction between the genetic make-up and the ultimate constitutional (physical traits and long-term predispositions to certain health and disease conditions) and behavioural characteristics. It follows that behavioural phenotypes are probabilistic constructs involving the heightened likelihood that people with a given genotypic make-up will end up exhibiting certain behavioural and developmental characteristics. When considering genetic syndromes, the notion of behavioural phenotype involves the likelihood that people with a given syndrome will present particular developmental sequelae relative to those without the syndrome (Dykens, 1995).

One major question regarding behavioural phenotypes is the extent to which they are specific. Dykens et al. (2000) envisage three possible answers to this question: no specificity, complete specificity, and partial specificity. As they note, the 'no specificity position' is associated with the view long held by behavioural researchers that organic disorders conducive to ID are non-specific in their effects. Dykens et al. (2000) quote Ellis, one of the leading figures in mental retardation research of previous decades, as writing 'Rarely have behavioural differences characterized different etiological groups' (Ellis 1969: 561). The reader will be in a position to evaluate the validity of Ellis's claim against the data presented in the present work. Complete specificity, on the other hand, in the sense of personality characteristics, cognitive or language profiles that would be unique (hence pathognomonic) to particular syndromes associated with ID, is exceptional. One can cite extreme self-mutilation in individuals with Lesch-Nyhan syndrome, extreme hyperphagia in individuals with Prader-Willi syndrome, and the 'cat cry' during infancy in individuals with a genetic subtype of cri-du-chat syndrome. Other behavioural characteristics do not seem to be good candidates for complete specificity in the present (obviously limited) state of knowledge. Partial specificity may be the answer, as suggested in this book. In partial specificity, several genetic disorders associated with ID may lead to particular behavioural outcomes but none of those is unique to only one disorder. In other words, given genetic conditions associated with ID may share a number of behavioural characteristics and yet differ regarding other series of traits.

The implications, both theoretical and practical, of the existence of behavioural phenotypes and their possible specificity, are most important, even if it is correct to say that the remarkable genetic advances that we have witnessed in recent years have yet to influence mental retardation research decisively. On the theoretical side, evidence of partial specificity between genetic syndromes associated with ID may indicate that some shared relationships exist between certain genes and some behavioural patterns, in a context of important variations. On the practical side, the verification of specific patterns of development and functioning within genetic syndromes relates to the strategic question of unique versus differential intervention approaches. Clearly, if, as we believe, partially specific patterns of behaviours and developmental courses can be demonstrated in individuals with various genetic ID syndromes then intervention strategies should be tailored precisely to the particular needs of the genetic groups leaving only the functional characteristics shared with other groups to common rehabilitative endeavours.

This book, then, aims, for the main part, to review and put into theoretical and applied perspectives the behavioural effects of different genetic aetiologies of ID.

The other major theme is school and social and community inclusion. At first glance, it might be thought that this rather non-specific and so far non-aetiological perspective might be at odds with the major emphasis of the book. This would be a shortsighted view of the general problem. Firstly, there is no guarantee that the aetiological perspective is necessarily relevant to the inclusion problem, either from a school perspective or a community perspective. It could be that a focus on behavioural characteristics shared by various conditions associated with ID would constitute a better strategy at these levels. Secondly, even assuming that the etiological perspective is relevant to the inclusion aspect, it would still remain to develop a reasonably sound empirical basis from which to implement this perspective in inclusion matters. Thirdly, as pointed out by Warren (2002), hybrid approaches in the field of ID – approaches that combine biological and behavioural interventions – are likely to be the most successful ones.

This book is divided into five chapters. Chapter 1, written by Hodapp and Dykens, analyses recent and current definitions and classifications of ID, as well as several of the continuing issues and controversies surrounding diagnosis. Chapter 2, again by Hodapp and Dykens, examines connections between genetic disorder and aetiology-related maladaptive behaviours and cognitive characteristics and individuals with ID (particularly people with Prader-Willi, Down, and Williams syndromes). They supply an in-depth definition of the notion of behavioural phenotype, and develop several themes for research on this topic (for example, particular strengths, weaknesses, and predispositions in specific syndromes, change in behavioural phenotypes with chronological age, within-syndrome variability and some of its sources). In Chapter 3, Rondal analyses and compares the language phenotype in 12 relatively frequent genetic syndromes of ID, demonstrating particular profiles of relative strengths and weaknesses regarding the various components of the language system. Rondal suggests that intersyndrome functional variability is related in major ways to syndromic differences in neurodevelopment and brain structures eventually affecting behavioural development and functioning. The second part of Chapter 3 is devoted to an analysis of individual language variability within syndromes. It ends with the claim that intra-syndrome variation is the primary causal factor of differences in brain development between individuals. The third part of the chapter describes and discusses language and cognition issues related to ageing in people with ID, including the possibility of earlier ageing and of a genetically based susceptibility to Alzheimer disease in Down syndrome.

Chapter 4 by Soresi and Nota highlights various themes related to the inclusion of ID children in mainstream schools. It gives a systematic analysis of relevant Italian law and the school system there, which are among the most generous in the world in their treatment of ID and benefit now from 25 years of experience. Soresi and Nota list critical points still to be addressed in order to ensure full acceptance and efficient inclusion of ID children in these schools (for example, regarding classroom interactions between typically developing (TD) and ID students, use of teachers, the role of social and health workers, and parental involvement). Lastly, Chapter 5, by Nota and Soresi, deals with social and community inclusion, participation of those with ID in community activities, empowerment, work inclusion and professional qualification, self-determination and quality of life for these people. They again discuss the relevant Italian laws and discuss actual outcomes and prospects related to the training of staff who can favour social and community inclusion.

References

Dykens E (1995) Measuring behavioral phenotypes: Provocations from the 'new genetics'. American Journal on Mental Retardation 99: 522–32.
Dykens E, Hodapp R, Finucane B (2000) Genetics and Mental Retardation Syndromes. Baltimore MD: Brookes.
Ellis N (1969) A behavioural research strategy in mental retardation: defense and critique. American Journal of Mental Deficiency 73: 566–77.
Nyhan W (1972) Behavioral phenotypes in organic genetic diseases. Presidential address to the Society for Pediatric Research, 1971. Pediatric Research 6: 1–9.
Rutter M (2002) Nature, nurture, and development. From evangelism through science toward policy and practice. Child Development 73: 1–21.
Sohn E (2001) Fragile X's missing partners identified. Science 294: 1809.
Warren S (2002) Presidential address 2002. Genes, brains, and behavior: the road ahead. Mental Retardation 40: 471–6.

Acknowledgements

This book grew out of personal encounters and exchanges between the authors within, around, and following the First National Symposium on Disability and Intervention, which took place at the University of Padua, in Northern Italy, at the end of May 2001. When planning the book and drafting the first chapters we were fortunate to attract the attention of Whurr Publishers. We are grateful to Whurr Publishers for their professionalism and the warm, human quality that characterized our relationships in the process of producing this book. We are also pleased to acknowledge the precious help of our secretaries and collaborators in the numerous tasks that are involved in the preparation of a large manuscript of this kind, covering a huge specialized literature that crosses the fields of behavioural genetics, mental retardation, language and cognitive development, and school, social, and community inclusion. Our special thanks go to Anastasia Piat-Di Nicolantonio.

There is only one science of which physics, biology,
and psychology are different aspects

J. B. S. HALDANE

Chapter 1
Intellectual disabilities: definitions and classification

Robert M Hodapp, Elisabeth M Dykens

To many people, the topic of intellectual disabilities (ID) seems clear and straightforward. Most would consider the person with ID to be slower, less intelligent and less able to negotiate the demands of everyday life. For many, ID might not even justify a book, far less an internationally based field of research or intervention.

Such sentiments – although undoubtedly widespread – neglect the many exciting findings and controversies inherent in the field of ID. Indeed, given the recent advances in studies of genetics, behaviour and interventions, intellectual disability research is booming. Over the past decade, this field has probably generated as much interest as any in psychology, psychiatry, or the social sciences in general. Thus, although many past writings have considered ID as something of a 'Cinderella' awaiting the social sciences ball (King et al., 1997; Tarjan, 1966), this time such predictions seem more likely to come true.

Why, exactly, does such interest and excitement abound? First, the field of human genetics has advanced greatly over the past two decades. As we discuss in Chapters 2 and 3, such successes have, in turn, led to important advances in understanding behaviour in different types of ID. To date, geneticists working on the human genome project have chemically 'mapped' virtually all of the 40,000 human genes (McGuffin et al., 2001). As time goes on, we will increasingly be able to know 'what most often leads to what' genetically; we are rapidly determining which environments, at specific times during development, have which effects on particular behaviours (Plomin, 1999). In short, we are on the cusp of a new frontier in understanding genetics, gene-environment interactions, and gene-brain-behaviour relations, and each of these understandings enriches our understanding of intellectual disabilities.

1

A second reason for excitement involves the advances and controversies surrounding the very definition of ID. How does one best characterize ID? How should ID best be defined? Which specific criteria differentiate individuals with ID from those without? Over the past two decades, such issues have become particularly contentious, with different professional groups, different countries, and even different states within countries subscribing to diverse definitions.

A third, and related, reason for excitement concerns the roles that persons with ID should play in society. As later sections of this book highlight, views have changed in most Western industrial societies toward persons with ID (Scheerenberger, 1983). Compared to 30 or 40 years ago, when many children with ID did not attend school and many adults resided in institutions, societal views have changed dramatically. In most Western countries, persons with ID increasingly take their place as full members of their society. They go to school and live at home as children, and, as adults, live in homes or apartments, work, marry, raise children, and fulfil all of the roles that each of us holds in our families, towns, and countries. Granted, such 'full integration' does not always work smoothly or simply but, overall, such inclusion of persons with ID into their societies must be considered a growing success.

For at least these three reasons, then, this is an exciting time in the ID field. As we hope to demonstrate in this book, despite some controversies, the field is making remarkable advances in both research and service delivery. Before describing a few such advances, however, we first describe some basic definitional and classificatory issues.

How does one define intellectual disabilities?

When asked to describe a person with intellectual disabilities, most people mention a person who has below-normal intelligence and deficient cognitive-mental processes, and that problems first appear in childhood, when development occurs at a slower rate. Furthermore, most adults clearly differentiate intellectual disabilities from mental illness, where people talk of emotional instability, anxiety, and erratic behaviour (Caruso and Hodapp, 1988).

Such informal characterizations are generally in line with more formal attempts to define intellectual disabilities, attempts that have persisted for over 150 years. Esquirol (1845) is credited as the first medical writer to have penned a definition and his seminal characterization of ID as a disorder of development instead of as a disease is maintained in all modern definitions (which require an onset during childhood or adolescence). Writing a century-and-a-half ago, Wilbur (1852; see Gardner, 1993) reasoned that intellectual disability was defined primarily by deficits in social or moral reasoning.

In line with the thinking of these and other early writers, several key features characterize most modern definitions. Granted, exact definitions vary from group to group (and even country to country), and at least three separate definitions and definition-classification manuals – the American Psychiatric Association, the American Association on Mental Retardation, and the International Classification of Disease (ICD-10 – World Health Organization, 1992) – all define intellectual disabilities slightly differently. To different extents, however, each diagnostic system focuses on the three criteria of deficits in intellectual functioning, deficits in social-adaptive functioning, and onset during the childhood years.

Deficits in intellectual functioning

In all definitions of intellectual disabilities, the first and most salient characteristic involves deficits in intellectual functioning. Both DSM-IV and ICD-10 specify an IQ of 70 or less in their diagnostic criteria for intellectual disability. In the 1992 version of the manual of the American Association on Mental Retardation, the authors defined the term 'significantly subaverage' as equivalent to 'IQ standard scores of approximately 70 or 75 and below' (p. 5). In the most recent diagnostic and statistical manual of the American Association on Mental Retardation (AAMR, 2002) this criterion has been changed to read intellectual deficits that are 'two or more standard deviations' below the mean.

As implied in these manuals, IQ scores are derived from standardized intelligence tests that meet appropriate psychometric criteria for reliability and validity. Tests that are commonly used to identify intellectual disability vary across different ages, languages, and the cognitive domains assessed. In general, diagnosticians should shy away from tests that tap a single domain (for example, receptive vocabulary) in favour of more extensive batteries that rely on performance across multiple cognitive domains.

Widely used English-language IQ tests include tests from among the Wechsler series (WISC-III; WAIS-R; WIPPSI), the Kaufman Assessment Battery for Children (K-ABC), and the Stanford-Binet-IV. All are tests that are individually administered, for children or adults within a certain age range. Recently, many such tests have provided scores for an individual's performance in verbal versus performance, sequential versus simultaneous processing, or other divisions of intellectual functioning (see Chapter 2).

Impairments in adaptive behaviour

In both formal and informal definitions, intellectual disabilities have generally been considered to be more than simply an 'intellectual problem'. That is, children and adults with intellectual disabilities are generally also deficient in their abilities to function in modern society.

Based on his pioneering work at the Vineland Training School in Vineland, New Jersey (USA), Edgar Doll (1934) was the first to develop a formal definition and measure of adaptive behaviour. Doll (1953: 10) noted that adaptive behaviour involved 'the functional ability of the human organism for exercising personal independence and social responsibility'. Two decades later, the American Association on Mental Retardation officially included deficits in adaptive behaviour in its definition of intellectual disability. Since that time, deficits in adaptive behaviour have been included formally in all definitions of intellectual disability. Definitions vary but adaptive behaviour is typically viewed as the performance of behaviours required for social and personal sufficiency. Such abilities involve communicating one's needs to others, performing daily living skills such as eating, dressing, grooming, and toileting, and being socialized to follow rules and to work and play with others.

Four aspects of the construct of adaptive behaviour seem central (Dykens et al., 1994). First, adaptive behaviour is a *developmental construct*. Thus, what is considered adaptive changes as children develop. One therefore expects much more – in terms of following rules, participating in social interactions, even eating or drinking – from a preschooler versus an infant. One expects even more from an adult.

Second, adaptive behaviour is a *social construct*. Adaptive behaviour, then, is defined by others' expectations of appropriate behaviour. But common perceptions of 'appropriate behaviour' are themselves in line with one's culture and sub-culture. Thus the adolescent living in an inner city of most Western countries faces different sets of demands from the adolescent in rural areas, or in rural areas of less industrialized societies.

Third, the performance of adaptive behaviour may *differ across various situations*. Any particular child, for example, may show appropriate adaptive behaviour in one circumstance (for example, school) but not in another (for example, home).

Fourth, adaptive behaviour is defined by *typical as opposed to optimal performance*. Thus, in most tests of adaptive behaviour, the examiner wants to know if the child routinely performs a particular behaviour, not whether that child can – under certain circumstances – do so.

In contrast to Doll's time, many instruments now exist that measure adaptive behaviour across multiple domains (such as community skills or personal grooming). A few such measures include the Vineland Adaptive Behaviour Scales (Sparrow et al., 1984), the Scales of Independent Behaviour (Bruininks et al., 1996), and the AAMR Adaptive Behaviour scales (Lambert et al., 1993). All are acceptable measures of adaptive behaviour in people with intellectual disabilities, yet the Vineland probably enjoys the most widespread use. Although most of these measures are administered as interviews with parents or other care providers, some of the newer measures are directly given to persons with intellectual disabilities. Central to all measures is the idea that adaptive behaviour is measured by typical, everyday performance as opposed to ability. If people with ID are able to perform certain behaviours, but for any reason do not routinely do so, then they necessarily have compromised adaptive functioning.

Onset during the childhood years

A third and final feature of intellectual disabilities is that it begins early in life. Thus, in order for a person to be diagnosed with ID, such diagnoses must occur early. For certain conditions (for example, some genetic disorders), diagnoses are made at or near birth. Although diagnoses for ID may occur up until age 18, adult-onset problems are not defined as intellectual disabilities. One would not, therefore, consider as ID any deficiencies caused by adult-onset degenerative diseases such as Alzheimer's disease or adult-onset head trauma.

Continuing issues and controversies concerning diagnosis

Although seemingly straightforward, the preceding diagnostic criteria hide several problems. Such problems have become fairly controversial, with different researchers, practitioners, and policymakers holding strongly to one or another position. These debates centre on the following issues.

Exact cut-off scores

As stated by the 1992 AAMR definition manual, intellectual impairments are defined by IQ scores of below 70 to 75. But most workers in the field of ID feel that a change to 'IQ standard scores of approximately 70 or 75 and below . . .' effectively changes the IQ criterion to IQs below 75. Although a five-point increase may seem small, the Gaussian (or bell-curve) nature of the IQ distribution makes this 'high-end' change in the definition of ID particularly important. MacMillan et al. (1993) noted that 'Small shifts in the upper limit have substantial consequences for the percentage of the population eligible to be diagnosed with [intellectual disability] (Reschly, 1992). *Twice as many people are eligible* when the cut-off is "IQ 75 and below" as when it is "IQ 70 and below"' (italics in original). This problem has now been addressed in the latest AAMR diagnostic-classificatory manual (AAMR, 2002) – which now talks of IQ deficits two or more standard deviations below the IQ mean of 100. Nevertheless, the issue of the exact cut-off score for the IQ criteria remains critically important in all definitions of ID.

Connections between IQ and adaptive behaviour

Although the two often occur together, deficits in IQ and in adaptive behaviour do not always go hand in hand. Proponents of adaptive behaviour argue that cognitive functioning and adaptive functioning are generally unrelated, with dramatically different theoretical underpinnings and measurement techniques. Indeed, some studies of people with mixed aetiologies for their ID find non-significant correlations between cognitive and adaptive functioning.

IQ and adaptive behaviour may be particularly unconnected in people with mild intellectual disabilities. Variable outcomes were seen, for example, when Ross et al. (1985) examined persons who had been diagnosed with intellectual disabilities during childhood 40 years earlier. Even though all subjects were at identical intellectual levels (with IQs between 55 and 69), 64 per cent of persons with mild ID functioned independently, whereas 24 per cent and 12 per cent were either partially or totally dependent on others. Edgerton (1967), who examined 48 residents of a large institution following their discharge and integration into the community, also observed that the IQ of any given individual said little about what to expect in the outside world.

In contrast, other studies find strong correlations between cognitive and adaptive behaviour, especially in people with moderate to profound intellectual disabilities. Significant correlations between IQ and adaptive behaviour are seen in studies of people with moderate ID of mixed aetiologies, as well as in studies of people with distinctive syndromes such as fragile-X syndrome, Down syndrome, Prader-Willi syndrome and 5p- (or cri-du-chat) syndrome (for a review, see Dykens, Hodapp and Finucane, 2000).

Definitions of intellectual and cognitive behaviour

Although the definition of IQ has long been debated, most of the current controversy in the ID field has focused on conflicting definitions of adaptive behaviour. In trying to give more weight to adaptive behaviour in its 1992 definition-classification manual, the AAMR decided to specify further the criteria of impairments in adaptive behaviour. The AAMR (1992: 1), as well as DSM-IV, thus defined intellectual disabilities as 'characterized by significantly subaverage intellectual functioning, existing concurrently with related limitations in two or more of the following applicable adaptive skill areas: communication, self-care, home living, social skills, community use, self-direction, health and safety, functional academics, leisure, and work.'

This definition thus proposes 10 areas of adaptive behaviour, including such rarely tested areas as leisure, health and safety, community use, and self-direction. But factor analytic studies of adaptive behaviour have consistently revealed from two to seven factors, with a single primary factor accounting for most of the variance (Harrison, 1987; McGrew and Bruininks, 1989). It thus seems inappropriate to test 10 areas when there is little empirical support to suggest that the construct has 10 separate domains.

A further problem is the absence of formal, psychometrically sound measures for several of these domains. For such areas as leisure, health and safety, and use of community resources, for example, it is unclear exactly how (or with which instrument) these domains are to be measured. The 1992 AAMR definition allows for clinical judgement to be used in these cases. In fairness, all other diagnostic manuals allow the use of clinical judgement in the evaluation of adaptive deficiencies, but problems associated with clinical judgement would seem exacerbated when there are so many domains, many of which are not well operationalized. Matters are complicated by the findings that many of these domains are not independent and that many are new to clinicians and other social service personnel. Still, whether one conceptualizes adaptive behaviour as having only a few or many separate domains, adaptive behaviour remains an important diagnostic criterion in all modern definitions of ID.

Testing considerations

A final set of issues revolves around testing itself. Bluntly stated, administering IQ tests to people with intellectual disabilities is quite challenging, both in terms of the testing situation itself and in the choice of an appropriate IQ test. Certain personality characteristics may also interfere with testing. Many people with intellectual disabilities, for example, look to others for solutions to difficult problems, and are quick to acquiesce, or become easily discouraged by failure (Zigler and Bennett-Gates, 1999). Certain techniques minimize these problems – for instance ensuring that the examinee succeeds with easy tasks before administering hard tasks, or providing positive incentives for effort.

Challenges also emerge with individuals who are non-verbal, and several IQ tests now exist that do not rely on expressive language (King et al., 2000). In addition, people with certain genetic syndromes (such as Williams syndrome, Down syndrome) also present unique test challenges, as many show syndrome-specific profiles of cognitive strength and weakness that are not easily described by a global IQ score (see Chapter 2). Persons with intellectual disability and co-occurring sensory or motor deficits also require adaptation to routine test procedures. Finally, examiners need to be extra cautious when testing individuals from minority groups, who may never have had the opportunities to be exposed to specific words, concepts, or experiences, or who may rarely have been exposed to a formal testing situation.

Classification within the ID population

Not all persons with ID are alike. The problem concerns how best to differentiate this diverse group. In this chapter's remaining pages, we present what have been called 'level of impairment' categories to classifying persons with ID. These categories have generally held sway with both researchers and practitioners for many years. Before proposing another way to categorize this population in Chapter 2, we first describe and critique the traditional level-of-impairment system.

Degree-of-impairment system

For close to a century, individuals with ID have been characterized by the level or degree of their intellectual impairment. Although the terms for such levels have varied over time and with different professional groups, most professionals in the ID field know and use the designation of persons with ID as having mild, moderate, severe, or profound degrees of impairment.

Mild intellectual disabilities (IQ 55 to 69)

These constitute the largest group of persons with intellectual disabilities, possibly as many as 90 per cent of the total ID population (APA, 1994). These individuals appear similar to typical, non-ID individuals, and often blend into the typical population in the years before and after formal schooling. As adults, some of these individuals hold jobs, marry, raise families and are indistinguishable from non-ID people – they may simply appear slow or need extra help in negotiating life's problems and tasks.

More persons with mild ID come from minority and low socioeconomic (SES) backgrounds than would be expected from their numbers in the general population (Hodapp, 1994; Stromme and Magnus, 2000). This so-called 'over-representation' of minority group members has been used to criticize measures of intelligence (see Reynolds and Brown, 1984), as well as to highlight the importance of both environmental-cultural (Ogbu, 1994) and genetic (Jensen, 1969) influences. Indeed, many of the most contentious issues in the ID field arise concerning this group.

Moderate intellectual disabilities (IQ 40 to 54)

This is the second most common level of impairment and it refers to those individuals who are more impaired intellectually and adaptively. More of these individuals are diagnosed as having ID during the preschool years. Many individuals with moderate ID show one or more clear organic causes for their intellectual disabilities. For example, many people with Down syndrome and with fragile-X syndrome function at moderate levels of impairment. Although some persons with moderate ID require few supportive services, most continue to require some help throughout life. In the 40-year follow-up study by Ross et al. (1985), for example, 20 per cent of persons with IQs from 40 to 49 lived independently, while 60 per cent were considered dependent and 20 per cent totally dependent on others. In a similar way, some of these individuals hold jobs in the community workforce as unskilled labourers, while others work in supervised workshop programmes.

Severe intellectual disabilities (IQ 25 to 39)

This refers to people with more severe impairments. The majority of these individuals suffer from one or more organic causes of ID. Many with severe ID show concurrent physical or ambulatory problems and others have respiratory, heart, or other co-occurring conditions. Most persons with severe ID require some special assistance throughout their lives. Many live in supervised group homes or small regional facilities, and most work in either workshop or 'pre-workshop' settings.

Profound intellectual disabilities (IQ below 25 or 20)

These are individuals with the most severe levels of intellectual and adaptive impairments. They generally learn only the rudiments of communicative skills, and intensive training is required to teach basic eating, grooming, toileting, and dressing behaviours. Persons with profound intellectual disabilities require life-long care and assistance. Almost all show organic causes for their ID, and many have severe co-occurring conditions that sometimes lead to death during childhood or early adulthood. Some persons with profound ID can perform pre-workshop tasks, and most live in supervised group homes or small, specialized facilities.

Issues and controversies

Two issues concern the degree-of-impairment classificatory system. The first revolves around the connections between the degree to which one is impaired and one's need for supportive services. In an effort to conceptualize intellectual disability more as an interaction between the person and the environment, the 1992 AAMR definition discarded the categories of ID based on levels of impairment. According to this system, individuals should no longer be considered to have mild, moderate, severe, or profound intellectual disabilities. Instead, individuals were categorized in terms of their need for supportive services. Supportive services are specified as intermittent, limited, extensive, and pervasive; these levels of environmental support are described for each area of adaptive skills (AAMR, 1992: 31–3).

In contrast, the field itself has continued to use such degree-of-impairment classifications. In examining how subject groups were described from 1993 through 1997 in three US-based journals (the *American Journal on Mental Retardation*; *Mental Retardation*; *Education and Training in Mental Retardation*), Polloway et al. (1999) found that 98.5 per cent of articles employed the level-of-impairment descriptors (mild, moderate, severe, and profound intellectual disabilities). In a similar way, most guidelines within the 50 states of the US plus the District of Columbia do not use the 1992 AAMR definition. In a nationwide survey, Denning et al. (2000) found that 44 states continued using diagnostic criteria of below-70 IQ and the mild-moderate-severe-profound degrees of impairment (four reported use of the 1992 AAMR manual as the basis of their regulations, and three remaining states used neither model). In short, degree of impairment continues to be used in research, practice, and policy.

A second issue concerns whether the degree-of-impairment system is the only, or the best, way to differentiate persons with ID. Although we discuss this issue in Chapter 2, we here note that, when one differentiates by degree of impairment, one groups together individuals with widely differing causes for their intellectual disability.

Conclusion

As seen in this chapter, the issues surrounding intellectual disabilities are neither simple nor straightforward. Granted, professionals in most Western countries have adopted the three-factor definition of impaired intellectual functioning, impaired adaptive behaviour, and onset during the childhood years. Beyond this general agreement, however, disagreements persist about the first two factors (impaired intelligence and adaptive behaviour). Similarly, professionals disagree about whether mild, moderate, severe and profound intellectual disabilities should be used to differentiate or classify persons with intellectual disabilities. With these issues and controversies as background, we now tackle the issue of aetiology, and the ways in which different genetic aetiologies of ID may predispose individuals to have different behavioural outcomes.

References

American Association on Mental Retardation (1992) Mental Retardation: Definition, Classification, and Systems of Supports (9th edn). Washington DC: AAMR.

American Association on Mental Retardation (2002) Mental Retardation: Definition, Classification, and Systems of Supports (10th edn). Washington DC: AAMR.

American Psychiatric Association (1994) Diagnostic and Statistical Manual (4th edn). Washington DC: APA.

Bruininks R, Woodcock R, Weatherman R, Hill B (1996) Scales of Independent Behaviour – Revised. Park Allen TX: DLM Teaching Resources.

Caruso DR, Hodapp RM (1988) Perceptions of mental retardation and mental illness. American Journal on Mental Retardation 93: 118–24.

Denning CB, Chamberlain JA, Polloway EA (2000) An evaluation of state guidelines for mental retardation: Focus on definition and classification practices. Education and Training in Mental Retardation 35: 226–32.

Doll EA (1934) Social adjustment of the mental subnormal. Journal of Educational Research 28: 36–43.

Doll EA (1953) Measurement of Social Competence: A Manual for the Vineland Social Maturity Scale. Circle Pines MN: American Guidance Scale.

Dykens EM, Hodapp RM, Leckman JF (1994) Behaviour and development in fragile X syndrome. Sage Series on Developmental Clinical Psychology and Psychiatry (No. 28). Newbury Park CA: Sage.

Dykens EM, Hodapp RM, Finucane BM (2000) Genetics and Mental Retardation Syndromes: A New Look at Behaviour and Interventions. Baltimore MD: Paul H Brookes Publishers.

Edgerton RB (1967) The Cloak of Competence: Stigma in the Lives of the Mentally Retarded. Berkeley CA: University of California Press.

Esquirol E (1845) Mental Maladies : A Treatise on Insanity. Translated from the French, with additions, by EK. Hunt. Philadelphia: Lea & Blanchard.

Gardner JF (1993) The era of optimism, 1850–1870: a preliminary reappraisal. Mental Retardation 31: 89–95.

Harrison P (1987) Research with adaptive behaviour scales. Journal of Special Education 21: 37–68.

Hodapp RM (1994) Cultural-familial mental retardation. In R Sternberg (ed.) Encyclopedia of Human Intelligence. New York: Macmillan, pp. 711–17.

Jensen AR (1969) How much can we boost IQ and scholastic achievement? Harvard Educational Review 39: 1–123.

King BH, Hodapp RM, Dykens EM (2000) Mental retardation. In HI Kaplan, BJ Sadock (eds) Comprehensive Textbook of Psychiatry (7th edn). Baltimore, MD: Williams & Wilkins, pp. 2587–613.

King BT, State MW, Shah B, Davanzo P, Dykens EM (1997) Mental retardation: A review of the past 10 years: Part I. Journal of the American Academy of Child and Adolescent Psychiatry 36: 1656–63.

Lambert N, Nihira K, Leland H (1993) AAMR Adaptive Behaviour Scales. Austin TX: Pro-Ed Press.

McGrew K, Bruininks R (1989) Factor structure of adaptive behaviour. School Psychology Review 18: 64–81.

McGuffin P, Riley B, Plomin R (2001) Toward behavioural genomics. Science 291: 1232–49.

MacMillan DL, Gresham FM, Siperstein GN (1993) Conceptual and psychometric concerns about the 1992 AAMR definition of mental retardation. American Journal on Mental Retardation 98: 325–35.

Ogbu J (1994) Culture and intelligence. In RJ Sternberg (ed.) Encyclopedia of Human Intelligence. New York: Macmillan, pp. 328–38.

Plomin R (1999) Genetics of childhood disorders: III. Genetics and intelligence. Journal of the American Academy of Child and Adolescent Psychiatry 38, 786–8.

Polloway EA, Smith JD, Chamberlain J, Denning CB, Smith TEC (1999) Levels of deficits or supports in the classification of mental retardation: Implementation practices. Education and Training in Mental Retardation 34: 200–6.

Reschly DJ (1992) Mental retardation: conceptual foundations, definitional criteria, and diagnostic operations. In SR Hynd, RE Mattison (eds) Assessment and Diagnosis of Child and Adolescent Psychiatric Disorders. Vol. II, Developmental Disorders. Hillsdale NJ: Erlbaum, pp. 23–67.

Reynolds C, Brown R (1984) Perspectives on Bias in Mental Testing. New York: Wiley.

Ross RT, Begab MJ, Dondis EH, Giampiccolo J, Meyers CE (1985) Lives of the retarded: a forty-year follow-up study. Stanford CA: Stanford University Press.

Scheerenberger RC (1983) A History of Mental Retardation. Baltimore, MD: Brookes.

Sparrow SS, Balla DA, Cicchetti DV (1984) Vineland Adaptive Behaviour Scales. Circle Pines MN: American Guidance Service.

Stromme P, Magnus P (2000) Correlations between socioeconomic status, IQ, and aetiology in mental retardation: A population-based study of Norwegian children. Social Psychiatry and Psychiatric Epidemiology 35: 12–18.

Tarjan G (1966) Cinderella and the prince: Mental retardation and community psychiatry. American Journal of Psychiatry 122: 1057–9.

World Health Organization (1992) The ICD-10 Classification of Mental and Behavioural Disorders. Geneva: WHO.

Zigler E, Bennett-Gates D (eds) (1999) Personality development in individuals with mental retardation. Cambridge: Cambridge University Press.

Chapter 2
Genetic and behavioural aspects: application to maladaptive behaviour and cognition

ROBERT M HODAPP, ELISABETH M DYKENS

Of all the recent advances within the ID field, arguably the most important concern genetics. As anyone reading the newspaper knows, modern-day geneticists are making discoveries at an incredibly rapid pace. Over the past few years, all 40,000 human genes have been chemically 'mapped', and connections are rapidly being drawn between one's genetic blueprint and ultimate behavioural outcomes. Indeed, the area of gene-brain-behaviour connections is booming, and such advances are affecting our very conceptualization of ID itself.

In this chapter, we begin examining connections between genetic disorders and behaviour. After describing how genetic disorders predispose one to particular aetiology-related behaviours, we briefly review the state of the art within behavioural research in intellectual disabilities and provide some general principles about how genes affect behaviour. We then provide two examples – of maladaptive behaviour/psychopathology and cognitive strengths and weaknesses – to illustrate aetiology-based approaches to behaviour in persons with intellectual disabilities. Then, in Chapter 3, we provide examples of aetiology-related findings in the area of language.

The genetic revolution

Today's genetic advances owe much to prior work, some as early as the mid-nineteenth century. In the 1860s, the Austrian monk Gregor Mendel demonstrated specific patterns that governed the inheritance of physical traits in garden pea plants. Although widely ignored at the time, Mendel's work was rediscovered in the early 1900s, starting a period of intense scientific and public interest in human genetics.

13

We now understand that every human cell is comprised of 23 pairs of chromosomes (one of each pair contributed from the mother, one from the father). Chromosomes are themselves composed of thousands of genes, arranged spatially up and down each chromosome, much like closely spaced knots along a rope. Each chromosome represents a continuous double chain of DNA (the rope), containing hundreds to thousands of distinct genes (the knots).

Chromosomes, and the genes they contain, are found in pairs within the body's cells: at the time of conception, one member of each chromosome pair is inherited from a person's mother, the other one from the father. Specific chromosomes can be distinguished from one another based on their size and banding (stripe) patterns. Most people have 46 chromosomes (23 pairs). The first 22 pairs are called *autosomes* and are similar in both males and females. Those in the 23rd pair are called the *sex chromosomes* because they determine a person's sex (male or female). In females, both sex chromosomes are alike and are called 'X' chromosomes; males have one 'X' and one 'Y' sex chromosome.

About 30 years ago, geneticists became able to 'see' chromosomes through a cytogenetic process called karyotyping. During the 1970s, the ability to stain chromosomes with darker and lighter coloured bands allowed geneticists to distinguish the various parts of each chromosome visually. More recently still, technologies have been developed that allow the chemical identification of individual genes (Jorde et al., 1997).

Given these new technologies, geneticists are now able to determine if a small area (or genetic region) is present or absent. Within the next decade, for anyone, geneticists will be able to determine if each of the 40,000 individual genes is present on all 23 pairs of chromosomes. Even now, when diagnosing such disorders as Williams syndrome (for example), small 'micro-deletions' can be observed using FISH (fluorescent *in situ* hybridization) and other molecular genetic techniques (Pober and Dykens, 1996). Such new molecular techniques allow for the identification of micro-deletions that could not be observed using the older cytogenetic techniques.

Geneticists have called this ability to see individual genes – in a molecular way – as 'the New Genetics'. Such advances led to an interesting moment. As geneticist David Comings (1980) noted over 20 years ago, 'we now have the ironic situation of being able to jump right to the bottom line without reading the rest of the page, that is, without needing to identify the primary gene product or the basic biochemical mechanism of the disease'. In essence, New Genetics advances allow us to identify instances of more, less, or rearranged genetic material, which in turn leads to an understanding of the 'beginnings' (the genes) and the 'endpoints' (the disorder) for a wide variety of genetic conditions.

In going from genes to endpoints, we also grow closer to specifying 'what leads to what'. Which single gene or group of genes predisposes an individual to early Alzheimer's disease, diabetes, high blood pressure, or obesity? Which gene or genes might lead to a genetic predisposition to alcoholism, or type A personality, or some other trait on the border between the biological and the behavioural (Plomin and Rende, 1991)? For our purposes, how do genes – and genetic disorders – influence the behaviours of affected individuals?

Behavioural phenotypes

As we consider the ways in which genetic disorders affect behaviour, we approach a topic that has been called 'behavioural phenotypes'. This name implies the movement from one's genetic endowment, or genotype, to some observable outcome, or phenotype. Since the outcome or phenotype here involves behaviour, aetiology-oriented behavioural researchers have coined the term 'behavioural phenotype'.

Unfortunately, there remains no single, agreed-upon definition of a behavioural phenotype. One definition, which is probably the most agreed-upon in the field, is offered by Dykens (1995: 523), who notes that behavioural phenotypes involve 'the heightened probability or likelihood that people with a given syndrome will exhibit certain behavioural or developmental sequelae relative to those without the syndrome'. This definition highlights several issues, each of which we discuss further below.

Many, but not all, individuals with a given syndrome will show the syndrome's 'characteristic' behaviours

In contrast to other definitions of behavioural phenotypes (for example, Flynt and Yule, 1994), Dykens' view of behavioural phenotypes highlights their probabilistic nature. That is, although many persons with a particular genetic intellectual disability disorder will show that disorder's 'characteristic' behaviour (or behaviours), rarely does every single person show the behaviour(s) in question. Nor will each individual show that behaviour to the same extent or to the same level of severity, or even at the same point during development. Some 'within-syndrome variability' exists within every genetic ID syndrome.

In noting that different individuals with a particular genetic disorder will not all show that disorder's 'characteristic' behaviour, we are applying to the domain of behaviour a few genetic principles that have long been applied to physical outcomes. Professionals and non-professionals alike, for example, consider epicanthal folds as the hallmark facial characteristic of persons with Down syndrome. At least during infancy, however, only 57 per cent of infants with Down syndrome show that disorder's characteristic epicanthal folds (Pueschel, 1990). In the same way, it is hardly ever the case that every individual with a particular syndrome shows that syndrome's characteristic behaviour or behaviours.

Although reasons for within-syndrome variability are undoubtedly complex, the larger issue concerns the ways in which the effects of genetic disorders are probabilistic. Thus, instead of a genetic disorder totally determining a behavioural outcome – such that all persons with that disorder show an identical, genetically caused behaviour or set of behaviours – genetic disorders are better conceptualized as predisposing the person to have one or another aetiology-related behaviour. For this reason, a particular behaviour or set of behaviours will occur more often (or more intensely) in a specific genetic disorder, but a disorder will rarely, if ever, produce a particular behaviour (or behaviours) in all affected persons.

Some aetiology-related behaviours will be unique to a single syndrome, whereas others are common to two or more syndromes

A probabilistic view of behavioural phenotypes says only that the behaviour in question occurs more commonly in a specific genetic syndrome than in groups with intellectual disability per se. The degree to which that behaviour or behaviours is found in only one syndrome, or is found in more than one syndrome, is left unclear.

Connections between genetic syndromes and specific outcomes sometimes appear to be unique and sometimes not (Hodapp, 1997). In the first, unique pattern, a genetic syndrome often results in a particular outcome that is not seen in other genetic disorders. At present, the following behaviours seem unique to one and only one syndrome:

- extreme hyperphagia (overeating) in Prader-Willi syndrome (Dykens, 1999);
- the 'cat cry' in 5p- syndrome (Gersh et al., 1995);
- extreme self-mutilation in Lesch-Nyhan syndrome (Anderson and Ernst, 1994);
- stereotypic 'hand washing' or 'hand wringing' in Rett syndrome (Van Acker, 1991); and
- body 'self-hugging' (Finucane et al., 1994) and putting objects into body orifices (Greenburg et al., 1996) in Smith-Magenis syndrome.

This list is fairly short, and probably only a few other instances exist in which a genetic disorder is unique in its behavioural effects. Flynt and Yule (1994: 667) also noted this peculiarity, nominating as unique only the self-mutilating behaviours in Lesch-Nyhan syndrome, overeating and abnormal food-seeking behaviour in Prader-Willi syndrome, and the hand wringing in Rett syndrome.

In other instances, however, aetiology-related behaviours are shared by two or more genetic disorders. To give but a few examples, a particular advantage in simultaneous (holistic, Gestalt-like) processing compared to sequential (step-by-step) processing has now been found in boys with fragile-X syndrome (Dykens et al., 1987; Kemper et al., 1988) and in children with Prader-Willi syndrome (Dykens et al., 1992). Similarly, compared to groups with intellectual disabilities in general, hyperactivity is more frequently found in children with 5p- syndrome (Dykens and Clarke, 1997) and in boys with fragile-X syndrome (Baumgardner et al., 1995). In both instances, a pattern of strengths and weaknesses or a particular type of maladaptive behaviour-psychopathology is found in a few genetic disorders to a much greater degree (or in higher percentages of individuals) than is commonly noted among others with intellectual disabilities.

As these examples also demonstrate, the situation is further complicated in that several unique and several specific behaviours often co-exist within the same syndrome. Groups with Prader-Willi syndrome are unique in that most individuals display hyperphagia, but persons with Prader-Willi syndrome join boys with fragile-X syndrome in showing simultaneous over sequential processing (which is not seen in groups with intellectual disabilities due to heterogeneous causes; Naglieri, 1985; Obrzut et al., 1987).

Finally, partially specific behavioural effects seem more in line with many areas of genetics, child psychiatry, and psychiatry. Across these different disciplines, researchers are now discussing the many pathways – both genetic and environmental – by which one comes to have a particular psychiatric disorder. Thus, many different genes, environments, and experiences may predispose an individual to become depressed or to have autism or schizophrenia. As the clinical geneticist John Opitz (1985: 9) notes, 'The causes are many, but the common developmental pathways are few'.

Aetiology-related behaviours occur across many behavioural domains

When considering behavioural phenotypes, most researchers think mainly of such salient maladaptive behaviours as hyperphagia in Prader-Willi syndrome or extreme self-mutilation in Lesch-Nyhan syndrome. With the possible exception of language in certain syndromes (for example, Williams syndrome, Down syndrome – see Chapter 3), most aetiology-based research has focused on maladaptive behaviour and psychiatric diagnoses in one or another genetic ID syndrome.

But behavioural phenotypes can be found that relate to many different domains of human functioning. Across a variety of genetic ID syndromes, aetiology-related behaviours have been noted in cognitive, linguistic, social, adaptive, and maladaptive areas. In certain cases, genetic disorders show behaviours that one would even hesitate to call a 'domain' per se. Many individuals with Smith-Magenis syndrome thus show a 'self-hugging' behaviour (Finucane et al., 1994), and recent studies show that children with Prader-Willi syndrome (particularly those having the deletion form) perform exceptionally well in putting together jigsaw puzzles (Dykens, 2002). However one defines the domains of psychological functioning, behavioural phenotypes need not be limited to maladaptive behaviour or psychopathology.

Genetic disorders also have indirect behavioural effects

Most discussions of the effects of genetic disorders concern the ways in which such disorders directly influence the behaviour of the individuals themselves. But genetic disorders might also produce 'indirect effects' that involve how others respond to aetiology-related behaviours (Hodapp, 1997). Genetic disorders thus predispose individuals with a syndrome to show specific behaviours (direct effects), which in turn bring about certain predictable reactions from others (indirect effects).

This model of indirect effects essentially applies Bell's (1968) inter-actional analyses to the domain of genetic ID disorders (Hodapp, 1999). In Bell's (1968; Bell and Harper, 1977) interactionism, mothers and children mutually affect one another. However, as Bell's theory arose partly in response to the prevailing socialization model – in which the main 'direction of effects' went from parents to children (and not vice versa) – much of the work involved looking at the ways in which children's behaviours or other characteristics (such as appearance or gender) affected parental behaviours and perceptions. This idea of children affecting their parents (and others in their environment) became more prominent following Bell's (1968) influential writings.

To take one example of how such indirect effects might work in genetic ID disorders, groups of children with Down syndrome general-ly display fewer behaviour problems compared to others with intellectual disability (Dykens and Kasari, 1997; Myers and Pueschel, 1991). At the same time, these children are considered to be sociable and upbeat in ratings and spontaneous reports from their mothers (Wishart and Johnston, 1990) and fathers (Hornby, 1995). Might not these children's relative lack of maladaptive behaviours and their more sociable, upbeat personalities positively affect others?

Although ages and comparison groups of various studies vary, moth-ers and fathers do seem positively affected by their children with Down syndrome, at least as compared to parents of children with autism, other psychiatric problems, or other types of intellectual disability (Hodapp et al., 2003). Compared to parents of other children with intellectual disabilities, these parents may even feel more reinforced by their children, particularly during the pre-teen years (Hodapp et al., 2001). Granted, Down syndrome is a fairly common and well-known syndrome, with a wide variety of active parent groups, materials, and support networks. As such, parents may find children with the syn-drome easier to parent solely due to such supports that go along with Down syndrome. Still, it seems quite likely that parental reactions are also partially influenced by these children's aetiology-related behav-iours.

Research on behavioural phenotypes: the state of the field

Before providing two examples of behavioural phenotypes, we first briefly summarize the current position of research concerning behavioural phenotypes of genetic ID disorders. Following this brief overview, we tackle two areas, using three aetiological groups to illustrate our points.

In thinking about 'where we are' in behavioural work on persons with genetic disorders of intellectual disability, one sees a tremendous amount of progress, in a fairly short space of time. At the same time, we have much, much further to go.

This mixed picture – essentially, the question of whether the glass is half full or half empty – can be shown by comparing today's state of affairs to only a decade or two ago. In the early 1990s, Hodapp and Dykens (1994) chronicled the 'two cultures' of behavioural work in ID. The metaphor of the two cultures was borrowed from CP Snow (1959/1963), a British scientist and novelist. Just as Snow had decried the lack of communication between mid-twentieth century artists and scientists, so too did it appear that the field of ID possessed two separate, rarely intersecting cultures.

In this case, the two cultures consisted of those behavioural researchers who adopted a 'degree of impairment' view toward intellectual disabilities versus those who were more aetiology-oriented. Degree-of-impairment researchers examined persons who had mild, moderate, severe, and profound intellectual disability, irrespective of how that individual came to have intellectual disabilities. As such, these workers generally knew and cared little about genetic advances, but were nevertheless among the most sophisticated workers in different types of psychology, family studies, special education, and other social science fields.

In contrast, the second group of workers – mostly including researchers from such biomedically oriented fields as genetics, paediatrics, and psychiatry – were exceptionally interested in different genetic IDs, but knew far less about behaviour. Specifically, the biomedical researchers were less sophisticated in the theory, measurement, and analyses of complex human behaviour.

At the time of the original Hodapp and Dykens (1994) article, surveys showed that approximately 80 per cent to 90 per cent of journals such as the *American Journal on Mental Retardation*, *Mental Retardation*, and the *Journal of Intellectual Disability Research* grouped their subjects by degree of impairment, not aetiology. In addition, with the exception of Down syndrome (which features a long and distinguished history of behavioural research), few genetic disorders had received much in-depth behavioural work.

In re-examining this issue over the past few years, we note that the situation has changed dramatically (Dykens and Hodapp, 2001). Granted,

the large majority of behavioural articles in the main ID journals continue to group subjects by their degree of impairment. But more and more,
researchers are beginning to look closely at several genetic ID syndromes.
For at least fragile-X, Prader-Willi, and Williams syndromes, the number
of behavioural research articles has increased dramatically. Figure 2.1
compares, from the 1980s to the 1990s, the numbers of empirical articles
on behaviour in fragile-X syndrome, Prader-Willi syndrome, and Williams
syndrome. As shown by that figure, the numbers of behavioural articles
on each of the three syndromes have increased several-fold. Even Down
syndrome, which has a 140-year history of behavioural research, shows
almost a doubling of research articles, from 607 articles during the 1980s
to 1,140 during the 1990s (Hodapp and Dykens, in press).

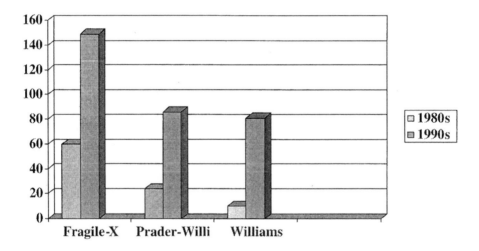

Figure 2.1 Aetiology articles, 1980s–1990s.

Shown in this way, aetiology-based behavioural research does appear to
be booming. Yet from another perspective, the situation remains less
clear. At the last count, over 750 genetic syndromes were thought to be
associated with ID (Opitz, 1996). To date, however, only 10 or so of these
groups have received much study. Thus, while we now know a fair
amount about behaviour in such syndromes as Down syndrome, Prader-
Willi syndrome, Williams syndrome, fragile-X syndrome, 5p- syndrome,
Smith-Magenis syndrome, and Rett syndrome, we know much, much less
about most other genetic ID disorders. To this day, it probably remains the
case that the majority of these 750+ syndromes have not been the subject
of even a single behavioural research article. Though the past decade has
witnessed remarkable advances in aetiology-based behavioural work, we
have a long way to go.

Behaviour in genetic ID syndromes: examples in two domains

Given this 'state of the art', we now illustrate behavioural phenotypes in two areas: maladaptive behaviour-psychopathology and intellectual profiles (we leave for the next chapter data on aetiology-related linguistic phenotypes). We also here focus on only three syndromes: Prader-Willi syndrome, Williams syndrome, and Down syndrome.

Maladaptive behaviour-psychopathology

In summarizing maladaptive behaviour-psychopathology, we first acknowledge that many persons with ID – from whatever cause – are prone to emotional-behavioural problems (Dykens and Hodapp, 2001). We also note the many problems in measuring maladaptive behaviour-psychopathology in ID groups, the many attempts to develop checklists, rating scales, interview and other measures, and the widespread disagreements among different professionals as to whether some or all psychiatric diagnoses are even relevant to the ID population (for discussions of these issues, see Dykens, 2000).

Prader-Willi syndrome

First identified in 1956, Prader-Willi syndrome affects about 1 in 15,000 births. As we detail below, the syndrome is best known for its food-related characteristics. Whereas babies invariably show hypotonia and pronounced feeding-sucking difficulties, young children between two and six years of age develop hyperphagia and food-seeking behaviour such as food foraging and hoarding (see Dykens and Cassidy, 1996 for a review). Hyperphagia is likely associated with a hypothalamic abnormality resulting in a lack of satiety (Holland et al., 1995; Swaab et al., 1995). Food preoccupations are lifelong, and without prolonged dietary management, affected individuals invariably become obese. Indeed, complications of obesity remain the leading cause of death in this syndrome.

Prader-Willi syndrome is also the first known human disease to show the effects of genomic imprinting, or the idea that genes are modified and expressed differently depending on whether they are inherited from the mother or the father. About 70 per cent of Prader-Willi syndrome cases are caused by a paternally derived deletion on the long arm of chromosome 15. Remaining cases are attributed to maternal uniparental disomy (UPD) of chromosome 15, in which both members of the chromosome 15 pair come from the mother. In either variant of Prader-Willi syndrome, there is an absence of the paternally derived contribution to this specific region of the genome. When missing information in this same region of chromosome 15 is maternally derived, it results in a completely different and more severe developmental disorder, Angelman syndrome.

Even compared to others with mental retardation, children and adults with Prader-Willi syndrome show high rates of a wide variety of behaviour problems. As shown in Table 2.1, most – but not all – individuals show temper tantrums, aggression, stubbornness, underactivity, excessive day-time sleepiness, and emotional lability (Dykens and Kasari, 1997). Coupled with food-seeking, these impulsive behaviours often lead people with Prader-Willi syndrome to need more restrictive levels of care than would be predicted by their mild levels of intellectual disability.

Table 2.1 Percentage of 100 individuals with Prader-Willi syndrome, ages 4–46 years, showing specific maladaptive behaviours (from Dykens et al., 2000)

Maladaptive behaviour	Percentage
Overeats	98
Skin picks	97
Stubborn	95
Obsessions	94
Tantrums	88
Disobedient	78
Impulsive	76
Labile	76
Excessive sleep	75
Talks too much	74
Compulsions	71
Anxious, worried	70
Prefers being alone	67
Is teased a lot	65
Peers don't like	60
Hoards	55
Steals (food, money for food)	54
Withdrawn	53
Unhappy, sad	51

Although, as shown in Table 2.1, those with Prader-Willi syndrome show high rates of many different maladaptive behaviours, during recent years several researchers have focused on obsessions and compulsions in this population. Obviously, people with Prader-Willi syndrome invariably are obsessed about food, but a remarkably high proportion of them also show non-food obsessions and compulsive behaviours. In one study, Dykens et al. (1996b) compared 43 adults with Prader-Willi syndrome with 43 individuals without ID but who had been diagnosed as having obsessive-compulsive disorder (OCD). The two groups of subjects did not differ in their mean number of compulsions, nor in the mean severity level of the compulsions that they did have. For example, whereas 33 per cent of individuals with Prader-Willi syndrome reported the need to clean excessively, the percentage was 37 per cent among the OCD subjects. For some symptoms – for example, hoarding of objects (PWS = 79 per cent;

OCD = 7 per cent) – higher percentages were shown in the Prader-Willi group; for others – for example, performing checking rituals (PWS = 16 per cent; OCD = 55 per cent) – the obsessive-compulsive disorder group was higher. But overall, the two groups were remarkably similar. In addition, just as in the OCD group, often these symptoms were associated with distress or adaptive impairment, suggesting marked risks of obsessive-compulsive disorder in this population (Dykens et al., 1996b). It now appears that obsessive-compulsive disorder is many more times likely in people with Prader-Willi syndrome than in the general population of people with intellectual disabilities.

It may also be the case that specific behavioural differences occur between Prader-Willi syndrome cases that are due to paternal deletion versus those caused by maternal UPD. Cases with deletions, for example, may show lower IQs, especially verbal IQs (Roof et al., 2000). Moreover, individuals with deletions may have more frequent and severe problem behaviours. Thus, in one study, the proportion of individuals considered by their parents to be withdrawn was 52 per cent in the group with deletions, but only 17 per cent among those with maternal disomy (Dykens et al., 1999). Similarly, deletion versus disomy cases differed in the percentages in each group who showed skin-picking (100 per cent deletion, 69 per cent disomy), overeating (96 per cent to 65 per cent); hoarding (65 per cent to 35 per cent); biting nails (61 per cent to 22 per cent), and sulking (50 per cent to 13 per cent). In every case, the percentage of persons showing the maladaptive behaviour was significantly higher in the deleted versus UPD sample. Although a dampening of symptom severity is suggested in many UPD cases, we also observe occasional cases of more severe problems in UPD, primarily autistic-like features and relatively low IQs.

Many people with Prader-Willi syndrome, then, are at increased risk for obsessive-compulsive, impulse-control, and other disorders. Yet even those who do not meet diagnostic criteria for these full-blown psychiatric disorders often show salient maladaptive behaviours that interfere with optimal adaptive functioning. Future research is needed to further clarify the ways in which psychiatric disorders or maladaptive behaviours differ across those with paternal deletions versus maternal UPD, when such problems occur, and which genetic, environmental, or family correlates relate to these problems and psychiatric conditions.

Williams syndrome

First identified in 1961, Williams syndrome is caused by a micro-deletion on one of the chromosome 7s that includes the gene for elastin, a protein that provides strength and elasticity to certain tissues such as the heart, skin, blood vessels, and lungs (Ewart et al., 1993). Affecting about one in 20,000 births, persons with Williams syndrome often show hyperacusis, hypercalcaemia, neuromusculoskeletal and renal abnormalities, and characteristic facial features described as elfin-like, cute and appealing (see

Pober and Dykens, 1996 for a review). People with Williams syndrome also typically show cardiovascular disease, especially supravalvular aortic stenosis, and these problems are probably associated with elastin insufficiency.

Williams syndrome is perhaps best known for its cognitive-linguistic profile. Many people with Williams syndrome show pronounced weaknesses in perceptual and visual-spatial functioning. Despite these difficulties, however, they often do well on facial recognition tasks. As described in Chapter 3, significant, relative strengths are often seen in expressive language, including vocabulary, syntax, semantics, and prosody (for example, Reilly et al., 1990; Udwin and Yule, 1990).

In contrast to work on cognitive-linguistic profiles, studies have yet fully to examine the personality or psychiatric features of people with Williams syndrome. Early descriptions of people with Williams syndrome hinted at a 'classic' Williams syndrome personality, described as pleasant, unusually friendly, affectionate, loquacious, engaging, and interpersonally sensitive and charming (for example, Dilts et al., 1990). Such qualities may change over the course of development, with adults being more withdrawn and less overly friendly than children (Gosch and Pankau, 1997).

Recent findings from our work on Williams syndrome expand these observations (Dykens and Rosner, 1999). Using the Reiss Personality Profiles (Reiss and Havercamp, 1998), we find that, relative to controls, adolescents and adults with Williams syndrome are more likely to initiate interactions with others (87 per cent of sample), to enjoy social activities (83 per cent), to be kind-spirited (100 per cent), caring (94 per cent), and to empathize with others' positive feelings (75 per cent) or when others are in pain (87 per cent) (Dykens and Rosner, 1999). At the same time, however, these subjects did not fare well in making or keeping friends, and were often dangerously indiscriminate in relating to others.

Indeed, although sociability in Williams syndrome has generally been viewed as a strength, these features also seem to reflect the type of social disinhibition that is characteristic of people who are anxious, impulsive, and overly aroused. Not surprisingly, salient problems in Williams syndrome include hyperactivity and inattentiveness and a proneness for ADHD, which may diminish with age (Gosch and Pankau, 1997; Pober and Dykens, 1996).

Recently, attention has begun to focus on anxieties and fears in this population. Generalized anxiety, worry, and perseverative thinking are commonly seen in Williams syndrome (see, for example, Einfeld et al., 1997), and people with the syndrome appear to show unusually high levels of fears and phobias. Relative to suitably matched controls, fears in persons with Williams syndrome are more frequent, wide-ranging, and severe, and are also associated with impaired social-adaptive adjustment. In one recent study, Dykens (2003) compared fears in 120 people with Williams syndrome (aged 6 to 48 years) to those with ID of mixed aetiologies. Only two fears – getting an injection and going to the dentist – were mentioned by over 50 per cent of the group with mixed causes of ID. In contrast, 48 different fears were mentioned by over 60 per cent of subjects with Williams syndromes. As shown in Table 2.2, such fears ran the gamut. Some involved interpersonal issues like being teased, being punished, or becoming involved in arguments with others. Others involved such physical issues as injections, being in a fire or being burned, or stung by a bee. Still others related to these children's hyperacusis or clumsiness (loud noises/sirens; falling from high places; thunderstorms). Thus, though not every person with Williams syndrome shows any or all of these fears, the vast majority do appear to be overly fearful compared to most others with intellectual disabilities.

Table 2.2 Fears mentioned by 60 per cent or more of subjects with Williams syndrome (from Dykens, 2003).

Fear	%	Fear	%
Falling from high places	92	Failure experiences	76
Fire	90	Being punished	76
Lost in a strange place	90	Shots, injections	76
Arguments between others	87	Being teased	76
Mean-looking dogs	87	Sharp objects	76
Being in a fight	87	Loud noises	76
Bee stings	84	Spiders	75
Thunderstorms	84	Earthquakes	74
Being hit by a car	84	Bombing attacks	74
Dark places	84	Roller coaster rides	74
Parents getting sick	82	Being sent to principal/boss	71
Electric shock	82	Uncertainty, ambiguity	71
Drugs	81	Snakes	71
Death, dead people	81	Ghosts, spooky things	71
Bears, wolves	81	Nuclear war	71
Nightmares	79	Poor grades, work evals	71
Being criticized	79	Going to the hospital	69
High places	79	Being alone	69
Burglar breaking in	79	Sight of blood	68
Getting a cut or injury	79	Not able to breathe	68
Strangers	79	Not fitting in with peers	66
Germs	79	Going to bed in dark	66
Guns	79	Getting sick	61
Being left behind	77	Cemeteries	60

Percentages of each fear endorsed by 46 persons with Williams syndrome. From Dykens, 2003.

Other emotional problems may also occur commonly in individuals with Williams syndrome. In addition to anxiety and fears, some young adults with Williams syndrome struggle with depression, sadness and low self-esteem (Pober and Dykens, 1996). Sociable personalities and strengths in facial recognition tasks suggest a low probability of psychiatric disorders in the Williams syndrome population involving an inability to read social and facial cues, such as autism or pervasive developmental disorder – not otherwise specified) (PDD-NOS; see Dykens and Volkmar, 1997 for a review). It is unknown how cognitive-linguistic or personality profiles might mediate the expression of other difficulties associated with Williams syndrome, including anxiety, fears, depression, inattention, and hyperactivity.

Down syndrome

As the most common chromosomal cause of intellectual disabilities, Down syndrome affects about one in 800 births, and increased risks of tri-somy 21 are seen among women with advanced maternal age. Down syndrome enjoys more behavioural research than all other ID syndromes combined (Hodapp, 1996).

Persistent personality stereotypes depict persons with Down syndrome as cheerful, friendly, eager to please and affectionate – the so-called 'Prince Charming syndrome'. Some findings, however, call this stereotype into question. Many mothers, for example, describe their children with Down syndrome as having a wide range of personality features (Rogers, 1987), and the temperaments of some children with Down syndrome are active, distractible, and difficult (Ganiban et al., 1990). Further, some studies find that children with Down syndrome are no easier to rear than children with other types of disabilities (Cahill and Glidden, 1996), although mothers generally do report that their children with the syndrome are more reinforcing and more acceptable (Hodapp et al., 2001). Similarly, fathers often spontaneously remark on their child's sociability (Hornby, 1995), and the temperaments of many children with Down syndrome have been described as easygoing (Ganiban et al., 1990). Even with these equivocal findings, the personality stereotype persists, with parents and researchers alike often remarking that children and adults with Down syndrome are extraordinarily charming and eager to please.

Yet these endearing features do not necessarily protect these same individuals from showing such behavioural problems as stubbornness, defiance, aggressive behaviour, and psychopathology. Children with Down syndrome have elevated behavioural problems relative to their siblings without developmental delay (Gath and Gumley, 1986; Pueschel et al., 1991). About 13 per cent to 15 per cent of children with Down syndrome appear to have significant behavioural difficulties, with prevalence estimates higher and more variable in studies of children and adolescents, ranging from 18 per cent to 38 per cent (Gath and Gumley, 1986; Myers and Pueschel, 1991). Primary problems include disruptive disorders such as ADHD, oppositional and conduct disorders, and occasionally, anxiety disorders.

In contrast to the 'externalizing' disorders of childhood, a particular vulnerability to depressive disorders seems to occur in adults with Down syndrome (see, for example, Collacott et al., 1992; Meyers and Pueschel, 1991). Such depression may be signalled by higher rates of internalizing symptoms in adolescents with Down syndrome; one recent study, for example, found higher levels of withdrawal and depressive symptoms among 14- to 19-year-olds as opposed to children and early teens with this disorder (Dykens et al., 2002). During adulthood, depression in Down syndrome is often characterized by passivity, apathy, withdrawal and mutism, and several cases of major depressive disorder have now been well described (for example, Dosen and Petry, 1993). Prevalence estimates of affective disorders among adults with Down syndrome range from 6 per cent to 11 per cent (Collacott et al., 1992; Myers and Pueschel, 1991), many times higher than the 1 per cent to 3 per cent rates seen in the general population of persons with intellectual disabilities (Lund, 1985).

It is not yet known why adults with Down syndrome appear vulnerable to depression. One hypothesis implicates dementia. Almost all persons with Down syndrome over age 35 to 40 show neuropathological signs of Alzheimer disease (Zigman et al., 1993). Yet not all adults with Down syndrome develop the behavioural correlates of Alzheimer-type dementia, and the risk for doing so dramatically increases with advancing age. Some researchers find rates of dementia as high as 55 per cent in persons aged 40 to 50 years, and 75 per cent in persons aged 60 years and older (Lai and Williams, 1989). Collectively, however, most studies suggest that less than 50 per cent of adults aged 50 years or more show symptoms of dementia (Zigman et al., 1993).

When considering maladaptive behaviour-psychopathology in individuals with Down syndrome, then, one must distinguish between children, adolescents, and adults. While only a relatively small number of children with Down syndrome show disruptive behaviour or other disorders, adolescents may be becoming more withdrawn, and adults definitely seem at considerable risk for depression and dementia. Aside from depression and dementia, the overall rate of psychiatric illness in the population of persons with Down syndrome is low relative to other groups of persons with mental retardation (Collacott et al., 1992; Dykens and Kasari, 1997; Grizenko et al., 1991). While sociable, charming personalities may be associated with lower rates of psychopathology, the interplay between personality and psychopathology has not yet been studied in children or adults with Down syndrome.

We see, then, that several syndromes do appear to differ in their susceptibilities to one or another type of maladaptive behaviour or psychiatric condition. We also see that such susceptibilities may vary with age. We return to issues of why and how within-syndrome variability occurs later, after we first examine cognitive profiles in these three conditions.

Cognitive profiles

Before we discuss cognitive profiles in Prader-Willi syndrome, Down syndrome, and Williams syndrome, a few issues must be considered. The first concerns the very nature of intelligence. To be blunt, various workers often vehemently disagree about what intelligence is, what the various domains of intelligence are, and whether intelligence is a single entity or instead is composed of more than one specific skill.

Such basic issues naturally extend to discussions of intellectual strengths and weaknesses within various ID syndromes. Strangely, as we show below, any single method of 'cutting the intellectual pie' into a particular set of domains that works well for one ID syndrome works less well for some others. Partly as a result, from the studies of these particular syndromes, we currently have no single answer concerning the question of what is the 'best' way to conceptualize different domains of intelligence.

A second issue relates to history within the ID field. As originally conceptualized within Zigler's 'similar structure hypothesis' (Weisz et al., 1982), people with intellectual disabilities were thought to be 'even' or 'flat' in their abilities from one domain to the next. To be fair, Zigler's (1969) similar structure hypothesis was first applied only to those with no clear organic cause for their intellectual disabilities – persons with so-called cultural-familial or sociocultural-familial ID. In recent years, however, it has become obvious that, in many genetic ID disorders, most persons with a particular syndrome show marked peaks and valleys in their intellectual functioning.

We now turn to analyses of Prader-Willi syndrome, Down syndrome, and Williams syndrome. Each shows clear strengths and weaknesses. Such striking profiles, in addition to demonstrating the ways in which different syndromes can show different profiles, also exemplify several other issues involving behavioural phenotypes.

Prader-Willi syndrome: simultaneous over sequential processing

Even as the nature of human intelligence continues to be debated, today's IQ tests have advanced greatly from earlier measures. Modern-day intelligence tests use various theories to determine a child's specific intellectual strengths and weaknesses; indeed, theory-based intelligence tests may constitute the greatest development within intelligence tests during the past two decades (Sparrow and Davis, 2000).

Prominent among these theory-based tests is the Kaufman Assessment Battery for Children, or K-ABC (Kaufman and Kaufman, 1983). Derived from Luria's (1980) neuropsychological perspective on intelligence, the K-ABC distinguishes between cognitive tasks involving simultaneous processing versus those requiring sequential processing. Simultaneous processing involves integration and synthesis of stimuli as a unified whole, and sequential processing involves consecutive, step-by-step order in problem solving (Das et al., 1975; Kaufman et al., 1984). Using this distinction, the K-ABC test is designed for children aged 2;6 to 12;6 years, but can also be used with older children with intellectual disabilities.

In several studies, K-ABC profiles of children and young adults with Prader-Willi syndrome show that these individuals have a particular weakness in sequential processing and a relative strength in simultaneous processing (Dykens et al., 1992). Thus, teens and young adults with Prader-Willi syndrome have special difficulties with sequential tasks such as imitating in order a series of hand movements and recalling a series of spoken digits. In contrast, these individuals do reasonably well on tasks requiring them to identify an entire picture from an incomplete drawing. Moreover, this relative weakness in sequential versus simultaneous processing is not shown by children with Down syndrome (Hodapp et al., 1992; Pueschel et al., 1986), nor by children with heterogeneous causes for their intellectual disabilities (Naglieri, 1985; Obrzut et al., 1987).

Such a simultaneous-over-sequential pattern is also shared with boys with fragile-X syndrome. As shown in several studies, boys with this disorder show higher performance on K-ABC subtests tapping Simultaneous Processing compared to those tapping either Sequential Processing or Achievement (Dykens et al., 1987; Kemper et al., 1988; Powell et al., 1997). In short, then, the 'Prader-Willi profile' is not unique to Prader-Willi syndrome, but seems to be shared with at least one other genetic ID disorder.

What may be unique, however, is the propensity of children with Prader-Willi syndrome to perform exceptionally well in jigsaw puzzles. This ability is primarily seen in children with only the deletion form of Prader-Willi syndrome. Although these children show relative strengths on standardized visual-spatial tasks such as Triangles (from the K-ABC) or Object Assembly (from the WISC-III), they perform exceptionally well only on jigsaw puzzles themselves. In one recent study (Dykens, 2002), children with Prader-Willi syndrome were asked to complete as much of a 40-piece jigsaw puzzle as they could in 3 minutes. Children with Prader-Willi syndrome correctly put together (on average) 28 pieces, whereas typically developing age-mates were able to put together only 10 pieces. Although the reasons for such a single extraordinary skill remain unclear, children with the deletion form of Prader-Willi syndrome – for whatever reasons – are exceptionally good at this single task.

It may also be the case that such simultaneous abilities may lead to specific strategies of intervention. Following from Kaufman et al.'s (1984) views of 'simultaneous' versus 'sequential' learners, children with Prader-Willi syndrome (as well as boys with fragile-X syndrome) are likely to have difficulty with phonics and decoding words; breaking down mathematics or science problems into their component parts; interpreting the parts or features of a design or drawing; understanding the rules of a game; following oral instructions; and remembering specific details and the sequence of a story. As extreme cases of 'simultaneous learners', children with Prader-Willi syndrome should find difficult any such task that involves dealing with information presented in a temporal or step-by-step manner.

In contrast, like those simultaneous learners without intellectual disabilities, children with Prader-Willi syndrome should show relative strengths when dealing with a different set of tasks. Presenting different interventions based upon whether a student is a simultaneous learner or a sequential learner, the K-SOS: Kaufman Sequential or Simultaneous (Kaufman et al., 1984) notes that simultaneous processing strengths may result in better sight word recognition; understanding overall maths or science principles using concrete, hands-on materials; and using diagrams, maps, or charts. Whenever the material is presented all at once, in a single, Gestalt-like manner, performance should be relatively high. By emphasizing the relative simultaneous processing strength of children with Prader-Willi syndrome, special educators may maximize student learning, thereby avoiding the frustration students may experience when presented with instruction requiring high levels of sequential processing.

Down syndrome: visual over auditory processing

A second example concerns Down syndrome. Children with Down syndrome display a different cognitive-linguistic profile – one that can also be linked to promising educational interventions. First, these children tend to have weak language skills. As detailed further in Chapter 3, these children often have difficulty with grammar, articulation, and expressive language in general. Conversely, children with Down syndrome display relative strengths in visual versus auditory short-term memory (Marcell and Armstrong, 1982; McDade and Adler, 1980). Children with Down syndrome perform much better on the visual versus the auditory subtests of the K-ABC (Hodapp et al., 1992; Pueschel et al., 1986), and this visual-over-auditory pattern is also seen on short-term memory subtests of the Stanford-Binet IV (Hodapp et al., 1999).

Like findings relating to maladaptive behaviour-psychopathology, such differences may also become more pronounced with increasing chronological age. In one recent study, Hodapp and Ricci (2002) re-examined sub-test performance on the Stanford-Binet IV (from Hodapp et al., 1999). When children of different ages were considered, it became apparent that the pattern of visual skills over auditory skills became more pronounced as children advanced in age.

Such differences across age are illustrated in Figure 2.2. In addition to average age-equivalent scores becoming increasingly discrepant, higher percentages of children with Down syndrome showed pronounced patterns of visual over auditory age-equivalent scores at each subsequent age group. Considering as 'pronounced' only those subjects showing a six-month or more visual-over-auditory discrepancy on the Bead Memory (visual) versus Memory for Sentences (auditory) subtests, 36 per cent of subjects (four of 11) showed such pronounced patterns when children were 5 to 10 years old, 60 per cent (12 of 20 subjects) when subjects were 10 to 15 years, and 75 per cent (9 of 12 subjects) when subjects were 15 to 21 years of age. Such increases in the degree to which such aetiology-related profiles occur as chronological age increases among boys with fragile-X syndrome (simultaneous over sequential processing; Hodapp et al., 1991), as well as in Williams syndrome (linguistic over visuospatial functioning; Jarrold et al., 2001). Although the exact content of intellectual profiles may vary from syndrome to syndrome, strengths in several syndromes get relatively stronger with increasing chronological age, while areas of weakness become relatively weaker over time.

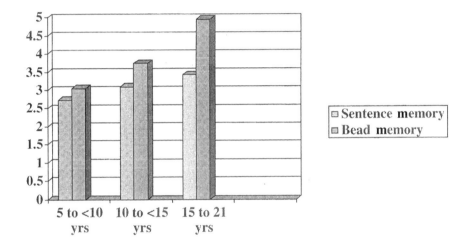

Figure 2.2 Changing profiles with age.

As with children with Prader-Willi syndrome, the profiles of cognition in Down syndrome may also lend themselves to aetiology-specific intervention techniques. Thus, rather than relying on their weaker auditory channel, children with Down syndrome might benefit most when information is presented visually. By pairing auditory input with visual cues (pictures, graphs), teachers can ensure that children with Down syndrome comprehend more content and circumvent their auditory processing and memory deficits (Laws et al., 1995).

Given both their weak expressive language skills and visual processing strengths, Sue Buckley (1995, 1999) and her colleagues have for many years promoted reading instruction for children with Down syndrome. In a study comparing 24 children with Down syndrome with a group of typical children who were average readers, Byrne et al. (1995) found that the children with Down syndrome had uneven cognitive profiles, with relatively advanced reading skills. In contrast, typically developing children scored significantly higher on all assessments except for reading, showing that children with Down syndrome can sometimes read at close to age-appropriate levels as their typical peers. Compared to non-readers with the syndrome, children with Down syndrome who were readers performed better on tests of receptive vocabulary, receptive grammar, auditory memory, and visual memory (Buckley, 1999).

During the preschool years, reading instruction may even constitute a 'way-in' to language for children with Down syndrome (Buckley, 1995). In following the progress of 15 preschool children for three years, Buckley found that the majority of children with Down syndrome could read single words by three or four years of age and sometimes earlier. This early reading instruction also had several benefits for the children's speech and language. Specifically, Buckley (1985) argued that

- the new words learned from flashcards soon emerged in the children's speech;
- two- or three-word utterances in reading helped accelerate similar utterances in speech;
- reading proper sentences led to the use of function words and correct grammar and syntax in speech;
- early reading instruction resulted in literacy attainments close to the children's chronological age; and
- reading practice improved phonology and articulation in children with Down syndrome.

Although each of these conclusions must be considered as tentative, it does appear that reading instruction constitutes a promising educational strategy for children with Down syndrome.

Williams syndrome: linguistic over visuospatial processing

In contrast to children with Down syndrome, children with Williams syndrome often show high levels of such linguistic skills as vocabulary, grammar, and storytelling (Bellugi et al., 1994). Although some early reports hinted that such skills were even at age-appropriate levels, such does not appear to be the case for most children (Mervis et al., 1999). Nevertheless, linguistic abilities remain a relative strength compared to other areas for most children with Williams syndrome (see also Chapter 3).

In contrast to their relative strengths in language, children with Williams syndrome perform particularly poorly on tasks involving visuospatial abilities (Udwin et al., 1987; Udwin and Yule, 1991). They seem unable to draw integrated figures, and such low-level performance may either involve problems in 'seeing the forest from the trees' (Bihrle et al., 1989) or extreme delays in their visuospatial abilities (Dykens et al., 2000). In either case, visuospatial tasks seem particularly difficult for these children.

Educationally, it may prove beneficial to use verbal language to teach a wide variety of tasks to these children (see Armstrong, 1994 for teaching methods for 'linguistically intelligent' children). These children should benefit from educational tasks involving telling stories and playing word and rhyming games. Tasks such as 'show and tell', group discussions, and other public, verbal tasks should also prove useful (Dykens and Hodapp, 1997). In contrast to, say, children with Down syndrome, children with Williams syndrome may respond best to phonetic approaches to reading; an emphasis on letter-sound correspondences may be easier for these children than whole-word (primarily visual) approaches (Dykens et al., 2000). Given the musical strengths and interests of many children with Williams syndrome (Lenhoff, 1998), it may also be possible to use music in many educational interventions.

In addition to having pronounced linguistic strengths and visuospatial weaknesses, children with Williams syndrome have also been described as friendly and outgoing. Dykens and Rosner (1999) report that, in their sample, parents considered all of their children with Williams syndrome as 'kind-spirited', 94 per cent were caring, and 90 per cent sought the company of others. At the same time, however, 76 per cent had few friends, 67 per cent were highly sensitive to rejection (Dykens and Rosner, 1999), and from 73 per cent to 79 per cent were considered to be unreserved or overly friendly with strangers (Gosch and Pankau, 1997; Udwin and Yule, 1990). Although such a 'hyper-social' and indiscriminately friendly orientation can be problematic (Davies et al., 1998; Udwin and Yule, 1990), teachers can capitalize on such personality traits by having children participate in cooperative learning groups, role playing, and 'acting out' academic content. Using linguistic, musical, and social interventions, many school-related tasks can be taught to the child with Williams syndrome.

Themes from research on behavioural phenotypes

In considering the booming field of behavioural phenotypes, we appreciate just how much we do – and do not – know about behaviour in these and other genetic ID syndromes. As this work progresses, however, we can also detect several overriding themes. We now turn to five such overriding themes.

Theme 1: particular strengths, weaknesses and maladaptive behaviours occurring in specific syndromes

This first theme seems obvious, but still needs to be stated. In short, even if to us it is obvious that different genetic disorders do indeed have particular behavioural sequelae, the data bring out this point compellingly. When considering maladaptive behaviour, we do see hyperphagia and obsessions and compulsions in Prader-Willi syndrome, high numbers of commonly held fears and anxieties in Williams syndrome, and – at least during adulthood – strong predispositions to both depression and dementia in Down syndrome. So too do we see compelling cognitive strengths and weaknesses in these three syndromes.

The point may not be that such clear problems and profiles exist, but rather that the ID field has been so slow to recognize them. Even in writings into the mid-1990s, one sees evidence that many fields continued to ignore such findings. In the field of special education, the authors of one of the field's main textbooks noted that, 'in general, the focus of educational programs varies according to the degree of the student's [intellectual disability]' (Hallahan and Kaufman, 1997: 138) – not etiology. Similarly, another stated that '. . . the cause of [intellectual disability] has little relevance in planning an educational program' (Blackhurst and Berdine, 1993: 425). Beyond the classroom, one found only sporadic evidence that genetic aetiology plays much of a role in special education empirical research. In the period from 1990 until 1998, only one empirical article (Powell et al., 1997) focused on genetic disorders in the *Journal of Special Education,* and there were no articles on genetic mental retardation disorders in *Exceptional Children.* Although such inattention to aetiology may be changing in special education (Fidler et al., 2002), and in other behavioural fields (Dykens and Hodapp, 2001), such changes have come about slowly. Especially given the fairly strong evidence that certain aetiologies do indeed lead to aetiology-related behaviours, we expect much more attention to aetiology across a wide variety of behavioural research fields in the years to come.

Theme 2: genetic disorders predispose affected individuals to both unique and partially specific behaviours and profiles

As shown even by the behaviours of these three syndromes, both unique and partially specific behaviours and profiles exist. Thus, we see that hyperphagia and exceptionally high abilities in jigsaw puzzles are found (to date) only in Prader-Willi syndrome – no other genetic disorder shows either such a strong propensity toward hyperphagia or toward such high levels of jigsaw puzzle skills as Prader-Willi syndrome. Similarly, at present individuals with no other genetic disorder seem as predisposed to anxiety and fears as do persons with Williams syndrome.

At the same time, however, some behaviours or profiles will be shared with others with ID in general, or with one or more ID syndromes. From our examples above, the relative strength in simultaneous processing and weakness in sequential processing seem to occur in several syndromes. So far, this simultaneous-over-sequential pattern has been shown in Prader-Willi syndrome (Dykens et al., 1992), in boys with fragile-X syndrome (Dykens et al., 1987; Kemper et al., 1988), and even in children and young adults with Smith-Magenis syndrome (Dykens et al., 1997).

Part of the issue here may simply involve the numbers of likely strengths and weaknesses given a limited number of domains. Similarly, there may only be so many ways in which one can express maladaptive behaviour-psychopathology. In short, logic alone – and the limited numbers of problems individuals can have or the numbers of strengths and weaknesses one can have across a limited set of domains – leads to the situation of many causes and few outcomes.

To us, however, the issue is more than simply one of logical limits. Instead, such examples of many roads converging on a single outcome may, at some future point, help us to understand the mechanisms at work that lead to various maladaptive behaviours, psychiatric conditions, or even cognitive, linguistic, adaptive, or other profiles. In spite of Comings' (1980) interesting situation of being able to progress directly from genetic beginning to behavioural endpoint, we increasingly want to know what's on the rest of the page of the gene-brain-behaviour story.

Theme 3: behavioural phenotypes change at different chronological ages

Increasingly, we are appreciating that behavioural phenotypes are not static. It is therefore probably incorrect to provide blanket statements such as 'persons with Prader-Willi syndrome are prone to hyperphagia' or 'persons with Williams syndrome show relative strengths in language and weaknesses in visuospatial skills'. When one examines them more closely, many of these behaviours or strengths and weaknesses are limited to children of a particular age. Thus, before the ages of two to five years, most children with Prader-Willi syndrome show failure to thrive and an inability to eat or gain weight. Similarly in Williams syndrome, the early language skills – and possibly the weaknesses in visuospatial skills – may not be as apparent during the early years.

As noted above, we have now witnessed such age-related changes in both maladaptive behaviours and in profiles. In boys with fragile X syndrome, early-occurring strengths in K-ABC simultaneous processing versus sequential processing skills become more pronounced with increasing chronological age (Hodapp et al., 1991). In Down syndrome, visual compared to auditory short-term memory advantages become more pronounced with increasing chronological age (Hodapp and Ricci, 2002). In Williams syndrome, the pattern of linguistic-over-visuospatial skills has been shown longitudinally and cross-sectionally (Jarrold et al., 2001). In each case, areas of cognitive-linguistic strength increase with age, whereas areas of weakness develop either slowly or not at all. As a result, areas of strength become relatively stronger (and areas of weakness, relatively weaker) as children grow older.

Although more such studies are needed, such research already provides a better sense of how behavioural phenotypes develop. Essentially, genes provide only the starting points in more complicated, multi-directional epigenetic pathways (Gottlieb, 2000). In the case of certain genetic disorders, the genetic anomaly seems to predispose some proportion of children with the aetiology to show early-occurring strengths and weaknesses. Such small, beginning strengths, in turn, subsequently strengthen even further as the child gets older.

But why such strengths become relatively stronger with age – and weaknesses relatively weaker – is less clear. Most likely, some combination of various factors is at work: children with a particular ID syndrome may be more likely to be stimulated in particular ways, to react favourably to such stimulation, and even to be motivated to partake of activities that use the particular skill. More frequent participation in particular activities may then lead to more practice, yielding better and better abilities.

In short, a cascade effect may be operating. Early propensities lead to greater interest; greater interest and time spent performing these activities lead to increased skills. As time goes on, then, pre-existing (slight) relative strengths thereby become more pronounced compared to other, less intrinsically interesting or less practised skills (Hodapp and Dykens, 2001).

Such cascade effects can even be seen in the everyday, leisure-time behaviours chosen by children with different ID syndromes. In one ongoing study, we asked parents of persons with Williams syndrome, Prader-Willi syndrome, and Down syndrome which activities their offspring engaged in (Rosner et al., 2003). As one might expect, children, adolescents, and even adults with Prader-Willi syndrome more often engaged in jigsaw puzzles and other visually based games, and individuals with Williams syndrome were more likely to listen to music and to play musical instruments. But, at least in Williams syndrome, individuals with this disorder also chose not to play visual games. In coding the content of various activities, a full 77 per cent and 60 per cent of subjects with Prader-Willi syndrome and Down syndrome, respectively, engaged in visual-motor activities (for example, puzzles, arts and crafts), compared to only 32 per cent of subjects with Williams syndrome. In short, persons with specific genetic disorders may have some sense of their stronger and weaker areas, after which they engage in activities for which they are already slightly better suited. Such unequal participation in strong versus weaker activities, over time, may lead to even more pronounced profiles of cognitive strengths and weaknesses.

Theme 4: within-syndrome variability comes about through a variety of sources

In addition to differences due to chronological age, there may be a wide variety of other sources within-syndrome variability in most genetic ID syndromes. We discuss two here, although many other possibilities also exist.

Genetic status

As genetic disorders are in some sense 'accidents of nature', it is not surprising that such accidents occur slightly differently in different people
with any particular ID syndrome. One need only examine various deletion
syndromes to understand how such person-to-person variability might
work. Deletion syndromes involve some small area of missing or deleted
genes along a particular chromosome. In most deletion syndromes, these
deletions vary slightly from person to person. Such variations can occur
either in the amount of missing (or deleted) genetic material (referred to
as the 'size' of the deletion) or in where, exactly, the deletion takes place
(the 'location' of the deletion).

Consider the case of 5p- syndrome. This syndrome was formerly called
'cri-du-chat' syndrome because of the characteristic, high-pitched 'cat cry'
shown by most children during the infancy years. Genetically, 5p- syndrome involves a deletion (designated by the minus sign) on the 'p-arm'
(for 'petite', or short arm) on chromosome 5 (the fifth biggest of the 22
autosomes). All individuals with 5p- syndrome, therefore, have a deletion
– of some size and at some particular location – on the short arm of chromosome 5.

As Gersh et al. (1995) demonstrated, however, only those individuals
who have deleted material at a specific part of the short arm of chromosome 5 show the syndrome's characteristic cat cry. In this case, the actual
amount of genetic material deleted (the size of the deletion) does not
seem to matter. Instead, those individuals who have deletions 'covering'
a certain specific portion of 5p (in this case, 5p15.3) show the cat cry.
There are even a few cases of persons who do not have intellectual disabilities but who do have a characteristic high-pitched cry. Further
examination shows that these people have deletions covering the 5p15.3
region, but not at 5p15.2. It seems that only deletions covering both areas
lead to the cat cry, intellectual disabilities, and the syndrome's various
facial features (for a review of 5p- syndrome, see Dykens et al., 2000:
233–40). Such differences in either size or location of a deletion, then,
may lead the individual to have slightly different behavioural outcomes.

In addition, certain ID syndromes have two variants. As noted above,
Prader-Willi syndrome can come about either because of a deletion on a
portion of the chromosome 15 inherited from the father (deletion) or
because one receives two chromosome 15s from the mother. In either
case, information is missing from the chromosome 15 inherited from the
father.

Although it was earlier thought that the deletion and maternal uniparental disomy forms of Prader-Willi syndrome predisposed affected
individuals to identical behavioural outcomes, some subtle differences
have been discovered in more recent studies. As noted above, persons
with the deletion form appear to have slightly higher IQs (possibly only
verbal IQs – Roof et al., 2000). Deletion cases – as opposed to maternal

disomy – also show more frequent or severe problem behaviours, such as skin picking, hoarding, temper tantrums, overeating, and social withdrawal (Dykens et al., 1999). In recent work, it appears that individuals with the deletion – but not with the maternal disomy – form of Prader-Willi syndrome excel at jigsaw puzzles. In short, genetic variation among affected individuals seems to be one source of inter-individual variation with many genetic intellectual disability syndromes.

Family background

A recent, relatively underexplored source of within-group variation may relate to family background. Particularly within the field of genetic psychiatry, researchers have long examined the family members of individuals who are affected with a particular psychiatric disorder. Suppose, for example, that a child is brought to a psychiatric clinic and is diagnosed with a particular psychiatric disorder (for example, depression; obsessive-compulsive disorder, or OCD; autism). Routinely, both researchers and clinicians now want to know whether the particular psychiatric disorder – often in less severe forms – 'runs in the family'. Thus, mothers, fathers, brothers, sisters – even grandparents or uncles and aunts – will be examined to see whether they have either that psychiatric disorder or even tendencies toward that disorder.

The reasons for obtaining such knowledge about immediate and extended families are fourfold. First, researchers in behaviour genetics are rapidly coming to appreciate that there is some degree of 'genetic loading' for various human traits (for example, intelligence; Plomin, 1999) and psychiatric disorders (Mathews and Freimer, 2000). Increasingly, it seems that many of these traits and disorders are genetic, but here we mean more that various genes, working together, predispose the person to have one versus another behaviour, trait, or disorder. Second (and related), researchers are now actively searching to identify these particular genes. Through analysis of cells from various family members and knowledge of which members do (and do not) have a particular problem, those specific genes can be determined that predispose any individual to a particular problem. For disorders such as obsessive-compulsive disorder, reading disabilities, depression, even autism (or autistic spectrum disorder), it now appears that many different genes – working in concert – lead one to have a particular psychiatric problem. The search for the many 'polygenes' making one more susceptible to such psychiatric problems is currently a major task of psychiatric genetics.

In recent years, the search for polygenes has extended to such traits as IQ. In a study that compared two separate groups of high-IQ children to normal IQ children, Chorney et al. (1998) identified a particular variant (allele) of a gene on chromosome 6 that differed widely between the two groups. Chorney et al. (1998) note that this particular gene accounts for only about 2 per cent of the variance in IQ (from among the 50 per cent or so of the variance associated with genes as opposed to environment).

For this reason, there may be many – even hundreds – of such genes that predispose one to high IQs. Nonetheless, as in research into psychiatric disorders, genetics – in this case, involving different variants of many different genes – will invariably become a part of many different behavioural fields in the years to come.

Why is the study of family genetic background relevant to understanding behaviour in genetic ID syndromes? Essentially, the idea is that some amount of within-syndrome variability might be due to family background. In certain families, children are already genetically predisposed (or not predisposed) to be anxious, or to have obsessions and compulsions. When an offspring then has Prader-Willi syndrome (concerning obsessions-compulsions) or Williams syndrome (concerning anxiety), one would predict that any particular person with a specific ID syndrome might show problems to greater or lesser intensities – or be protected from such problems (or show them at lesser intensities) – partly due to the family's genetic background.

Such forays into understanding one's genetic background also tell us much about one's family's environmental background. Indeed, as with many human behaviours, the perceptions, behaviours, and even family practices common in one versus another family also are more likely to lead one to – or protect one from – various types of psychopathology. So, too, for offspring with genetic ID syndromes. Family environmental background – as well as family genetic background – will both partially influence the presence of and/or intensity to which one shows particular behaviours, profiles, or problems.

In discussing the entire issue of why within-syndrome variation occurs, we preview what may be the next generation of aetiology-based research. The past 15 to 20 years have mainly featured group-difference findings – those showing that a specific disorder displays a pattern of maladaptive behaviour or cognitive-linguistic strengths and weaknesses compared to MA- or CA-matched typical children or to other persons with mental retardation. In the future, one important job will be to understand better those individuals with a particular syndrome who do not show aetiology-related behaviours. Age-related changes, genetic variants of the same disorder, and one's family genetic and environmental background all barely constitute the tip of the iceberg for what we need to know about why, exactly, different individuals with the identical ID syndrome differ behaviourally one from another.

Theme 5: aetiology-related behaviours may have implications for intervention

In addition to the importance of aetiology-related behavioural information for increasing basic scientific knowledge, data on behavioural phenotypes can be put to immediate good use in treatment and intervention. Behavioural phenotypes guide treatment priorities, providing novel adaptations to more standard clinical care.

Consider the increased risk of non-food compulsivity in people with Prader-Willi syndrome. This vulnerability suggests that many people with Prader-Willi syndrome need particular help becoming 'unstuck'. Persons with this syndrome may particularly benefit from environmental or pharmacological interventions to help their transition from one thought or activity to the next (see, for example, Dykens and Hodapp, 1997). While many people with developmental disabilities need help with transitions, such help may be particularly necessary in Prader-Willi syndrome.

In another example, the sociability and keen interests in others shown by many people with Williams syndrome may be especially well suited to group therapies, social skills training, and the use of team or buddy systems at school or work. Further, to the extent that verbal comprehension and expressivity are indeed strengths in Williams syndrome, such individuals may be able to express their thoughts and feelings accurately in individual or group therapy.

Without such support and training, the extreme, even disinhibited, sociability displayed by many individuals with Williams syndrome may lead to increased risks of impulsivity, exploitation and abuse. In one study, Davies, Udwin, and Howlin (1998) noted that 94 per cent of adults with Williams syndrome were considered socially disinhibited, with 59 per cent engaging in inappropriate touching, hugging, and kissing others. Among these adults, a full 10 per cent of their sample had reported sexual assaults to police, and an additional 10 per cent made allegations of assault that had not been reported. Although sexual abuse (as well as other types) occurs from three to four times more often in disabled versus non-disabled populations (Sullivan and Knutson, 2000), it may be that children and adults with Williams syndrome may be at particularly high risk and in need of more intensive preventative training in this area.

Finally, researchers and practitioners are increasingly becoming interested in the possibilities of aetiology-based educational interventions (Hodapp and Fidler, 1999). As noted earlier, several syndromes show aetiology-related patterns of cognitive strengths and weaknesses. Capitalizing on the idea that educational interventions might 'play to the strengths' of children with one or another aetiology, such strategies might be used to teach a wide variety of skills to (most) children with several specific etiologies. Although the ultimate value of all such aetiology-related interventions – pharmacological, psychotherapeutic, or educational – remains unknown at the present time, all seem promising for more tailored, more effective interventions.

Conclusion

As we ponder the entire field of behavioural phenotypes in genetic ID disorders, a few points become clear. First, the genetic revolution in the ID field has only just begun. That revolution's progress – while enormous –

in many respects barely represents the tip of the iceberg. Thus, we now know about a few domains of behaviour, in a few genetic ID disorders. For at least these disorders, then, we have some sense of Comings' (1980) beginnings (genetic disorder) and endings (behavioural phenotype).

But just as we lack even the most rudimentary knowledge about many of the 750+ genetic ID disorders, so too do we have almost no understanding of the 'rest of the page' for any syndrome. Even in Down syndrome, by far the most researched of all genetic ID syndromes, we do not know why linguistic, visual, auditory, or other domains progress as they do, or why certain domains show faster progress than others. Even beyond the psychological level, we know very little – or suspect that we know very little – about the exact molecular sequelae of having a third chromosome 21, of how protein production is affected by that extra 21st chromosome, or how such protein changes somehow become 'translated' into ultimate behavioural functioning.

Indeed, at this point, one can hazard only the vaguest of guesses about how any genetic ID disorder operates. As genes make proteins, proteins come together to make neurological (and other bodily) structures, and neurological structures operate to cause behaviour, we know in some general sense that we are looking at a developmental path from genes, to brain, to behaviour. Beyond this vague statement, however, we know very little.

Let's consider a few of the questions about which we know almost nothing. How, precisely, does a particular deletion (as in Prader-Willi or Williams syndrome) or trisomy (as in Down syndrome, trisomy 21) affect the production of protein? Which protein is being affected, and where does that protein 'reside' in the brain? Once in the brain, what does that protein do? Considering even more dynamic questions, how does all of this work over the child's development, and how does the environment in general – or specific environments (at specific times) – alter this developmental pathway? How do the affected child's family genetic and family environmental backgrounds relate to the presence or absence of any behavioural phenotype, and even how does the child's own choice of behaviours and activities – every day over a many-year span – affect behavioural outcomes? Such are only a few of the challenging questions that must be answered – for specific ID syndromes – in the years to come.

To reach even further we, like all researchers, would ultimately like our findings to have implications for intervention or therapy. To date, we have proceeded in our thinking about intervention more in terms of symptoms than of causes. If individuals with Prader-Willi syndrome have obsessive compulsive disorder (OCD), might not those medications be useful that are helpful for OCD patients in general? Similarly, given the various educational ideas about 'playing to the child's strengths', we borrow those educational techniques that teachers have begun to use with children who show simultaneous over sequential processing, or visual over auditory processing, or linguistic over visuospatial processing. But are such strategies always (or even usually) more effective than others that might be used with these children? We do not know.

In short, the present state of the behavioural phenotype field engenders both humility and excitement. As attested to by this almost endless list of unanswered questions, we simply need to know much more – about genes, about the proteins they make, about the location and operation of proteins in the brain, even about the effects of different environments at different times during development. We do not even really know about behaviour per se: What are, ultimately, the 'real' domains of intelligence, or of any other of the traditional domains by which we divide up complex human functioning?

Simultaneously, however, we sense that we are witnessing a new frontier, a new dawn in our understandings of many different genetic ID syndromes. As social scientists, we marvel at the new advances in such areas as 'behavioural genomics' (how genes influence behaviour – Plomin and Crabbe, 2000). We become excited by the many advances in finding genes predisposing people to various psychiatric conditions, and are in awe of just how many advances have been made, in such a short space of time, by so many professionals in such a wide variety of fields. With each passing day, we realize that, while geneticists may have chemically 'mapped' all 40,000 genes in the human genome, the most interesting, exciting, and useful work in the ID field has only just begun.

References

Anderson L, Ernst M (1994) Self-injury in Lesch-Nyan disease. Journal of Autism and Developmental Disorders 24: 67–81.

Armstrong T (1994) Multiple Intelligences in the Classroom. Alexandria, Virginia: Association for Supervision and Curriculum Development.

Baumgardner TL, Reiss AL, Freund LS, Abrams MT (1995) Specification of the neurobehavioural phenotype in males with fragile X syndrome. Pediatrics 95: 744–52.

Bell RQ (1968) A reinterpretation of direction of effects in studies of socialization. Psychological Review 75: 81–95.

Bell RQ, Harper LV (1977) Child Effects on Adults. Hillsdale NJ: Erlbaum.

Bellugi U, Wang P, Jerrigan T (1994) Williams Syndrome: An unusual neuropsychological profile. In SH Broman, J Grafman (eds) Atypical Cognitive Deficits in Developmental Disorders. Hillsdale NJ: Erlbaum, pp. 23–56.

Bihrle AM, Bellugi U, Delis D, Marks S (1989) Seeing either the forest or the trees: dissociation in visuospatial processing. Brain Cognition 11: 37–49.

Blackhurst AE, Berdine WH (1993) An Introduction to Special Education. New York: HarperCollins.

Buckley S (1985) Attaining basic educational skills: reading, writing, and number. In D Lane, B Stratford (eds) Current Approaches to Down's Syndrome. Eastbourne,England: Holt, Rinehart & Winston, pp. 315–43.

Buckley S (1995) Teaching children with Down syndrome to read and write. In L Nadel, D Rosenthal (eds) Down Syndrome: Living and Learning in the Community. New York: Wiley-Liss, pp. 158–69.

Buckley S (1999) Promoting the cognitive development of children with Down syndrome: the practical implications of recent psychological research. In JA Rondal, J Perera, L Nadel (eds) Down's syndrome: A review of current knowledge. London: Whurr, pp. 99–110.

Byrne EA, Buckley S, MacDonald J, Bird G (1995) Investigating the literacy, language, and memory skills of children with Down's syndrome. Down's Syndrome: Research and Practice 3: 53–8.

Cahill BM, Glidden LM (1996) Influence of child diagnosis on family and parent functioning: Down syndrome versus other disabilities. American Journal on Mental Retardation 101: 149–60.

Chorney MJ, Chorney K, Seese N, Owen MJ, Daniels J, McGuffin P, Thompson LA, Detterman DK, Benbow C, Lubinski D, Eley T, Plomin R (1998) A quantitative trait locus associated with cognitive ability in children. Psychological Science 9: 159–66.

Collacott RA, Cooper SA, McGrother C (1992) Differential rates of psychiatric disorders in adults with Down's syndrome compared with other mentally handicapped adults. British Journal of Psychiatry 161: 671–4.

Comings DE (1980) Presidential address. The American Society of Human Genetics 31st Annual Meeting, New York.

Das JP, Kirby J, Jarman R (1975) Simultaneous and successive synthesis: An alternative model for cognitive abilities. Psychological Bulletin 82: 87–103.

Davies M, Udwin O, Howlin P (1998) Adults with Williams syndrome. British Journal of Psychiatry 172: 273–6.

Dilts CV, Morris CA, Leonard CO (1990) Hypothesis for development of a behavioral phenotype in Williams syndrome. American Journal of Medical Genetics 6: 126–31.

Dosen A, Petry D (1993) Treatment of depression in persons with mental retardation. In RJ Fletcher, A Dosen (eds) Mental Health Aspects of Mental Retardation: Progress in Assessment and Treatment. New York NY: Lexington, pp. 242–60.

Dykens EM (1995) Measuring behavioral phenotypes: provocations from the 'new genetics'. American Journal on Mental Retardation 99: 522–32.

Dykens EM (1999) Prader-Willi syndrome. In H Tager-Flusberg (ed) Neurodevelopmental Disorders. Cambridge MA: MIT Press, pp. 137–54.

Dykens EM (2000) Psychopathology in children with intellectual disability. Journal of Child Psychology and Psychiatry 41: 407–17.

Dykens EM (2002) Are jigsaw puzzles 'spared' in persons with Prader-Willi syndrome? Journal of Child Psychology and Psychiatry, 43: 343–52.

Dykens EM (2003) Anxiety, fears, and phobias in Williams syndrome. Journal of Developmental Neuropsychology, 23: 291–316.

Dykens EM, Cassidy SB (1996) Prader-Willi syndrome: genetic, behavioral and treatment issues. Child and Adolescent Psychiatric Clinics of North America 5: 913–28.

Dykens EM, Clarke DJ (1997) Correlates of maladaptive behaviour in individuals with 5p- (cri-du-chat) syndrome. Developmental Medicine and Child Neurology 39: 752–6.

Dykens EM, Hodapp RM (1997) Treatment issues in genetic mental retardation syndromes. Professional Psychology: Research and Practice 28: 263–70.

Dykens EM, Hodapp RM (2001) Research in mental retardation: toward an etiologic approach. Journal of Child Psychology and Psychiatry 42: 49–71.

Dykens EM, Kasari C (1997) Maladaptive behavior in children with Prader-Willi syndrome, Down syndrome, and nonspecific mental retardation. American Journal on Mental Retardation 102: 228–37.

Dykens EM, Rosner BA (1999) Refining behavioural phenotypes: personality-motivation in Williams and Prader-Willi syndromes. American Journal on Mental Retardation 104: 158–69.

Dykens EM, Volkmar FR (1997) Medical conditions associated with autism. In DJ Cohen, FR Volkmar (eds) Handbook of Autism and Pervasive Developmental Disorders (2nd edn). New York: John Wiley, pp. 388–407.

Dykens EM, Hodapp RM, Leckman JF (1987) Strengths and weaknesses in intellectual functioning of males with fragile X syndrome. American Journal of Mental Deficiency 92: 234–6.

Dykens EM, Hodapp RM, Walsh KK, Nash L (1992) Profiles, correlates, and trajectories of intelligence in Prader-Willi syndrome. Journal of the American Academy of Child and Adolescent Psychiatry 31: 1125–30.

Dykens EM, Finucane BM, Gayley C (1996a) Cognitive and behavioral profiles in persons with Smith-Magenis syndrome. Journal of Autism and Developmental Disorders 27: 203–11.

Dykens EM, Leckman JF, Cassidy SB (1996b) Obsessions and compulsions in Prader-Willi syndrome. Journal of Child Psychology and Psychiatry 37: 995–1002.

Dykens EM, Finucane BM, Gayley C (1997) Brief Report: Cognitive and behavioural profiles in persons with Smith-Magenis syndrome. Journal of Autism and Developmental Disorders 27: 203–11.

Dykens EM, Cassidy SB and King BH (1999) Maladaptive behavior differences in Prader-Willi syndrome due to paternal deletion versus maternal uniparental disomy. American Journal on Mental Retardation 104: 67–77.

Dykens EM, Hodapp RM, Finucane BM (2000) Genetics and Mental Retardation Syndromes: A New Look at Behaviour and Interventions. Baltimore, MD: Paul H. Brookes Publishers.

Dykens EM, Rosner BA, Ly TM (2001) Drawings by individuals with Williams syndrome: are people different from shapes? American Journal on Mental Retardation 106: 94–107.

Dykens EM, Shah B, Sagun J, Beck T, King BY (2002) Maladaptive behaviour in children and adolescents with Down Syndrome. Journal of Intellectual Disability Research, 46: 484–92.

Einfeld SL, Tonge BJ (1992) Manual for the Developmental Behaviour Checklist: Primary carer version. Sydney: School of Psychiatry, University of New South Wales.

Einfeld SL, Tonge BJ, Florio T (1997) Behavioural and emotional disturbances in individuals with Williams syndrome. American Journal on Mental Retardation, 102: 87–103.

Ewart AK, Morris CA, Atkinson D, Jin W, Sternes K, Spallone P, Stock AD, Leppert M, Keating MT (1993) Hemizygosity at the elastin locus in a developmental disorder, Williams syndrome. Nature Genetics 5: 11–16.

Fidler DJ, Hodapp RM, Dykens EM (2002) Behavioural phenotypes and special education: parent report of educational issues for children with Down syndrome, Prader-Willi syndrome, and Williams syndrome. Journal of Special Education, 36, 80–8.

Finucane BM, Konar D, Haas-Givler B, Kurtz MD, Scott LI (1994) The spasmodic upper-body squeeze: a characteristic behaviour in Smith-Magenis syndrome. Developmental Medicine and Child Neurology 36: 78–83.

Flynt J, Yule W (1994) Behavioural phenotypes. In M Rutter, E Taylor, DL Hersov (eds) Child and Adolescent Psychiatry: Modern Approaches (3rd edn). London: Blackwell Scientific, pp. 666–87.

Fodor J (1983) Modularity of Mind: An Essay in Faculty Psychology. Cambridge MA: MIT Press.

Ganiban J, Wagner S, Cicchetti D (1990) Temperament and Down syndrome. In D Cicchetti, M Beeghly (eds) Children with Down Syndrome: A Developmental Perspective. New York: Cambridge University Press, pp. 63–100.

Gath A, Gumley D (1986) Behaviour problems in retarded children with special reference to Down's syndrome. British Journal of Psychiatry 149: 156–1.

Gersh M, Goodart SA, Pasztor LM, Harris DJ, Weiss L, Overhauser J (1995) Evidence for a distinct region causing a cat-like cry in patients with 5p- deletions. American Journal of Human Genetics 56: 1404–10.

Gosch A, Pankau R (1997) Personality characteristics and behaviour problems in individuals of different ages with Williams syndrome. Developmental Medicine and Child Neurology 39: 527–33.

Gottlieb G (2000) Environmental and behavioural influences on gene activity. Current Directions in Psychological Science 9: 93–7.

Greenberg F, Lewis RA, Potocki L, Glaze D, Parke J, Killian J, Murpha MA, Williamson D, Brown F, Dutton R, McCluggage C, Friedman S, Sulek M, Lupski JR (1996) Multidisciplinary clinical study of Smith-Magenis syndrome (deletion 17p11.2). American Journal of Medical Genetics 62: 247–54.

Grizenko N, Cvejic H, Vida S, Sayegh L (1991) Behaviour problems in the mentally retarded. Canadian Journal of Psychiatry 36: 712–17.

Hallahan DP, Kauffman JM (1997) Exceptional children: introduction to special education (7th edn). Boston MA: Allyn & Bacon.

Hodapp RM (1996) Down syndrome: developmental, psychiatric, and management issues. Child and Adolescent Psychiatric Clinics of North America 5: 881–94.

Hodapp RM (1997) Direct and indirect behavioural effects of different genetic disorders of mental retardation. American Journal on Mental Retardation 102: 67–79.

Hodapp RM (1999) Indirect effects of genetic mental retardation disorders: theoretical and methodological issues. International Review of Research in Mental Retardation 22: 27–50.

Hodapp RM, Dykens EM (1994) Mental retardation's two cultures of behavioural research. American Journal on Mental Retardation 98: 675–87.

Hodapp RM, Dykens EM (2001) Strengthening behavioural research on genetic mental retardation disorders. American Journal on Mental Retardation 106: 4–15.

Hodapp RM, Dykens EM (in press) Studying behavioural phenotypes: issues, benefits, challenges. In E Emerson, C Hatton, T Parmenter, T Thompson (eds) International Handbook of Applied Research in Intellectual Disabilities. New York: John Wiley & Sons.

Hodapp RM, Fidler DJ (1999) Special education and genetics: connections for the 21st century. Journal of Special Education 33: 130–7.

Hodapp RM, Ly TM (in press) Visual processing strengths in Down syndrome: a case for reading instruction? In S Soraci, K Murata-Soraci (eds) Perspectives on Fundamental Processes in Intellectual Functioning. Vol. 2. Visual Information Processing. Stamford CT: Ablex.

Hodapp RM, Ricci LA (2002) Behavioural phenotypes and educational practice: the unrealized connection. In G O'Brien, O Udwin (eds) Behavioural Phenotypes in Clinical Practice. London: MacKeith Press, pp. 137–51.

Hodapp RM, Dykens EM, Ort SI, Zelinsky DG, Leckman JF (1991) Changing patterns of intellectual strengths and weaknesses in males with fragile X syndrome. Journal of Autism and Developmental Disorders 21: 503–16.

Hodapp RM, Leckman JF, Dykens EM, Sparrow SS, Zelinsky D, Ort SI (1992) K-ABC profiles in children with fragile X syndrome, Down syndrome, and nonspecific mental retardation. American Journal on Mental Retardation 97: 39–46.

Hodapp RM, Dykens EM, Masino LL (1997) Families of children with Prader-Willi Syndrome: Stress-support and relations to child characteristics. Journal of Autism and Developmental Disorders 27: 11–24.

Hodapp RM, Evans D, Gray FL (1999) What we know about intellectual development in children with Down syndrome. In JA Rondal, J Perera and L Nadel (eds) Down's syndrome: A Review of Current Knowledge. London: Whurr, pp. 124–32.

Hodapp RM, Ly TM, Fidler DJ, Ricci LA (2001) Less stress, more rewarding: parenting children with Down syndrome. Parenting: Science and Practice 1: 317–37.

Hodapp RM, Ricci LA, Ly TM, Fidler DJ (2003) The effects of the child with Down syndrome on parental stress. British Journal of Developmental Psychology, 21: 137–51.

Holland AJ, Treasure J, Coskeran P, Dallow J (1995) Characteristics of the eating disorder in Prader-Willi syndrome: implications for treatment. Journal of Intellectual Disability Research 39: 373–81.

Hornby G (1995) Fathers' views of the effects on their families of children with Down syndrome. Journal of Child and Family Studies 4: 103–17.

Jarrold C, Baddeley AD, Hewes AK, Phillips C (2001) A longitudinal assessment of diverging verbal and non-verbal abilities in the Williams syndrome phenotype. Cortex 37: 423–31.

Jorde LB, Carey JC, White RL (1997) Medical Genetics. St Louis MO: Mosby.

Kasari C, Freeman SFN (2001) Task-related social behaviour in children with Down syndrome. American Journal on Mental Retardation 106: 253–64.

Kasari C, Freeman SFN, Mundy P, Sigman M (1995) Attention regulation by children with Down syndrome: coordinated joint attention and social referencing. American Journal on Mental Retardation 100: 128–36.

Kaufman AS, Kaufman NL (1983) Kaufman Assessment Battery for Children (K-ABC). Circle Pines MN: American Guidance Service.

Kaufman AS, Kaufman NL, Goldman BZ (1984) K-SOS: Kaufman Sequential or Simultaneous. Circle Pines MN: American Guidance Service.

Kemper MB, Hagerman RJ, Altshul-Stark D (1988) Cognitive profiles of boys with fragile X syndrome. American Journal of Medical Genetics 30: 191–200.

Lai F, Williams RS (1989) A prospective study of Alzheimer disease in Down syndrome. Archives of Neurology 46: 849–53.

Laws G, Buckley S, Bird G, MacDonald J, Broadley I (1995) The influence of reading instruction on language and memory development in children with Down's syndrome. Down's Syndrome: Research and Practice 3: 59–64.

Lenhoff HM (1998). Information sharing. Insights into the musical potential of cognitive impaired people diagnosed with Williams syndrome. Music Therapy 16: 33–6.

Lund J (1985) The prevalence of psychiatric morbidity in mentally retarded adults. Acta Psychiatrica Scandanavica 72: 563–70.

Luria AR (1980) Neuropsychology in the local diagnosis of brain damage. Clinical Neuropsychology 2(1): 1–7.

McDade HL, Adler S (1980) Down syndrome and short-term memory impairment: a storage or retrieval deficit? American Journal of Mental Deficiency 84: 561–7.

Marcell M, Armstrong V (1982) Auditory and visual sequential memory of Down syndrome and nonretarded children. American Journal of Mental Deficiency 87: 86–95.

Matalainen R, Airaksinen E, Mononen T, Launiala K, Kaarianen R (1995) A population-based study of the causes of severe and profound mental retardation. Acta Pediatrica 84: 261–6.

Mathews CA, Freimer NB (2000) Genetic linkage analysis of the psychiatric disorders. In BJ Sadock, VA Sadock (eds) Comprehensive Textbook of Psychiatry. 7th edn. Vol. 1. Philadelphia PA: Lippincott Williams & Wilkins, pp 184–98.

Mervis CB, Morris CA, Bertrand J, Robinson BF (1999) Williams syndrome: findings from an integrated program of research. In H Tager–Flusberg (ed.) Neurodevelopmental Disorders. Cambridge MA: MIT Press, pp 65–110.

Myers BA, Pueschel SM (1991) Psychiatric disorders in persons with Down syndrome. Journal of Nervous and Mental Disease 179: 609–13.

Naglieri JA (1985) Assessment of mentally retarded children with the Kaufman Assessment Battery for Children. American Journal of Mental Deficiency 89: 367–71.

Obrzut A, Nelson RB, Obrzut JE (1987) Construct validity of the Kaufman Assessment Battery for Children with mildly mentally retarded students. American Journal of Mental Deficiency 92: 74–7.

Opitz JM (1985) Editorial comment: the developmental field concept. American Journal of Medical Genetics 21: 1–11.

Opitz JM (1996) Historiography of the causal analysis of mental retardation. Speech to the 29th Gatlinburg Conference on Research and Theory in Mental Retardation and Developmental Disabilities, Gatlinburg TN, March.

Plomin R (1999) Genetics of childhood disorders: III. Genetics and intelligence. Journal of the American Academy of Child and Adolescent Psychiatry 38: 786–8.

Plomin R, Crabbe J (2000) DNA. Psychological Bulletin 126: 806–28.

Plomin R, Rende R (1991) Human behavioural genetics. Annual Review of Psychology 42: 161–90.

Pober BR, Dykens EM (1996) Williams syndrome: an overview of medical cognitive and behavioural features. Child and Adolescent Psychiatric Clinics of North America 5: 929–43.

Powell L, Houghton S, Douglas G (1997) Comparison of etiology-specific cognitive functioning profiles for individuals with Fragile X and individuals with Down syndrome. Journal of Special Education 31: 362–76.

Pueschel SM (1990) Clinical aspects of Down syndrome from infancy to adulthood. American Journal of Medical Genetics [Suppl 7]: 52–6.

Pueschel SM, Bernier JC, Pezzullo JC (1991) Behavioural observations in children with Down's syndrome. Journal of Mental Deficiency Research 35: 502–11.

Pueschel SR, Gallagher PL, Zartler AS, Pezzullo JC (1986) Cognitive and learning profiles in children with Down syndrome. Research in Developmental Disabilities 8: 21–37.

Reilly JS, Klima E, Bellugi U (1990) Once more with feeling: affect and language in atypical populations. Development and Psychopathology 2: 367–91.

Reiss S, Havercamp SH (1998) Toward a comprehensive assessment of functional motivation: factor structure of the Reiss profiles. Psychological Assessment 10: 97–106.

Rogers C (1987) Maternal support for the Down's syndrome personality stereotype: The effect of direct experience on the condition. Journal of Mental deficiency Research 31: 271–8.

Rondal J (1995) Exceptional language development in Down syndrome. New York: Cambridge University Press.

Roof E, Stone W, MacLean W, Feurer ID, Thompson T, Butler MG (2000). Intellectual characteristics of Prader-Willi syndrome: comparison of genetic subtypes. Journal of Intellectual Disability Research 44: 25–30.

Rosner BA, Hodapp RM, Fidler DJ, Sagun J, Dykens EM (2003) Social competence in persons with Prader-Willi, Williams and Down syndromes. Submitted for publication.

Rutter M, Simonoff E, Plomin R (1996) Genetic influences on mild mental retardation: concepts, findings and research implications. Journal of Biosocial Science 28: 509–26.

Snow CP (1959/1963) The two cultures. Rede Lecture given at Cambridge University, 7 May 1959. Republished in CP Snow (1993) The Two Cultures. Cambridge: Cambridge University Press.

Sparrow SS, Davis SM (2000) Recent advances in the assessment of intelligence and cognition. Journal of Child Psychology and Psychiatry 41: 117–31.

Sullivan PM, Knutson JF (2000) Maltreatment and disabilities: a population-based epidemiological study. Child Abuse, Neglect 24: 1257–73.

Swaab DF, Purba JS, Hofman MA (1995) Alterations in the hypothalamic paraventricular nucleus and its oxytocin neurons (putative satiety cells) in Prader-Willi syndrome: a study of five cases. Journal of Clinical Endocrinology and Metabolism 80: 573–9.

Udwin O, Yule W (1990) Expressive language of children with Williams syndrome. American Journal of Medical Genetics 6: 108–14.

Udwin O, Yule W (1991) A cognitive and behavioural phenotype in Williams syndrome. Journal of Clinical and Experimental Neuropsychology 13: 232–44.

Udwin O, Yule W, Martin N (1987) Cognitive abilities and behavioural characteristics of children with idiopathic infantile hypercalcaemia. Journal of Child Psychology and Psychiatry 28: 297–309.

Van Acker R (1991) Rett syndrome: a review of current knowledge. Journal of Autism and Developmental Disorders 21: 381–406.

Weisz JR, Yeates K, Zigler E (1982) Piagetian evidence and the developmental–difference controversy. In E Zigler, D Balla (eds) Mental Retardation: The Developmental-Difference Controversy. Hillsdale NJ: Erlbaum, pp. 213–76.

Wishart JG, Johnston FH (1990) The effects of experience on attribution of a stereotyped personality to children with Down's syndrome. Journal of Mental Deficiency Research 34: 409–20.

Zigler E (1969) Developmental versus difference theories of mental retardation and the problem of motivation. American Journal of Mental Deficiency 73: 536–56.

Zigman WB, Schupf N, Zigman A, Silverman W (1993) Aging and Alzheimer disease in people with mental retardation. International Review of Research in Mental Retardation 19: 41–70.

Chapter 3
Intersyndrome and intrasyndrome language differences

Jean A. Rondal

The study of language intellectual disabilities (ID) has a long history (Rondal, 1975), from the early speech and language studies of the 1950s and 1960s (and before) to the psycholinguistically oriented works of the 1970s and later. This includes cognitively motivated accounts of ID such as those of Luria and Vinogradova (1959), Inhelder (1968), O'Connor and Hermelin (1963), and the studies of Lenneberg (1967) and Lenneberg et al. (1964) and studies stressing biological and maturational factors in language development of ID subjects (see Rondal and Edwards, 1997, for a historical sketch). Predominantly non-aetiological conceptions have dominated the ID field for a long time for a variety of reasons assumed to be good ones – for instance: syndrome labels are unnecessary as people with different syndromes behave basically the same, and labels may be socially and educationally harmful (see Dykens et al., 2000, for a discussion). The situation remained unchanged even after the discovery of the chromosomic aetiology of Down syndrome (DS) in the late 1950s (Lejeune et al., 1959). This latter fact appears to be something of a paradox. Actually, the increase in knowledge of DS (language and otherwise) that followed (and has continued until the present time) often led to this condition being considered as prototypical of ID (sometimes with the proviso that, as a rule, it was more detrimental to language development and functioning than other ID entities known or, most of the time, undiagnosed – cf. Zisk and Bialer, 1967).

Whereas DS remains today by far the best-known ID entity from a variety of points of view (with its 140-year scientific history and extended tradition of behavioural and biological research), the notion that this entity is fully representative of moderate and severe ID can hardly been sustained any more. Numerous data (in continuous and rapid expansion) show not only that DS is not prototypical of ID (having its own genetic, physical, and behavioural characteristics) but also that there is substantial variation across ID syndromes, which warrants further investigation. It also seems (cf. Rondal and Edwards, 1997) that intelligence quotient (IQ), mental age (MA), or other general cognitive variables have only little explanatory value when it comes to accounting for the differences between ID syndromes in terms of language, for example. In this respect, schemes differentiating between various levels of ID (such as Luria's 1961 comparison between so-called oligophrenes with lighter cognitive handicaps and organic retardates; Zigler's 1969 distinction between cultural-familial and organic mental retardation, or Inhelder's 1968 classification of ID subjects according to whether they had reached the so-called intellectual sensory-motor level, the preoperatory, or the concrete operatory level, derived from Piagetian theory of cognitive development) are in a difficult position, because the new descriptions of language and cognitive development and problems in the rapidly growing list of ID syndromes cut across these classifications for the major part.

Among the ID syndromes, the genetic ones seem particularly interesting and worth careful study. They account for about one-third of all occurrences of ID (Matalainen et al., 1995). This chapter will be devoted, for the most part, to these syndromes. They represent an enormous challenge for the field of intellectual disabilities. According to Moser (1992), there exist several hundreds of syndromes leading to ID. Shprintzen (1997) lists more than 200 genetic conditions conducive to language, speech, or communication disorders – this list includes a large number of ID syndromes of genetic origin. In the introductory part of his book on genetics syndromes and communication disorders, Shprintzen (1997: viii) writes:

> Perhaps the acceptance of genetics as a powerful force influencing human behaviour has grown along with the incredible expansion of the science of genetics. Unfortunately, those of us working in the field of communicative science have been left behind [and] scientists who work in the genetic sciences probably know as little about speech, language, and hearing as communication scientists [most often] know about genetics.

The amalgamation of the communication sciences and genetics, called for by Shprintzen, may materialize in the near future. Precursors can already be observed indicating that the wishful move has been initiated. The present contribution may be located within that orientation.

In this chapter, I will first deal with the usual speech and oral language problems of a number of ID genetic syndromes, the most researched so far. I will then turn to the most interesting cases of so-called exceptional language development and functioning in ID subjects reported in the recent specialized literature. Theoretical and practical implications will be drawn from the above studies. I will propose that an explanation both for the large intersyndromic and interindividual variabilities exposed should be sought in a neurogenetic perspective having little to do with the usual classificatory considerations in ID.

The chapter will also deal with the language problems of ageing persons with ID. Lastly, attention will be given to presenting and discussing some of the major principles that may be ascribed to language remediation in intellectual disabilities.

Genetic syndromes of intellectual disability

Among the many syndromes conducive to ID, only a few have been thoroughly studied from a language point of view. This is the case overall for Down syndrome, Williams syndrome, and fragile-X syndrome. A few other syndromes (for example, cri-du-chat, Prader-Willi), although less well documented, have motivated sufficient data gathering to justify at least preliminary comparative analyses. In what follows, the section on language in DS is the most extensive. As indicated, this is not because DS could be regarded in any way as prototypical of ID but because, being the best-known syndrome to date, it readily serves for meaningful comparisons with other ID genetic syndromes.

Down syndrome (DS)

Down syndrome is the most common non-herited chromosomal ID condition (Clarke et al., 1985) with a prevalence estimated by Dolk et al. (1990) to be 1 in 750 births, equally affecting both sexes. It may be close to 1 in 1,500 in a number of developed countries due to the conjunction of early diagnosis procedures and abortive practices. Aetiologically, DS is due to increased gene copy number (gene dosage) regarding a number or all of the 225 genes composing the DNA (deoxyribonucleic acid) sequence for chromosome 21 (Capone, 2001).

No major language differences have been demonstrated between the three main aetiological subcategories of DS (standard trisomy 21 accounting for 97 per cent of the cases; translocations, 2 per cent; and mosaicism, 1 per cent; in these latter cases, the embryos develop with a mosaic of normal and trisomic cells), except for a possible slight referential lexical superiority of mosaic DS, who generally tend to have higher IQs (Fishler and Koch, 1991).

Prelinguistic development shows significant delays in DS infants. Turn-taking skills, basic for future conversational exchanges, are slow to develop. The type of prelinguistic phrasing that can be observed in typically developing (TD) babies, beginning around three months of age (intermittent babbling, approximately 3 s long, with phrase-ending syllables lasting longer than other syllables), is different in DS babies. They take longer to finish a phrase. The sounds of babbling are mostly similar in types and tokens in non-disabled (TD) and DS infants (Smith and Oller, 1981). However, the onset of reduplicated babbling (production of speech-like syllables – 'bababa', 'dadada', and so forth – a precursor to meaningful speech) is delayed in DS infants (eight months versus six months in TD infants). Articulatory development is typically slow and difficult in DS children. In the most serious cases (with markedly reduced speech intelligibility), one may probably suspect a developmental apraxia (Kumin and Adams, 2000; Kumin, 2001) or (better) dyspraxia of speech. The overall speech progression, however, parallels that of TD children, even if many DS children exhibit more inconsistent segmental development (Dodd and Leahy, 1989) (but is more consistent than TD children with a phonological disorder – Dodd and Thompson, 2001). Vowels, semivowels and nasal and stop consonants are produced and mastered first. Fricatives and affricates are more difficult to articulate, later to appear, and in some cases never stabilize. Major phonological strategies seem to be similar in TD and DS children (for example, Stoel-Grammon, 1980, in press).

Many DS children do not demonstrate consistent production of conventional words before two or three years chronological age (CA). Their shortcomings in motor development (Wishart, 1988) favour the delays. The articulatory difficulties mentioned above also contribute to the lexical retardation. Semantic development is delayed in DS in proportion to the general cognitive impairment characteristic of the condition. Down syndrome infants exhibit delays (one month on average) in the onset of sustained eye-contact with the mother, and further delays (two months on average) in the setting of high levels of this behaviour (Gunn et al., 1982). Delays in imitative, verbal, and gestural abilities (Gutman and Rondal, 1979; Sokolov, 1992) may also contribute to the slower pace of development of meaningful speech in DS. Early lexical development (both productive and receptive) generally shows a positive linear relation with mental age (MA) increase (Barrett and Diniz, 1989; Rondal and Edwards, 1997). However, the rate of DS children's acquisition of new words does not keep up with that of non-disabled (ND) children and the equations describing both vocabulary learning curves gradually differ more and more as to slope (Miller, 1999). The gap continues to widen with increasing CA particularly for productive lexicon (Cardoso-Martins et al., 1985). The existence of noticeable individual differences in rate of vocabulary acquisition among DS children must also be acknowledged. Based on a sample of 43 DS children studied at the University of Wisconsin, using parental report (the MacArthur Child Development Inventory), Miller (1999) reports 65 per cent of his DS subjects scoring below their MA-ND peers whereas 35 per cent were learning vocabulary at a rate consistent with 80 per cent of their MA-ND peers.

The first multi-word productions are often observed around three or four years CA in DS children. When they begin to combine two and three words within the same utterance, DS children appear to express the same range of relational meanings or thematic roles and relations as reported by the students of early combinatorial language in the ND child and pertaining to the semantic structures of the natural languages. Examples of early thematic relations expressed by mentally retarded children (MR), as well as by ND, children are notice of existence, denial, disappearance, recurrence, attribution, possession, location, instrument, conjunction, agent-action, action-object and agent-action.

Mean length of utterance (MLU) is widely used as a criterion variable for assessing language development. Up to a certain level of development, each morphosyntactic acquisition is directly reflected in the MLU count. Mean length of utterance development in DS shows a good linear relationship with CA until early adolescence (Rondal and Comblain, 1996). Mean length of utterance values of 1 are usually observed around 2 years. Between 2 and 9 or 10 years, MLU goes from values of 1 to 4 approximately. Mean lengths of utterance of 5 or 6 units are often observed from 12 years. Non-Down syndrome children reach MLU levels of five units and more around 6 years. In conversational speech between ND adults, average MLU values are close to 12. The slowness and limitation of MLU development in DS correspond to lasting shortcomings in morphosyntax. Productive use of grammatical words (articles, prepositions, pronouns, conjunctions, auxiliaries) and morphological marking of gender, number, tense, mode and aspect are limited. Many DS subjects are restricted to monopropositional sentences. Subordinate clauses are rare. Word order in those languages relying on strict sequential devices to express thematic relations (for example, English, French) is usually correct (Rondal, 1978; Rosenberg and Abbeduto, 1993).

Even at corresponding MLU levels, DS children may not demonstrate exactly the same kind of lexico-syntax as their ND peers (Rondal, 1978; see Fowler et al., 1994, however, for a more positive evaluation claiming close percentages of use of grammatical morphemes in MLU-matched ND and DS children). For example, when matched for MLU with ND children, DS children tend to use fewer complex verb groups and advanced types of indefinite pronouns.

Numerous reports point to serious limitations of DS children and adolescents in the comprehension of morphosyntactic structures and their lagging behind MA-matched ND controls in this respect (cf. Rondal, 1975, 1985; Rondal and Edwards, 1997). Kernan (1990) has documented the difficulty of young adults with DS in processing temporal sentences, particularly those in which clause order did not match the order of the events (for example, 'John left after Mary signed the contract'). Rondal et al. (1988) have studied the comprehension of declarative monopropositional sentences varying according to voice and semantic transitivity features (see Hopper and Thompson, 1980). Their results show that in a large majority of cases, DS adults do not correctly understand the morphosyntactic and the semantic aspects associated with the passive voice. However, reversible declarative active sentences are correctly understood in a good proportion of the cases, particularly when action verbs are used and at relatively higher IQ levels (between 45 and 55 points).

A marked superiority of language comprehension over language production has sometimes been claimed for DS individuals. Miller (1999), for example, suggests a typical discrepancy between comprehension and production favouring the first function. The differences in lexical comprehension may not amount to more than the usual imbalance between productive and receptive vocabulary repertoires in ND people. Concerning morphosyntax, one will recall (with Caplan, 1993) that there are three routes to sentence meaning:

- a syntactic route that computes a full syntactic representation for a sentence and uses this representation to assign aspects of sentential meaning;
- a heuristic route using a reduced syntactic structure (for example, word order) for the same purpose; and
- a lexico-pragmatic (lexico-semantic) route that infers aspects of sentence meaning from single word meaning and knowledge of real-world events.

The specialized processing mechanisms assigning syntactic structures to sentences are (normally) unique to the left cerebral hemisphere; the right one being able to understand sentences using semantic relations between single words and world knowledge – that is, following the lexico-semantic-pragmatic route. Miller's suggestion may reflect the use by DS individuals of the heuristic and/or lexico-pragmatic route rather than a genuine morphosyntactic treatment of which many if not most of them are incapable – as demonstrated by Rondal (1995) in experimentally controlled tasks involving comprehension of reversible passives, relative, causative, and temporal clauses, excluding the heuristics above.

There is a growing literature on language pragmatics in DS (Abbeduto and Keller-Bell, in press). Young DS children (1 to 4 years) use one-word utterances to request objects located out of reach (Greenwald and Leonard, 1979). Few differences exist between MA-matched or MLU-matched ND and DS children in the frequency of speech acts, for example, question-answer, assertion, suggestion, request, command (Coggins et al., 1983). Preschoolers with DS and ND toddlers matched for expressive language make the greatest use of the speech act 'answering' when interacting with their mothers (Owens and MacDonald, 1982). The turn-taking behaviour of DS adolescents is mostly rule governed and systematic. Limitations are observed, however, in the use of linguistic forms that ND people find appropriate for the expression of particular speech acts. Many DS children and adolescents have difficulty in using conventional forms for softening their requests (for example, using indirect requesting). Topic contribution and topic continuation in conversation have been studied less. Down syndrome subjects keenly desire to keep topics going and develop them when conversing and to contribute significantly to verbal exchanges. But they often lack the appropriate and refined formal language skills to do so.

Two major dimensions of discourse (text) are macrostructures and cohesion. I take macrostructure to mean the larger discursive framework in opposition to the semantic propositional and morphosyntactic levels (discursive microstructures). Discourses vary as to their basic organization corresponding to implicit knowledge shared between people. It is possible to distinguish between four major types of discourse: narrative, argumentative, descriptive, and theoretical or explanatory (less relevant in the present context). Narratives are typically organized in chronological order. One may modify that order but the interlocutor has to be warned (so-called markedness of the expression). By default, one expects the speaker to start the story at the beginning and go through it chronologically, optionally terminating with a personal comment. Argumentative texts are not necessarily organized according to a particular chronology (although they may be). The key feature is coherence. A good argument is one that is relevant and does not contradict itself. Descriptive texts must be referentially adequate – they must correspond in major ways to the objects or events under description.

Discourse macrostructures are clearly cognitive in nature and as such could be expected to cause problems for DS people. A study by Boudreau and Chapman (2000) on linguistic expression of event representation in narratives suggests that DS adolescents and young adults deal with event structures in narratives in the same way as MA-matched TD children. Regarding use of linguistic devices and cohesion, however, the DS individuals perform more poorly than MA-matched controls. According to Halliday (1985), textual cohesion is realized in four major ways:

- *reference:* a participant or circumstantial element introduced at one place in the text can be taken as a reference point for something that follows (for example, 'the boy' . . . 'he' . . . 'him', and so forth – pronominal use in such cases implies correct application for the co-reference rule between noun and pronoun);
- *ellipsis:* a clause or part of a clause once formulated may be presupposed and omitted at a subsequent place in text;
- *lexical cohesion:* discursive continuity may also be established by the choice of words that may take the form of word repetition, the presence of key words, or the choice of words that are related semantically to previous ones; and
- *conjunction:* a clause or some longer portion of text may be related to what follows by one of a set of particular words (adverbs, conjunctions) carrying relational or hierarchical meaning (for example, 'than', 'in such a way that', 'therefore', 'but', 'because', 'for').

Other works (such as Chapman et al., 1991; Reilly et al., 1991) confirm the particular difficulty of DS children and adolescents in various aspects of online story telling and processing. Despite expressive lexical and syntactic limitations, adolescents and young adults with DS have been found to express more narrative content and develop higher-level story schemas than MLU-matched TD controls (Miles and Chapman, 2002), which could be the result of the DS subjects' longer experience with story content (listening to stories).

Williams syndrome (WS)

This is a rare congenital metabolic disorder (prevalence: one case in approximately 25,000 births – Martin et al., 1984). The condition is associated with hemizygous deletion (concerning only one chromosome in the pair) of a set of genes (18 identified so far), including the elastin locus at 7q11.23 (Korenberg et al., 2000). Hemizygosity of the elastin gene accounts for the vascular abnormalities typical of the syndrome (particularly, supravalvular aortic stenosis – a narrowing of the arteries that reduces bloodflow). The genes contributing to other features of the syndrome, such as infantile hypercalcaemia, dysmorphic faeces, hyperacusis, and cognitive defects (between mild and moderate mental retardation), remain to be identified (Galaburda et al., 1994). A proposal has been made by Frangistakis et al. (1996), based on the genotypic-phenotypic analysis of rare cases of partial WS deletions, to link impaired visuo-spatial construction abilities in WS to hemizygosity of LMK1 gene, encoding a protein (kinase) that is expressed in the developing brain. However, a subsequent study by Tassabehji et al. (1999) failed to confirm Frangistakis et al.'s hypothesis.

Many adolescent and adults with WS have good referential lexical abilities (Bellugi et al., 1990). However, early vocabulary development is usually as delayed in WS as it is in DS (Bellugi et al., 2000). Later, and in an as yet unexplained way, things improve considerably from a lexical point of view for many if not most WS subjects. Vocabulary scores of many adolescents and young adults with WS may be closer to their CAs than their MAs (Bellugi et al., 1988; Stevens, 1996, cited by Stevens and Karmiloff-Smith, 1997). However, this is disputed by Volterra et al. (1994). The latter authors insist that language in WS is not ahead of MA. They document – and this may explain the conflicting reports – marked interindividual differences among WS subjects (see also Pezzini et al., 1999). This is already obvious in the distribution of IQs in WS – ranging from 40 to 90, close to normal distribution with a mean IQ of approximately 55 (Bellugi et al., 2000). Individual variations are also demonstrated in a vocabulary study by Patterson et al., quoted by Bishop (1999). They gave the Peabody Vocabulary Picture Test – revised (a labelling test) to 127 WS individuals aged four to 52 years. Only a small minority of adults exhibited CA-appropriate vocabulary levels. Williams syndrome infants exhibit overall delays in terms of the first words (observed between 18 and 24 months) and the onset of canonical babbling (recorded 2 to 3 months prior to the onset of first words, as is the case of typically developing infants), as observed by Masataka (2001).

Williams syndrome children have difficulties with lexical access as demonstrated in online experimental tasks and are less sensitive to word frequencies than ND controls (Tyler et al., 1997). A study by Stevens and Karmiloff-Smith (1997) further suggests that the relatively high vocabulary scores displayed by many WS individuals do not necessarily reflect a normal development pathway. These authors compared a WS group and a ND MA-matched control group in the range of CA 3–9 years in different experiments, testing for processing constraints on word learning. As argued in the literature (for example, Markman, 1990), in construing the meaning of new words, ND children display mutual exclusivity (an object cannot have more than one name), whole object (a novel word heard in the presence of a novel object refers to the whole object rather than to its substance, properties, or component features), and taxonomic constraints (lexical categories are constituted of entities or events of the same types as opposed, for example, to thematic or linear associations).

Whereas WS children show fast mapping and mutual exclusivity, they do not seem to abide by the whole object and taxonomic constraints. This suggests that despite sometimes advanced vocabulary ages, the processes underlying lexical acquisition and organization in semantic memory may follow a path somewhat different from that of ND individuals. It is, of course, tempting to relate the apparent absence of the whole object constraint in the lexical learning of WS children to their serious difficulties in visuospatial integration (Bellugi et al., 1990; Atkinson et al., 1997; Stiles et al., 2000).

Speech in WS is usually fluent with correct articulation and prosody. The voice may be hoarse. Sentence comprehension and use of morphosyntactic devices are not intact (Capirci et al., 1996; Bellugi et al., 2000) contrary to preliminary suggestions, even if globally the productive syntax of many WS subjects appears relatively advanced. Careful scrutiny (Thomas et al., 2001) reveals that WS subjects are CA-delayed (but not MA-delayed or much less MA-delayed) in the acquisition of past-tense forms in English (irregulars worse than regulars). Studies by Karmiloff-Smith et al. (1997, 1998); Clahsen and Almazan (1998); and Stojanovik et al. (2001) indicate that WS individuals have difficulties in production as well as in comprehension of subcategory constraints (such as 'intransitive verbs cannot take a direct object'), embedded structure sentences, reversible passives, and gender assignment across sentence elements.

Discursive ability seems to be relatively preserved in WS (Wang and Bellugi, 1994). Reilly et al. (1991) compared cognitively matched WS and DS adolescents in a story-telling task. In contrast to DS subjects, the WS adolescents told cohesive and complex narratives making good use of affective prosody. The WS, but not the DS, subjects enriched the referential contents of their stories with particular narrative devices such as mental verbs, intensifiers, emphatic forms, negative markers, and from time to time, onomatopoeic forms. The same authors report, however, that the WS subjects would use the same level of expressivity regardless of how many times they have told the same story and irrespective of the audience, indicative of a difficulty taking into account other people's presence and point of view. Losh et al. (2000) have compared WS children (5 through 10 years old) and TD children matched with the WS children either for CA or MA in a story-telling task from a wordless picture book. The children with WS committed significantly more morphological errors and used less complex syntax than comparison children. However, they tended to use many more evaluative devices, assigning meaning and emotional salience to particular events and behaviours, than either the CA- or the MA-matched controls and they exhibited preferences for those types of evaluation serving as social engagement devices. Losh et al. interpreted these indications as reflecting WS children's proclivity for intensive sociability. This is all the more troublesome as a suggestion because these children are often described as having particular difficulties in engaging and sustaining normal social interactions.

Pragmatics is often the area of major weakness in WS. This is paradoxical as these individuals are generally described as very social ('overfriendly' or even 'hypersocial') with engaging personalities (see, for example, Jones et al., 2000). These children have difficulties with topic introduction, topic maintenance, turn taking, and in maintaining appropriate eye contact in dyadic face-to-face interactions. They sometimes appear to be talking nonsense. Their speech is often odd, socially inappropriate, and repetitive with incessant questions. At times, they may echo the interlocutor's utterances with limited apparent understanding (Volterra et al., 1994). It is conceivable that at least a part of the pragmatic limitations of WS subjects could stem from their difficulties in integrating semantic information. Thomas et al. (2001) have proposed an account of language in WS in which development occurs with greater weight placed on phonological and formal information and less weight on semantic knowledge. However, Stojanovik et al. (2001) have reported conversational data showing not only semantic and pragmatic difficulties (for example, verbosity and utterances providing too little information in interactive settings) but also limitations in expressive syntax.

Fragile-X syndrome

Fragile-X syndrome (FXS) is an X-linked disorder passed on through generations. It is the leading inherited cause of ID with a prevalence of one in 4,000 males (Turner et al., 1996). Surveys (for example, Webb et al., 1986) show that FXS accounts for 2 per cent of ID among males. The cytogenetic expression of the fragile site is Xq27.3. It is caused by a trinucleotide repeat mutation that is associated with methylation and resultant transcriptional silencing of the FMR gene (Verkerk et al., 1991). FMR protein expression varies substantially between cases with either mosaicism, either partially methylated or fully methylated. This variation accounts for a small but significant amount of variance in levels of motor, social, adaptive, cognitive, and language early developments in males with FXS (Bailey et al., 2001). Fragile-X syndrome is one genetic abnormality following an unusual pattern that is not yet completely understood (see Phelps, 1998). Twenty per cent of males with the errant gene present no pathological symptom (are non-penetrant). The rest of the affected males are moderately to severely mentally retarded (Maes et al., 1994). Approximately, one-third of the females are affected with a phenotypic variant of the syndrome determining learning difficulties. A minority is impaired with mild to moderate ID (Hagerman, 1995). These females have inherited FX from a carrier mother. Premutation carriers have trinucleotide repeats in the 50 to 200 range, whereas individuals with a full mutation have more than 200 repeats (Pennington, 1995). Autistic-like behaviours have been reported in males with FXS. Many of them show a particular pattern of gaze (characterized by avoidance-approach sequences). However, the whole behavioural picture in these subjects does not conform with autism (cf. Dykens et al. 2000, for a discussion). Psychomotor development in FXS males carrier females lags behind the norm from birth on, with twice as long a time expected for these infants to sit alone and walk unassisted (Prouty et al., 1988).

The language picture for the males affected with FXS may be summarized as follows (the corresponding state of affairs for the affected and the carrier females is still less clear). Speech tends to be fast, repetitive, perseverative, with cluttering and fluctuating rates, increased loudness, and sometimes oral apraxia (Newell et al., 1983; Wolf-Schein et al., 1987). Unusual voice effect, dysrhythmia, echolalia, speech impulsiveness, disrupted prosody, cluttering, and poor intelligibility, have been noted (Borgraef et al., 1987). Some FXS children speak in a high-pitched voice. Fragile-X syndrome subjects frequently omit or substitute vocalic or consonant phonemes (Vilkman et al., 1988). Receptive vocabulary is relatively preserved (Gérard et al., 1997). However, word-finding difficulties have been reported (Spinelli et al., 1995).

Utterance formulation is restricted and productive morphosyntax deficient (Sudhalter et al., 1991). Receptive language is also deficient and slow to develop but less so than expressive language (Roberts et al., 2001).

The language of FXS subjects is pragmatically limited with poor topic maintenance and turn-taking difficulties (Sudhalter et al, 1991; Abbeduto and Hagerman, 1997). They may exhibit deviant repetitive language (Madison et al., 1986). In a study by Belser and Sudhalter (2001), repetitive speech was found to be more prevalent among children, adolescents, and young adults with FXS compared with subjects with autistic disorder or intellectual disability not caused by FX. The authors suggest that the repetitive speech seen in FXS is not the result of either general developmental delay as undiagnosed autistic disorder (as has been proposed), but rather has much to do with the effects of a physiological arousal (poorly regulated by the autonomic nervous system) determined by hypersensitivity and greater reactivity to social stimuli and situations. Discourse is often poorly constructed and lacking in cohesion (Sudhalter et al., 1991). Additionally, Simon et al. (2001) suggest the existence in FXS women of a deficit establishing coherence (illustrated in selecting appropriate endings to jokes relative to stories) correlating strongly with the X activation ratio and measures of working memory. An interesting study with two monozygotic twin boys with FXS has been conducted by Sheldon and Turk (2000). These authors had the two boys undergo a thorough genetic, psychiatric, neurological and psycholinguistic evaluation at 10 years of age. They both demonstrated physical features, speech and language difficulties, social problems, and attention deficits that are common in the FX condition. However, one of the twins exhibited more language dysfunction (lexical, grammatical, and discoursive) and less social interaction than the other twin, suggesting that the Xq27.3 anomaly responsible for FXS may not be sufficient to account for all the behavioural phenotypic features of the syndrome, nor even the neuroanatomical features given that the first twin boy had markedly larger caudate volumes.

Cri-du-chat (cat-cry) syndrome (CDCS)

This is a rare syndrome (prevalence: approximately one case in 50,000 newborns, not varying according to sex – Niebuhr, 1978; Pueschel and Thuline, 1991) caused by a loss of chromosomal material from the region 5p (Lejeune et al., 1963). Twenty per cent of the cases are familial, with parental translocation accounting for the majority of these. The rest of the cases occur spontaneously by a genetic mutation. Gersch et al. (1995) have determined that two distinct chromosomal regions are associated with differential phenotypic manifestations. Deletions in 5p15.3 result in the high-pitched cry characteristic of the syndrome. The typical facial dysmorphias are lacking and cognitive impairment is mild to moderate. In contrast, the loss of region 5p15.2, designated the cri-du-chat critical region (Overhauser et al., 1994), results in the full spectrum of CDCS.

A significant number of these individuals reach puberty and survive into adulthood (Niebuhr, 1978). The typical phenotype presents a characteristic monochromate cry at birth (due to a laryngomalacia in most subjects but not persisting beyond two years in 30 per cent of them; the rest of the subjects may present an acute and monochromatic tone of voice all their life); other characteristics include dysmorphic craniofacial features with microcephaly, dental malocclusion, hypotonia, psychomotor retardation, slower rate of growth, respiratory and ear infections, and orthopaedic malalignment. Neurological examinations suggest hypoplasia of the cerebellar vermis associated with dysgenesis of the corpus callosum (Michele et al., 1993). Level of ID varies from profound to severe.

Longitudinal data (Carlin 1988a,b; 1990) indicate that the prognosis for most parameters of health development and longevity in CDCS is more optimistic today than has been presented in previous sources of medical information. For example, the risks of major organ anomalies and decreased survival are actually low. As for other ID syndromes, home rearing and early intervention are key variables to the improved outlook.

Despite large variations in the size and location of the chromosome deletions, a remarkable phenotypic consistency exists. Early growth failure, microcephaly, psychomotor retardation and respiratory and ear infections, are observed in all individuals. Almost 100 per cent of them have hypotonia, at least in the early months of life. In later years, about 50 per cent retain some degree of hypotonia and experience limitations in their range of motion at certain articulation joints. Attention deficits are general. Most individuals are friendly and enjoy interacting with other people.

People with CDCS demonstrate cognitive, language, and motor deficits. Lack of speech may be observed in some cases. Limited verbal abilities and severe language problems are cursorily noted. However, many children with CDCS have the ability to develop at least some language, but onset usually is markedly delayed (Sohner and Mitchell, 1991). Cornish and Munir (1998) assessed the receptive and expressive abilities in a cohort of 14 CDCS individuals (males and females) aged four to 14 years. Except in one case, no subject's score on the British Picture Vocabulary Scales (Dunn et al., 1982) was CA appropriate. Three children failed to reach the two-year baseline. All subjects were delayed in receptive grammar – some failed to reach the CA 4 years baseline – assessed with the Test of the Reception of Grammar (TROG, Bishop, 1983). Expressive language was markedly delayed (by several years) – equivalent scores on the Reynell Developmental Language Scales revised (Reynell, 1985). At the time of testing, only one subject could speak in sentences of four or more words. A common pattern in CDCS is for receptive language skills to be better preserved than expressive ones across the various language components. Even if expressive oral language is limited in typical CDCS, some forms of sign language, including the child and his family's idiosyncratic gestures, may be successfully used by a large number of these children (Carlin, 1990; Cornish and Pigram, 1996).

Prader-Willi syndrome (PWS)

Prader-Willi syndrome has a prevalence of 1 in 10,000 to 1 in 15,000 births (Cassidy, 1997) or 1 in 15,000 to 1 in 30,000 equally affecting both sexes (Daniel and Gridley, 1998). About 70 per cent of the cases are associated with a silencing (technically labelled genomic imprinting when one of the two allele genes is silenced whereas the other is expressed) of a number (not yet defined with precision) of genes on the chromosome 15 (region q11-13) of maternal origin together with the simultaneous deletion of the same part of the chromosome 15 of paternal origin (Butler et al. 1986). As a consequence, the maternal alleles cannot compensate for the deleted paternal genes given that they have been silenced (Everman and Cassidy, 2000). In 25 per cent of the cases, both chromosomes 15 originate from the mother (maternal uniparental disomy) and the regions q11-13 of these chromosomes are silenced (Nicholls et al., 1989).

The syndrome is characterized by dysmorphic features, hypotonia, and intellectual disability (but not in all cases). According to a survey conducted by Curfs (1992), about one-third of PWS subjects have IQs above 70, another third show mild ID, 27 per cent have moderate ID and the remaining ones severe to profound intellectual impairment.

Many people with PWS demonstrate obsessions and eating compulsions that may be pathognomonic for the syndrome. Overeating in PWS may be related to a hypothalamic dysfunction involving a set of neurons related to satiety (Swaab et al., 1995). Beyond food preoccupations, they also show sleep disturbances, obsessive symptoms including hoarding (for example, paper, pens, books), ordering and arranging objects to certain rules, and compulsive telling or asking (Dykens et al., 1996; Dykens and Kasari, 1997). Maladaptive behaviours seem to be less numerous and less severe in PWS cases due to maternal uniparental disomy than those originating in paternal deletion (Dykens et al., 1999).

Psychomotor development is retarded. Eye difficulties, particularly strabismus, are noted. By school age, if not before, cognitive, language, and behavioural deficits, become apparent (Dykens et al., 1992). Language studies are still insufficiently numerous in PWS. Multiple articulation errors (consonant distortions, probably associated with hypotonia), voice difficulties (including impairment of frequency levels and resonance), and hypernasality are reported markedly lowering speech intelligibility (Kleppe et al., 1990; Defloor et al., 2002). Oral motor functions, pitch level and resonance are disturbed. This is related to cerebral dysfunction and a characteristic anatomy of the mouth and the larynx (Akefeldt et al., 1997). Aerodynamic capabilities are often poor (Defloor et al., 2002) and dysfluencies are common but do not seem to conform completely to the pattern of stuttering. A mixed clinical picture emerges with features characteristic of stuttering (for example, within-word dysfluencies such as part-word repetitions, whole-word repetitions, blocks, prolongations, broken words; dysfluencies occurring more frequently on the first words of a sentence and being more prevalent in lexical than in function words) but none of the secondary symptoms of stuttering, such as bodily movements (Defloor et al., 2000). Hearing problems are common. Receptive and expressive lexical and syntactic levels are found below CA expectations (Akefeldt et al., 1997). Language pragmatic skills and communicative efficiency are problematic (for example, excessive talkativeness and verbal perseverations on a narrow range of topics (Dykens et al., 1996; Kleppe et al., 1990; but see Boer and Clarke, 1999, for a more positive appreciation). However, individual differences may be quite important (Kleppe et al., 1990).

Noonan syndrome (NS)

This is a genetic congenital disorder occurring approximatively once in 1,000 births (Noonan and Ehmke, 1963). Its primary aetiology is autosomal dominant with the mutations concerning a set of genes mapped to 12q22. Characteristics associated with NS include cardiac defects, short stature, ear anomalies, hypertelorism (wide-spaced eyes), short webbed neck, arched palate, velar hypotony, dental malocclusions, genital malformations, impaired intellect in the majority of cases, and delayed gross motor development.

Onset of language is usually markedly delayed (first words around three years). Individuals with NS present articulation problems (in the majority of cases), phonological deficits (such as stopping and cluster reduction, final consonant deletion), poorly intelligible speech, and hearing impairment (in a minority of cases) (Nora et al., 1974). Reduced receptive and expressive vocabulary is observed. However, semantic structural relations typically follow with corresponding cognitive development. Morphosyntactic development is delayed and remains incomplete. Basic sentence constituents are produced in monopropositional sentences. Few complex sentences are typically attempted (Wilson and Dyson, 1982). At the pragmatic level, the basic speech acts (such as labelling, giving information, requesting actions and information, describing events) are usually correctly performed.

Angelman syndrome (AS)

This is another syndrome, like PWS, showing the effects of genomic imprinting. It has a prevalence of 1 in 20,000 to 1 in 30,000 births (Angelman, 1965) or 1 in 12,000 to 1 in 25,000 (Kytterman, 1995).

In 60 per cent to 70 per cent of the cases, AS is caused by the silencing of a number of genes in the q11-13 region of chromosome 15 of paternal origin (Christian et al., 1995) and the simultaneous deletion of the same genes on the maternal copy of the same chromosome (Lombroso, 2000). In a small percentage of the cases (from 2 per cent to 5 per cent), the condition is the result of paternal uniparental disomy (inheritance of two copies of the above locus from the father and none from the mother; the pathology occurs when the whole region q11-13 or a part of it is silenced). In 5 per cent to 8 per cent of the cases, the molecular basis of the condition is found in mutations of one of the genes of the region q11-13 (UBE3A) that appears to be specifically expressed in the brain (Kishino et al., 1997; Everman and Cassidy, 2000).

Neurological examinations reveal microcephaly, brain ventricular enlargement, anomalous cortical growth, abnormal patterns of the electroencephalography (EEG), hyperactivity, restlessness, eating problems, sleep disturbances, frequent seizures, ataxia, and apraxia (Nicholls et al., 1992). Phenotypic differences exist to varying degrees across the genetic subtypes. The subjects with the deletions are those who exhibit the typical symptoms listed. More variability and a milder phenotypic picture may characterize the AS individuals with paternal uniparental disomy (Smith et al., 1998).

Level of intellectual disability varies from moderate to profound. Developmental delays are severe. Parent ratings of maladaptive behaviour using the Aberrant Behaviour Checklist (Aman and Singh, 1986) suggest, however, happier demeanour and better sociable disposition in AS by comparison with groups of children and young adults with developmental disabilities of mixed aetiology (Summers and Feldman, 1999). Another study using the same parental checklist signals, however, shows a curious fascination with water in 68 per cent of the AS children studied and episodes of inappropriate laughter in 57 per cent of the AS subjects studied (Clarke and Marston, 2000).

Noticeable in AS is the absence or severe reduction of speech and oral language, together with oral dyspraxia (Penner et al., 1993), widely spaced teeth and protruding tongue. Non-verbal techniques of communication have been tried with limited success, suggesting that the capacity for language (not only speech) may be gravely impaired (Summers et al., 1995). Already at the prelinguistic level, major difficulties exist in joint attention, babbling, reciprocal interaction with caretakers, sound imitation, and imitation of mouth and lip movements (Jolleff and Ryan, 1993; Brun Gasca et al., 2001). However, Clayton-Smith (1993) and Williams et al. (1995) have reported more positive indications regarding babbling, use of gestures and signing (for example, Makaton signed vocabulary) turn taking, joint action, and even receptive lexicon, but with no or limited expressive ability in 30 per cent of the cases. Andersen et al. (2002) report expressive verbal vocabulary consisting of less than two words in 50 per cent of their cohort of AS (boys and girls aged 2 to 14 years), two to three words in 33 per cent of the children, and four to five words in the remaining ones.

Neurofibromatosis 1 (NF1)

Neurofibromatosis 1 (Von Recklinghausen type) is a neurocutaneous disorder appearing in childhood and due to a single gene defect (Cale and Myers, 1978). The incidence is approximately 1 in every 4,000 births (Stumpof et al., 1988). Mutations of the NF1 gene (on chromosome 17q11.2) result in abnormal control of cell growth and differentiation of tissues, especially in the central and peripheral nervous systems. The protein controlled by this gene (neurofibromin) is thought to function as a tumour suppressor.

Physical features of NF1 include macrocephally, gliomas and optic nerves enlargement, skin tumours, and dysmorphic features.

Cognitive problems (particularly visuospatial) and learning disability are frequent (occurring in 30 per cent to 40 per cent of cases), even if the prevalence of ID in NF1 does not exceed 5 per cent (Legins et al., 1994). For a long time, NF1 was considered as not causing language difficulties. Actually, the language skills of many children with NF1 are less developed than those of unaffected siblings (Solot et al., 1990). Some NF1 subjects demonstrate both expressive and receptive language difficulties whereas others exhibit solely difficulties in expressive language. The limitations are particularly marked at the pragmatic and discoursive levels. Speech disorders, including stammering and abnormal fluency, hypernasality, abnormal prosody and rate of articulation, mispronunciations, incorrect sequencing of sounds, and voice problems (pitch, hoarseness), are present in 30 per cent to 40 per cent of the cases. Lexical reduction and receptive morphosyntactic limitations are found too (Mazzocco et al., 1995; Saint-Arroman and Alozy, 1998).

The precise neurological substrates of these impairments have not been defined yet. Mazzocco et al. (1995) suggest that the NF1 phenotype is specific in its inclusion of visuospatial and linguistic deficits in subjects either with normal intelligence, learning disability, or mild intellectual disability. It is indeed remarkable that serious language problems may coexist with normal intelligence or only minimal MR.

Turner syndrome (TS)

Turner syndrome occurs in approximately 1 per 1,500 (Palmer and Reichmann, 1976) or 1 per 2,500 births in females (Ross et al., 2000). About 60 per cent of the females born with TS are missing one X chromosome (45X0 formula), whereas the remainder have a partial X chromosome or a mosaic chromosomal pattern (complete or partial monosomy). 47XXX cases also exist (Pennington et al., 1980; Ginther and Fullwood, 1998). All full, partial, and mosaic TS subjects lack ovarian oestrogens production as the result of the absence of definite gonads (Park et al., 1983). They therefore allow the particular biological effects of oestrogen and X chromosome on brain development and subsequently on language and cognition to be studied. Depressed foetal hormones may affect brain development and specifically the development of early hemispheric asymmetry including the patterns of maturation of the cerebral hemispheres, which are left without the natural biologic influence observed in typical development. Comparing women with mosaic and full TS, Murphy et al. (1997) have demonstrated 'X chromosome dosage' effects in left cerebral temporal and parietal metabolism, and global language ability with mosaic TS intermediate to control and full TS subjects.

Turner syndrome females present a reduced stature and abnormal upper to lower body ratio, various affections of the renal and cardiovascular systems, and occasional strabismus. The individuals with 45X0 and 47XXX exhibit both gross and fine motor dysfunction (measured at the Bruininks-Oseretsky Test of Motor Proficiency by Salbenblatt et al., 1989). The same authors confirm the existence of consistent delays in motor development and sensory-motor integration in these subjects (from already a delay in the age of independent walking) associated with moderate language dysfunction in some cases; ID is uncommon but particular cognitive deficits are found in visuospatial processing (Ross et al. 1995). Oral language skills have often been described as usually preserved (Walzer, 1985, for a review; Ross et al., 1995). Van Borsel et al. (1999), however, report frequent voice disorders, articulation problems, occasional stuttering, and overall delayed language development, in a sample of 128 girls with TS ranging in age from 2 years 4 months to 5 years 8 months. Murphy et al. (1994) signal lower scores in tests of oral language (particularly category naming and syntax comprehension) in some TS individuals. Some TS females also have difficulty in tasks of verbal fluency (Money and Alexander, 1986). Mosaic TS subjects, however, exhibit better cognitive and verbal abilities (Bender et al., 1984). Pennington et al. (1980) have indicated that 47XXX females do present early with important language delays together with delays in first walking, and later verbal as well as non-verbal deficits (longitudinal study conducted with unselected girls between birth and 14 years). Corresponding data regarding the existence of a significant deficit in verbal IQ in 47XXX children have been supplied by Netley and Rovet (1982). Regarding memory, test scores (in story recall and visual recognition and reproduction tasks) were found to be reduced independently of X chromosome dosage in all the TS subjects studied by Murphy et al. (1994).

Traditional neuropathological measures (for example, EEG) have failed to identify consistent anomalies in TS individuals (Elliott et al., 1996). However, brain imagery studies reveal structural anomalies including decreased volumes of hippocampus, caudate, ventricular, and thalamic nuclei, and parieto-occipital brain matter, parieto-occipital asymmetry with left-brain regions having greater volumes than right ones in adults (Murphy et al., 1994).

Results of dual-listening tasks suggest that females with TS are left-hemisphere dominant for the language functions (Lewandowski et al., 1985). Such findings have motivated a 'right hemisphere dysfunction' hypothesis in TS, which probably needs some reformulation in view of the above indications.

Clark et al. (1990) have found lower rates of glucose metabolism in the occipital and parietal lobes in TS subjects compared to controls and PET findings by Elliott et al. (1996) suggest that hypometabolism in the parietal and occipital lobes may be common among TS girls exhibiting some degree of cognitive impairment but is not evidenced by those without such impairment. The Murphy et al. (1997) PET study documents the coexistence of a significant absolute hypermetabolism (mean global grey matter metabolic rate) in most brain areas of young adults with TS (compared to healthy controls) and a significant relative hypometabolism in the insula and the association cortices bilaterally.

The global picture in this syndrome is complex and remains partially unclear. It seems likely, however, that the X chromosome plays a role in brain development, with reference, among other skills, to verbal abilities, possibly through an involvement in the development of the temporo-parietal regions (Murphy et al., 1994).

Klinefelter syndrome (KS)

This is a genetic disorder found exclusively in males with one, two, or even three extra X chromosomes (47XXY, 48XXXY, 49XXXXY), one extra Y chromosome (47XYY), or one extra X and one extra Y chromosome (48XXYY). The aneuploidies may be partial or complete and mosaicism may be involved. It affects one in 1,000 births (Mandoki et al., 1991). The additional X chromosome is of paternal origin in 50 per cent to 60 per cent of the XXY births, with maternal origin occurring in the remaining cases. Klinefelter syndrome is characterized by a tall stature, decreased muscle tone, average intelligence, learning disability, or mild ID (Walzer et al., 1991). Language problems are common, particularly on the expressive side. Auditory processing deficits are characteristic, although language receptive skills are usually within the normal range. Verbal IQ tends to be depressed compared to non-verbal IQ (Netley and Rovet, 1982). Delayed speech development during early childhood is frequent with prosodic difficulties. Word selection and sentence organization are problematic in some cases (Leonard et al., 1979). There is an increased incidence of reading difficulties, dyslexia (Samango-Sprouse, 2001) and learning disability (Rovet et al., 1996).

The oral language difficulties are also a characteristic of adults with 47XXY, with scores significantly below controls in lexical abilities and verbal processing speed in a study of KS subjects aged 16 to 61 years by Brauer Boone et al. (2001). In this study, however, older age was significantly correlated with an intriguing increase in verbal IQ for which the authors had no explanation.

Males with 49XXXXY have better visuospatial skills than verbal skills (Curfs et al., 1990). Curfs et al. (1990) and Lomelino and Reiss (1991) noted a decline in intellectual ability with age in 49XXXXY males. Severe retardation in language development in the same patients has been described by Curfs et al. (1990). This was confirmed in a study of individual cases of 49XXXXY including a 5-year-old and 9-year-old male. They exhibited expressive language skills lower than receptive ones, an observation also made by Moric-Petrovic et al. (1973). These indications go in the same direction as those from other sex chromosome aneuploidies (anomalies in the number of chromosomes), for example, TS (see above).

The observations regarding the cases of individuals with KS suggest that one major contributory factor may be the chromosome X or Y because in the polysomy disorders of KS, there is only one active X or Y, and the additional X, Xs or Y undergo inactivation to some extent

(Willard, 1995), whereas a number of genes on chromosomes X and Y are altered by the existence of the polysomy (Geschwind et al., 2000).

A neurogenetic perspective of the kind can simultaneously explain the differences between XO (TS) and other sex chromosome anomaly disorders as well as the basic similarities among disorders such as XXY, XXXY, XXXXY, XYY, and XXYY. The variability in individuals with KS may also be related with the impact of gonadal steroids (Patwardhan et al., 2000). As in TS, but mutatis mutandis, depressed foetal hormones may alter the development of hemispheric asymmetry in boys with KS. This is probably related to the smaller head circumference often observed in this syndrome denoting a delay or slowing down of cell division during prenatal development (Stewart et al., 1986).

Rett syndrome (RS)

Rett syndrome is peculiar for it is a progressive disorder. It affects 1 in 10,000 to 15,000 individuals. Mutations in the gene MECP2 at Xq28, encoding the methyl-CpG-binding protein 2 seem to be the major cause (but possibly not the only one) of this X-linked dominant neurodevelopmental disorder occurring almost exclusively in females (Amir et al., 1998; Xiang et al., 2000), the severity of the condition depending on the loci of mutation (Uchino et al., 2001) and the type of mutation (see below). The mutations are found in 100 per cent of the patients with classic RS. Their prevalence in atypical RS is still uncertain (Auranen et al., 2001) but they could relate in major ways to the MECP2 gene in this Rett variety as well (Yamashita et al., 2001).

Most infants with RS develop within expected limits until six to 12 months of age or so (Kerr and Corbitt, 1994; Dunn, 2001). Regression occurs (between one and three years) drastically affecting language, motor, and cognitive acquisitions. Failure of locomotion in late infancy is often the primary (and pathognomonic symptom) (Segawa, 2001). Thus the impairment of the neural systems underlying locomotion may be the primary lesion in the pathophysiology of RS. Progressive cardiac dysfunction is common in classic RS (but much rarer in the so-called preserved speech variant – PSV-type) which may be associated with the sudden unexpected deaths observed in 26 per cent of the 1.2 per cent annual mortality rate in the syndrome (in comparison, the incidence of sudden unexpected death in the general population between 1 and 22 years is 1.3 per 100,000 individuals per year) (Guideri et al., 2001). Life expectancy, however, is not necessarily drastically reduced in RS. No systematic data are available on this question, but genetically ascertained cases of RS women aged 30 years and more have been documented. One of the oldest people with RS may be a 77-year-old woman (of the classic RS form) studied by Nielsen et al. (2001).

By 7 years of age, RS children are severely intellectually disabled (Witt-Engerstrom, 1987). In many RS children (with the classic Rett syndrome) language rarely develops beyond prelinguistic acquisition and single words. Hand skills peak between 10 and 12 months CA followed by the loss of purposeful hand use and the appearance of stereotyped hand movements and by ataxia (Kerr et al., 1987). In some cases, there is a complete failure to develop language (alalia – Trevathan and Moser, 1988) subjects not even showing behaviours interpretable as elementary intentions to communicate (for example, joint attention, gaze shifts and turns) (Coleman et al., 1988; Sandberg et al., 2000). It could be that RS patients with the classic variant could be divided into subgroups according to the age of disease onset, for example before and after the age of one year, with speech and motor functions significantly more severely affected in the earlier onset cases (Gratchev et al., 2001).

However, some RS girls (around 5 per cent – Kerr et al., 2001) (of the PSV-type) keep an ability to use at least some grammatical language, produced with articulation difficulties (Zapella, 1997). Zappella et al. (2001) have reported a clinical analysis of 18 PSV cases (aged from 10 to 30 years); 10 of them presented a MECP2 mutation. The course of their disorder was in stages, as in classic RS. All patients had a slow recovery of verbal and praxic abilities, and exhibited autistic behaviours. Six subjects had MAs of 2 to 3 years and were able to speak in sentences. Four subjects had MAs not beyond 1 to 2 years and spoke in single or two-word utterances. Analyses suggest that different types of mutations may be associated with the poorer Rett prognosis and the PSV variants. The classical Rett variant may be directly related to early truncating mutations whereas the PSV could be the result of late truncating mutations, plus the presence of one or more modifier genes interacting with the MECP2 protein.

Rubinstein-Taybi syndrome (RTS)

The RTS (Rubinstein and Taybi, 1963) is a rare syndrome (prevalence: one in 125,000 births – Hennekam et al., 1991) linked to a gene deletion on the short arm of chromosome 16 (16p13.3) in about 12 per cent of individuals (Lacombe et al., 1992 ; Wallerstein et al., 1997; Taine et al., 1998). Other genetic mechanisms are involved in the aetiology but they have escaped the investigations so far. Cases with confirmed deletions at 16p13.3 do not appear to be clinically distinguishable from those without detected deletions (cf. Wallerstein et al., 1997).

Current physical and medical features of RTS include congenital heart defects, urinary tract problems, palate abnormalities, dental problems, ocular problems, broad thumbs and first toes, undescended testes, frequent ear infections, and a tendency to be overweight (Stevens et al., 1990).

Intelligence quotient scores in RTS range from 3 to 79 points, with a mean of 51 (Stevens et al., 1990). Many RTS subjects are described as having short attention spans, difficulties in concentrating, impulsiveness, and poor coordination (Hennekam et al., 1992). Mood abnormalities and self-injury have been reported (Boer et al., 1999). Most children with RTS exhibit delay in speech development and some have articulation problems (Stevens et al., 1990). Lexical acquisitions are delayed with receptive vocabulary developing better than expressive vocabulary (Hennekam et al., 1992). Syntax is reduced with short utterances and sentences (MLU close to 3 in average values; Hennekam et al., 1992). The pragmatic abilities of RTS subjects also seem limited. Boer et al. (1999) signal repetitive speech and repetitive movements, verbal abuse, and overfriendliness with strangers.

Partial syndrome specificity

Table 3.1 displays the language profiles of the twelve genetic syndromes presented in the preceding section. Some of these syndromes are relatively well documented (although the extent of individual variations still needs to be more thoroughly analysed). Other syndromes demand more systematic investigations. The comparative analysis attempted in Table 3.1 and the following considerations must be considered as tentative. However, these data already allow for some interesting considerations.

Table 3.1 Typical language binary feature distribution in 12 ID syndromes

Syndromes	Phonetico phonological	Lexical	Morpho- syntactic	Pragmatic	Discursive
Down	– –	–	– –	+	– –
Williams	+ +	+	+	– –	+
Fragile-X (affected males)	– –	+	–	– –	–
Cri-du-chat (cat cry)	–	–	–	+	?
Prader-Willi	– –	–	–	–	–
Noonan	– –	–	–	+	?
Angelman	– –	– –	– –	– –	– –
Neuro- fibromatosis 1	–	–	–	–	–
Turner	?	+	+	+	+
Klinefelter	–	–	–	?	?
Rett (classic)	– –	– –	– –	– –	– –
Rubinstein- Taybi	–	–	– –	–	?

Key: +(+) relative strength; –(–) relative weakness; ? insufficient or contradictory data; classic Rett (i.e. the non-preserved speech variant.

As shown in Table 3.1, the extent of variation between the 12 genetic syndromes of ID considered (admittedly a limited sample in view of the estimated number of ID genetic syndromes) is substantial. It must be recalled that, whatever the syndrome, the range of IQ and MA are about the same (with the exceptions of Rett and Angelman syndromes drifting towards lower IQ levels, and Neurofibromatosis 1, Turner, and Klinefelter syndromes, towards higher IQ ranges). As group variables, IQ, MA, and other global cognitive measures do not seem well suited to accounting for the language differences between syndromes (even if, individually, they may predict the language levels, particularly regarding the more conceptual aspects of language – lexicon and semantics). Instead the documented differences plead for an aetiological approach to ID (see also Dykens et al., 2000; and Dykens and Hodapp, 2001). Such an approach has great potential for studying the organic underpinnings of the recurrent language problem in the various ID entities in greater depth, helping to define and design more specific and hopefully more efficient remediation strategies and, last but not least, helping significantly to enhance the knowledge of the relationships between genotypes and organic and behavioural phenotypes in the field of intellectual disability and the neurosciences. The syndrome differences amount to partial syndromic specificity in the field of language, at least for those syndromes of genetic origin. Additional research is needed to analyse the above comparisons in more detail, make full sense of their theoretical and practical implications and extend the search for language specific (or partially specific) profiles in other ID syndromes.

Partial syndrome specificity means that the non-aetiological conceptions of the past are not completely outmoded and could still be used to justify some generalizations and global remediation indications. It also implies that they must be complemented and, in some cases, supplemented by particular aetiological considerations. Viewed from the limited data available to date, full syndromic specificity already appears unlikely if not plainly impossible. Syndrome pathognomonic features do not seem to be in existence in the field of language and ID. Even outside of language, pathognomonic symptoms (according to Stedman's Medical Dictionary, 1990, characteristics of a disease denoting one or more symptom(s) or pattern(s) of abnormalities specific for a given disease and not found in any other condition) are exceptional in ID. Bellugi et al. (1990) have suggested that preserved performance in facial discrimination may be a specific neuropsychological marker of WS. Actually, this is the good performance on facial discrimination in the context of impaired spatial cognition (and partially preserved language function) that may constitute a particular characteristic of WS. What matters are syndrome profiles and systemic characteristics and not (or much less) syndrome individual features.

True, so to speak, pathognomonic markers may exist, however, but they are exceedingly rare. Cases in point are the extreme hyperphagia and food obsession typically found in PWS (Dykens and Cassidy, 1996) and the extreme self-mutilation behaviours described in Nesch-Nyhan syndrome (Nyhan, 1972), which are not found in other ID syndromes to anywhere the same degree.

From the above data and analyses it is clear that language remediation and work with DS and WS children ought to be organized according to differing aetiological priorities beyond common generalities. Down syndrome children, overall, need phonological, lexical, and morpho-syntactic remediation. Individuals with Williams syndrome are mostly in need of pragmatic, communication training and only secondarily of grammatical intervention. Correspondingly, it would be more beneficial for remediation with CDCS children to focus on their relatively better language receptive skills rather than relying on expressive techniques. Regarding AS and RS, it would be indicated to devote full attention to prelinguistic acquisitions at the beginning of the remediation procedure. These are a few quick examples awaiting more systematic analysis of the remediation implications of partial syndrome specificity. Behavioural remediation work typically seeks the subjects' weaknesses and tries to improve them, reducing the developmental delay and/or bringing about new and better phenotypic organization. However, aetiology-oriented work helps setting aside not only the typical syndrome weaknesses but also, and most importantly, the relative strength in each syndrome. These stronger aspects can then be used as scaffoldings for promoting further development.

The time of general remediative practices compulsorily identical in all ID cases with no serious syndrome consideration has probably passed. For the sake of efficiency, language therapists should also abide by aetiological specificities.

Explaining syndrome specificity

One reasonable possibility is that the intersyndrome variability corresponds in major ways to differences in neurodevelopment and brain structures. Individuals with DS are known to have central nervous system dysfunctions. Examination of DS brains reveals reductions in weight of the hemispheres, brain stem, and cerebellum, smaller overall brain and cerebellar volumes, relatively larger subcortical grey matter volumes, delays in myelinization (primarily in the association cortex), reductions in number of neurons in the whole cerebral cortex and particularly in some cortical layers (Pinter et al., 2001). DS persons have reduced synaptic density and abnormal synaptic morphology and contacts (Wisniewski and Kida, 1994). The presence of the above abnormalities from an early age in DS (cf. Pinter et al., 2001, using a higher-resolution magnetic resonance imagery – MRI – study) suggests that foetal or early postnatal differences with normal neurogenesis underlie the observed patterns and abnormalities. The abnormal neurogenesis in DS may primarily reflect genetically determined altered brain programming.

Available studies already point to important neurological differences between syndromes originating in different genetic bases that may explain the specific fractionation of language functions observed in the phenotypes. Research suggests that functional differences between WS and DS individuals correspond to syndromic variation at brain level. Bellugi et al. (1990) compared the neurological profiles of WS and DS adolescents matched for CA and IQ. The WS subjects demonstrated generalized hypotonia, tremor, midline balance problems, and motor abnormalities, suggestive of cerebellar dysfunction. Down syndrome adolescents showed minimal hypotonia, little evidence of palaeocerebellar signs, and better performance on oromotor functions. Both groups exhibited equal degrees of microcephaly, cerebral hypoplasia, reduced cerebral volume, and decreased myelination; but the overall brain shapes of each group proved distinct. DS brains exhibit important degrees of hypofrontality, whereas WS individuals show relative preservation of anterior cortical areas but have decreased posterior width with reduction in size of the forebrain posterior to the rolandic sulcus – the posterior parietal, temporal (with relative preservation of mesial-temporal, however) and occipital cortical regions. Individuals with WS have elongated posterior to anterior length compared with normal brains, a greater ratio of frontal to posterior (parietal-occipital) tissue, and disproportionate volume reduction of the brainstem (Reiss et al., 2000). Hypofrontality of neocortex in DS subjects, together with reduction in the frontal projections from the corpus callosum, was further demonstrated in a magnetic resonance imagery study by Wang et al. (1992). These authors relate this neuroanatomical indication to a profile of frontal lobe dysfunction in DS corresponding to poor verbal fluency, perseverative tendencies, and greater difficulty on tasks requiring flexible problem-solving strategies. Individuals with DS, however, have relatively preserved basal ganglia and diencephalic structures (Bellugi et al., 2000). In contrast, WS subjects exhibit better front- al, superior temporal gyrus volumes, and temporal limbic structures (Jernigan et al., 1993). In WS, there is also evidence of dysregulation of the control of neuronal and glial numbers, as illustrated by increased cell packing density at the cytoarchitectonic level (Galaburda et al., 1994). This may reflect an interference with naturally occurring cell death and the presence of neurotrophic factors (possibly linked to abnormal extracellular calcium levels). A study by Schmitt et al. (2001a, b) throws further light on the anatomy of the corpus callosum in individuals with WS. Compared to CA-matched ND controls, WS subjects (aged between 19 and 44 years) showed significantly reduced total midsagittal corpus callosum. However, the splenium and isthmus areas were disproportionately reduced in WS beyond the absolute reduction of the entire corpus callosum. The reductions may be set in concordance with the decreased parieto-occipital volumes and functionally with the observed visuospatial problems existing in WS. Electrophysiological studies (for example, using the event-related potential technique of sentence processing) suggest abnormal patterns of cerebral specialization for language treatment in persons with WS (Bellugi et al., 1999; Mills et al., 2000).

The cerebellar volume in DS subjects is approximately 77 per cent of the equivalent in young normal controls, versus 99 per cent in WS subjects. Although cerebellar size is intact and the neocerebellum largely preserved or even enlarged in WS (Schmitt et al., 2001a, b), some other neurological findings are suggestive of cerebellar dysfunction. The posterior fossa structures of the WS and DS subjects were further examined by Bellugi et al. (1990), leading to the identification, in WS, of an anomalous pattern, with neocerebellar vermal lobules showing hyperplasia in the context of low-normal palaeocerebellar vermal development and significantly reduced forebrain size. Such an aberrant cerebrum/cerebellum volume ratio could serve to distinguish WS neurologically from other syndromes such as DS (Courchesne et al., 1988). Bellugi et al. (1990) speculate (in agreement with suggestions by Leiner et al. 1991, 1993, and Fabbro et al., 2000, regarding the possible role of human neocerebellar structures in linguistic functions) that the observed hyperplasia of specific vermal lobules in the context of cerebellar maldevelopment may be related to the language profile of WS subjects. Bellugi et al. (1990) further remark that their WS subjects were behaviourally grossly similar to unilateral right-hemisphere damaged (normal) adults, whereas the DS individuals were more like left-hemisphere damaged aphasics, demonstrating language impairment and a marked tendency towards more global information processing. Atkinson et al. (1997) examined the neural basis of the deficit in visuospatial integration, action (for example, locomotion over uneven surfaces), and manipulation of objects, as opposed to preserved (and even often better than normal) visual (particularly face) recognition in WS individuals. They suggest that the cerebral dorsal cortical 'stream' function, which processes the information required for the visual guidance of actions, particularly the precise control of hand and the analysis of the positions of objects or parts of objects relative to each other and relative to the observer, is deficient in WS, whereas the 'ventral stream' transmitting other information to temporal lobe structures involved in the recognition of objects and faces is largely preserved or even overfunctioning (also Atkinson et al., 2001). It is attested, indeed, that in the midst of serious perceptual-cognition problems (relating particularly to the integration of visual stimuli and spatial cognition), face processing and recognition is preserved in WS and sometimes even better than in ND controls (Rosen et al., 1995; Bellugi et al., 2000).

Brain systems specific to face recognition seem to exist. One important line of evidence comes from brain-injured patients with prosopagnosia. The lesions that produce this disorder, consisting in an inability to recognize familiar faces without a concomitant decrement in other forms of object recognition, are usually bilateral (with a greater involvement of the right than the left cerebral hemisphere) and extend along temporal and occipital regions (Damasio et al., 1990). Accordingly, it is possible that these brain areas are largely preserved or even enlarged and more functional in WS individuals than in ND people. A precise link from neuroanatomy to the genes is still lacking, but it is, no doubt, amenable to discovery in the near future as more genes with brain developmental effects are identified within the WS aetiological deletion.

Neurological differences in other genetic syndromes have been less studied. In many male subjects with FXS, decreased posterior cerebellar vermis size is observed (Hagerman, 1996). As this neurological structure is involved with processing sensory stimuli and modulating motor activity, the above indication is consistent with the motor deficits (Friefeld and MacGregor, 1993), as well as with the inattention, hyperactivity, and hypersensitivity to stimuli, seen in many FXS males (Mostofsky et al., 1998). Decreased amounts of FMRP (the FMR-1 protein) impair the development of the cerebellum Purkinje cells, the cholinergic neurons innervating the limbic system (involved in emotional and mood regulation), and other neuronal tissues (grey matter particularly) that normally exhibit high concentrations of FMRP. Conversely, in males and females with FXS, there are enlargements of some brain structures such as the hippocampus (a major convergence zone in the cortex involved, among other things, in the storage and consolidation of long-term declarative memories), the ventricles, the thalamus, and the caudate nucleus (Reiss et al., 1995). These findings may be associated with perseverations, stereotypies, hyperactivity, attentional impairment, and other problems in planning and executive functions such as inhibiting responses, regulating affect and motor activity (Abrams and Reiss, 1995). Head circumference is typically large in male FXS individuals, in contrast to the microcephaly found in DS and many other ID syndromes. This suggests a failure of neuronal priming mechanisms at early stages of brain development (Hagerman, 1996).

In RS, electrophysiology demonstrates progressively abnormal electro-encephalograms. Neurometabolic factors including reduced levels of dopamine, serotonin, noradrenaline, and choline acetyltransferase in the brain have been documented (cf. Dunn, 2001). Hyperfunction of the aminergic neurons (noradrenaline, serotonin, and dopamine in the brainstem and midbrain) has been suggested as the main cause of dysfunction of the neuronal systems involving primarily locomotion and hand use, and secondarily the development of language and cognitive functions (Segawa, 2001).

Regarding KS, Geschwind et al. (2000) propose that altered left-hemisphere functioning, whether causing or due to altered functional and anatomical cerebral dominance, is at the core of KS individuals' language problems. But, of course, the interaction of neurogenetic syndrome needs to be further explored. A study by Patwardhan et al. (2000) offers an important elaboration on the effect of supernumerary X chromosome material in men. These authors have measured regional brain volumes with high-resolution magnetic resonance imagery (MRI) in a cohort of 10 young adults with (47XXY) KS and 10 CA controls. They document a significant lower volume in left temporal grey matter volumes in KS subjects when compared with normal control subjects. Differences in left temporal grey matter volumes were also significant between the KS subjects treated with exogenous testosterone supplementation since puberty and those KS subjects who did not receive this treatment. The former group of subjects significantly outperformed the second group in verbal fluency scores obtained from a test of word associations – the COWAT (Controlled Oral Word Association Test).

For TS, Murphy et al. (1997) suggest that the generalized brain hypermetabolism they observed in young female adults reflects global abnormalities in neuron packing whereas the lower regional metabolism observed in the association cortices reflects neuronal abnormalities related to the cognitive deficits typical of the condition.

Individual language variability

Individual differences within syndromes have been little studied systematically, and even less accounted for theoretically. This is the case in the field of language as well as in any other field of intellectual disability. Recent research on rare cases of exceptionally favourable language development and functioning in ID reveal that the individual variability may be extensive toward the positive pole of the distribution. Regarding the negative pole, I know of no systematic study. Clinical experience has it that there are difficult cases, fortunately rare, where speech and/or language limitations are severe. Looking at the whole distribution of language abilities in ID syndromes will probably make it appear quite large, much larger than the usual (but little specified too) span of interindividual differences in the language of ND people.

Table 3.2 lists a number of selected cases of exceptionally favourable language development in ID individuals (for a full review and other cases, see Rondal 1995, and Rondal and Edwards, 1997).

U. Bellugi (personal communication, 3 March 1997) has suggested that the three cases documented in her 1988 paper (together with Marks, Bihrle and Sabo) may be standard for WS. Van, Crystal, and Ben demonstrated correct phoneme discrimination and articulation, receptive vocabulary at the 9- to 12-year level, and advanced receptive and expressive morphosyntactic abilities, although not quite at CA level. Their speech included full passives, embedded relative clauses, conditionals, and multiple embeddings. They were able to correct ungrammatical

Table 3.2 Exceptional cases of language development and functioning in ID individuals

Study	Subjects	Aetiology	CA[a]	IQ[b]	MA[c]	MLU[d]	Cognitive Level
1. Bellugi, Marks, Bihrle and Sabo (1988)	Van	WS[e]	11	50		8.6	Preoperatory[f]
	Crystal	WS	15	49		13.10	Preoperatory
	Ben	WS	16	54		10.00	Preoperatory
2. Curtiss (1989) Yamada (1990)	Antony	Unknown	6	50	2.9 years		Preoperatory
	Rick	Unknown	15				Preoperatory
	Laura	Unknown	16	32			Preoperatory
3. Cromer (1991, 1993)	DH	Unknown	Adolescent	< 35			Severely retarded
4. Vallar and Papagno (1993)	FF	DS[g]	23	63			Grossly defective in reasoning[h]
5. O'Connor and Hermelin (1991); Smith and Tsimpli (1995)	Christopher	Unknown	29	42–67[i]			Severe problems in spatial cognition. Failure on tasks of number conversation
6. Rondal (1995)	Françoise	DS	32	60	5.8 years		Late preparatory to early operatory

Notes:
a. CA: chronological age (in years) at beginning of study.
b. IQ: nonverbal intellectual quotient according to standard intellectual scales.
c. Mental age (in years and months).
d. Mean length of utterance (computed in a number of words plus inflectional morphemes).
e. Williams syndrome.
f. According to Piagetian criteria and with reference to Piaget's cognitive developmental theory.
g. Down syndrome (the two cases are standard trisomy 21).
h. Raven Progressive Matrices and Wisconsin Card Sorting Test.
i. Christopher was given the WAIS (Wechsler, 1958) several times, the resulting IQ varying between 42 and 67. Empty boxes in Table correspond to pieces of information not supplied by the authors in the original sources.

sentences due to violations of subcategorization features, phrase structure rules, or errors in reflexive pronoun usage. As indicated before, numerous WS adults enjoy relatively good language abilities. Their vocabulary acquisition, however, may not be fully normal and their sentence comprehension and use of morphosyntactic devices are not intact. Contrary to Bellugi's suggestion, therefore, the language skills of Van, Crystal, and Ben may be particularly favourable even when compared with other WS adolescents or adults.

The three subjects studied by Curtiss (1989) and Yamada (1990) exhibited extreme dissociations between cognitive and language levels. Antony's speech was well formed phonologically, and morphosyntactically appropriate with fully elaborated inflectional and derivational bound morphology and free grammatical morphemes. It included syntactic structures involving movement, embedding, and complementation. In contrast, his language was semantically deficient. Antony often used words incorrectly and failed to grasp the full meaning of his own and others' utterances. He had poorly developed topic maintenance skills, was only moderately sensitive to the interests of his interlocutors and apparently little concerned with the need to be relevant or informative in conversation.

Rick's language paralleled that of Antony. Rick had well-developed phonological, morphological, and syntactic abilities, alongside poorly developed lexical and semantic abilities. He had difficulties in correctly understanding the meaning of the utterances addressed to him and made mistakes in his lexical and propositional utterances.

Laura's linguistic profile is similar to those of Rick and Antony, with the proviso that her lexicon was richer, in particular containing more quantifiers and adverbs. Laura's level on the PPVT was 6 years and 1 month. Despite her larger vocabulary, she presented semantic, pragmatic, and discursive deficiencies akin to those of Rick and Antony. However, Laura's language was phonologically correct, fully elaborated morphologically, and contained complex and well-formed syntactic structures. She produced full passives, sentences with coordinated and subordinated clauses, including WH-relatives, multiple embeddings, infinitival complements, and complement containing participial forms. Receptively, the picture was different. Laura demonstrated genuine grammatical difficulties in comprehension. On the Curtiss-Yamada Comprehensive Language Evaluation (CYCLE, 1992), her receptive performance was poor in syntax. She performed at or below the 2-year-old level on most subtests, including the object manipulation version of various tasks (for example, active and passive voice word order, WH-questioning of grammatical subject and object in relativization tests). In her spontaneous speech, Laura produced many of the structures that she failed to understand on the comprehension tests. On the Token Test (De Renzi and Vignolo, 1962), which evaluates the ability to understand sentences of varying syntactic complexity, Laura scored below the mean score of ND children aged 3 years 6 months. Her comprehension of grammatical morphemes likewise was reduced. On the CYCLE battery of morphology, she demonstrated mastery over only two grammatical morphemes (tense/aspect marker -ing and comparative -er). It is remarkable that she spontaneously and correctly produced some of the same forms that she could be proved not to understand in controlled receptive tasks.

Cromer (1991, 1993) has reported the case of DH, a spina bifida adolescent girl with arrested hydrocephalus. She has been unable to learn to

and general cognitive level comparable to ND two-year-olds that their grammar starts developing (Singer et al., 1994). These data are consistent with the view that a cognitive-semantic basis amounting to what is known by ND children around 20 to 24 months and severely and moderately MR children around 4 to 5 years CA (MA around 24 months), is needed for the grammatical component to start working, when such a component is indeed available.

The preceding discussion should not be taken to mean that particular cognitive mechanisms could not, in principle, have a role in phonological and grammatical development. One such mechanism may be short-term (or working) memory (Baddeley, 1990). Gathercole and Baddeley (1993) have suggested that auditory-vocal short-term memory (AV-STM) – one of the basic components, together with visuospatial short-term memory (VS-STM), and a central executive and attentional system, in Baddeley's (1990) working memory model – is directly involved in several aspects of language acquisition. Correlational evidence for a link between non-word repetition ability (known to depend on the proper functioning of the phonological loop, a subcomponent of AV-STM) and size of receptive vocabulary in children and teenagers has been reported (see, for example, Gathercole et al., 1992; Laws, 1998; see Bowey, 1996, 1997, however, for a criticism arguing that previous work on the subject has failed to separate the phonological memory component from the phonological processing components of the non-word repetition task involved in constructing a phonological representation of a spoken non-word and reconstructing this representation into speech output). A mechanism possibly accounting for this relationship is that the longer the new word is held in short-term storage, the greater its chance of being learned. This might help explain the difficulty of language-disordered children in learning new words despite normal conceptual development (Gathercole and Baddeley, 1990). These children could have poor short-term phonological storage capacities, which would render learning new words more difficult. The same reasoning may be applied to ID individuals (Jarrold et al., 1999). Typical moderately and severely ID children, adolescents, and adults have important limitations in AV-STM (MacKenzie and Hulme, 1987; Rondal, 1995; Rondal and Comblain, 1999), which could be responsible in part for their difficulties in vocabulary learning. A noisier functioning of the phonological loop, less efficient rehearsal strategies (whether purely articulatory, auditory, or both; and slower speech rhythm – Rondal, 1995 – given that immediate memory span corresponds to the number of items that can be uttered in about two seconds – Baddeley, 1990; Cowan, 1992), could render unstable the organization of phonological representations of new words in STM, which could hinder the construction of long-term memory representations. These difficulties would add to the conceptual deficits to make vocabulary development problematic. However, Jarrold et al. (2000) have expressed doubts regarding the sufficiency of the limitations cited in

order to explain the poor verbal memory of DS individuals. They suggest
an additional explanation: encoding difficulties. If the information entering the phonological store is of a lower quality, recall would necessarily be
poorer even if the phonological loop and the AV-STM processes were
intact. Jarrold et al. correctly acknowledge that an encoding deficit of this
sort places the locus of impairment partially or totally outside of the STM
system. I have long suspected that articulatory difficulties and early lexical
limitations negatively interact with AV-STM development in DS. One
should not exclude quicker trace fading, modality notwithstanding, given
that VS-STM in DS is similarly reduced or only slightly better than AV-STM
(Marcell and Armstrong, 1982; Marcell and Weeks, 1988; Jarrold and
Baddeley, 1997; Rondal, 1995, 1998; Rondal and Comblain, 1999). One
could indeed hypothesize that speech encoding and even language development as a whole play as important a role in the development of working
memory as the components charted in Baddeley's standard model. Data
published by Seung and Chapman (2000) supply a beginning empirical
basis for this claim. These authors report that language production level
(for example, MLU) accounted for substantial variance in digit span of individuals with DS.

Considering language-atypical ID individuals, it is unlikely that the
same phonological memory limitations as for typical ID subjects could be
advocated to explain their lexical limitations. Curtiss's Antony and Rick
have AV-STMs at the 6- to 7-year-old level. Yet they demonstrate marked
productive and receptive lexical difficulties. The same is true of Laura,
studied by Yamada. But Laura's AV-STM span does not exceed three items.
Part of her lexical difficulties may have to do with limitations in phonological memory. Françoise's AV-STM span is four items (digits, words,
non-words). She has near-normal AV-STM processes (attested by phonological similarity, word-length, and Brown Peterson effects, when recalling
verbal material – cf. Baddeley, 1990) and she uses rehearsal strategies relying on semi-private speech. The relative underdevelopment of her lexicon
cannot be explained in terms of phonological memory limitations. Nor
can it be suggested (following Jarrold et al., 2000) that the lexical limitations of Françoise and those of other atypical-language ID individuals
stem (even partially) from speech encoding or language difficulties. The
lexical deficits exhibited by Curtiss's subjects, as well as the milder lexical
limitations of Françoise, must be traced primarily to their conceptual
shortcomings, mutatis mutandis for regular ID/DS individuals. This suggests that the impact of the conceptual limitations on vocabulary
development are underestimated in Jarrold et al.'s (2000) analysis.

Vallar and Papagno (1993) claimed that their subject FF's better AV-STM
span (5.75) and articulatory rehearsal explain her good acquisition of the
Italian vocabulary. This is not convincing in the absence of systematic
vocabulary assessment. The authors may have based their suggestion on
the standardized score (8 points; population mean 10) obtained by FF on

the vocabulary subtest of the WAIS (actually a metalexical task consisting in defining vocabulary items).

A positive contribution of AV-STM to vocabulary development, due to a better functioning of the phonological loop, cannot be ruled out in some language-atypical ID individuals. Given the data exposed, however, such a contribution must be conceived of as quite limited.

Working memory has also been claimed to play a role in language comprehension (Baddeley, 1990). The phonological store might have a buffering role in retaining strings of incoming words for a period of time pending the construction of more durable representations of the sentence. This could prove particularly so with longer sentences. Again, relevant data from the ID language-atypical subjects do not concur with such a hypothesis. As indicated, Françoise's AV span is four units. Her sentence span is 14 words, however. At times, she can repeat correctly sentences containing up to 20 words. This is near-normal functioning (Craik and Massani, 1969). In contrast, typical DS adults, used as controls, could not repeat correctly sentences containing more than five to eight words. In controlled tasks, Françoise had no problem correctly interpreting (centre-)embedded subject and object relatives when the relative pronouns and their coreferring nouns were separated by several incoming words. Nor did she have difficulties in establishing pronominal coreference across sentences in non-ambiguous paragraph interpretation, or with personal pronouns and coreferring nouns separated by incoming words. The contribution of Françoise's immediate phonological memory to sentence treatment may therefore be considered minimal.

Explaining intrasyndrome variation

There is no indication that particular remedial procedures were responsible for the formal language abilities of the exceptional ID individuals. Therefore one has to look for internal variables in order to make sense of atypical formal language abilities demonstrated in ID people. Yamada (1990) suggested that the formal language abilities of her exceptional subject Laura had much to do with the fact that Laura was left-hemisphere dominant for the language functions (as are the vast majority of ND people – see Bresson, 1991). Such is also the case of Françoise (unfortunately, no corresponding data have been published for the other ID subjects with atypical linguistic talent). However, this evidence is not sufficient to warrant the validity of Yamada's hypothesis. Indeed, I have reported (Rondal, 1995) corresponding data for 24 DS adults with typical language abilities for DS (15 males and 9 females, aged 21 to 36 years) in a dichotic-listening task and 19 of the same DS adults in a dual-task study (Kinsbourne and Hiscock, 1983). A large number of these subjects showed interference between verbalization and right-hand movements in the dual task, compatible with the hypothesis of a left-hemisphere (LH) dominance for speech production. In the dichotic-listening task, three females exhibited a right-ear advantage (from 30 per cent to 70 per cent), suggesting LH dominance for speech reception. Six males also exhibited a right-ear advantage (from 10 per cent to 63 per cent). Retaining those individuals for whom the right-ear advantage was equal to or in excess of 50 per cent, one had two female and one male individuals. All three subjects demonstrated a positive relative amount of interference in the dual task, suggesting LH dominance for speech production. They could be considered homogeneous as to cerebral hemispheric dominance for the speech functions. This was also the case for Françoise. However, the language abilities of the above three DS adults were only average for DS persons. Left-hemisphere dominance may be a necessary condition for advanced language development in favourable natural conditions (outside early focal brain possibly determining a (partial) transfer of the language control from the left perisylvian areas to areas of the right cerebral hemisphere – Verger and Junque, 2000; theoretically such a situation does not concern ID/DS individuals who are not supposed to present unilateral focal brain lesions as a primary result of their condition). Left-hemisphere dominance, however, cannot be a sufficient condition for exceptionally favourable formal language development in people with ID.

I have suggested elsewhere (Rondal, 1998, in press) that the major determinants of morphosyntactic and phonological differences between atypical and typical ID individuals probably operate at brain level. The brain areas responsible for the expressive and receptive treatments of the formal aspects of language in ND adults involve the posterior perisylvian sector of the left-cerebral hemisphere with respect to the processing of speech sounds, phoneme assembly into words, and selection of word forms; the anterior perisylvian sector of the left hemisphere with respect to receptive and expressive morphosyntax (Damasio and Damasio, 1989).

As indicated earlier in this chapter, brain studies in individuals with DS, WS and FXS reveal major anomalies. Currently, no other genetic syndromes leading to ID have been the object of systematic neuroanatomical investigation. The macroscopic brain structures devoted to the treatment of the formal aspects of language (as opposed to the more conceptual ones) may be spared to a large extent in those ID individuals with atypical language abilities, whereas the same brain structures remain underdeveloped in typical ID people. I have further suggested (Rondal, 1998, in press) that atypical ID individuals with genetic syndromes escape the latter fate for reasons related to favourable phenotypic effects of genetic variation. Geneticists agree that there is substantial variation at the genetic level between people within DS, WS, and other genetic causes of ID (Dykens, 1995). Most genetic influences on phenotypes are not discrete. The inheritance patterns may be a blend between single gene and polygenic influences (Smith et al., 1996). Complex traits show a quantitative variation in their presentation. Major sources of variation are: first, major genes involved in a phenotype showing variable penetrance (the proportion of individuals affected with a given susceptibility); second, variable expression of a single major or of a number of genes involved in a phenotype, due to the modifying influence of other genes or environmental factors; third, a major gene can have several possible mutations (alleles) that may differentially affect the corresponding phenotype and, fourth, imprinting effects – variability of gene expression associated with parental origin (father versus mother) of the genetic material.

Genetic research is yielding more precise gene identification and mapping of a number of chromosomes. Korenberg et al. (1994) have indicated that DS, aetiologically linked to chromosome 21, is a contiguous gene syndrome, meaning that many adjacent genes contribute to the specific phenotype. This weighs against any single chromosomal region being responsible for the DS features. Down syndrome and its phenotypes are the result of the overexpression and subsequent interactions of a subset of the genes located on chromosome 21. Korenberg et al. (1994) designate a region of 2-20 megabases between region p11.2 and 22.3 on the distal part of the long arm of chromosome 21 as containing the genes responsible for 25 features considered typical of DS. This conception is consistent with the rich variety of phenotypes and the variability in both penetrance and expression of the DS features. Correspondingly, for WS syndrome (defined as a contiguous gene deletion syndrome), 18 genes, including the elastin locus at chromosome 7q11.23, have been identified (Korenberg et al., 2000), the hemizygous deletion of which is responsible for the characteristics of this syndrome.

It is conceivable that there could be significant within-syndrome variability at brain level in the language area of DS, WS, and other individuals with genetic syndromes, consequent upon genetic variation. The brain-gene perspective has the advantage of proposing a single explanation for the variability currently observed in the language of typical ID people and the extremes of such variability in atypical cases. It is also compatible with the explanatory orientation proposed earlier for the syndrome differences identified. The genotype-brain phenotype perspective defined here supplies a coherent theoretical framework for dealing with the new research data in the field of intellectual disability.

Lastly, it should be kept in mind that language-exceptional ID subjects are atypical mostly with respect to the phonological and morphosyntactic aspects of language. Their lexical abilities are less impressive (with the possible exception of Christopher). The conceptual and the formal language difficulties of ID people have different roots. The former originate in their cognitive limitations and are unavoidable as such. The latter do not stem from limitations in general cognition, as proved by the atypical cases. They probably arise from basic impairments in brain structures responsible for particular functions.

Ageing persons with intellectual disabilities

People with intellectual disabilities live longer these days than was the case before (for example, the average DS lifespan has sextupled since the beginning of the twentieth century). Recent estimates for Down syndrome (for example, Baird and Sadovnick, 1995; Jancar and Jancar, 1996) suggest a life expectancy beyond 68 years for over 15 per cent and 55 years for over 50 per cent of people with DS. Strauss and Eyman (1996) estimate the life expectancy in people with DS to be around 55 years in average value. Between the years 2000 and 2025, the number of adults with DS will likely double. No corresponding estimates are currently available for other ID syndromes. That is why the remaining part of this section will be devoted almost exclusively to DS. Except for the question of a greater susceptibility in this syndrome to a form of Alzheimer disease (AD) in ageing people (see below), the problem of a possible language deterioration in older ID people with other syndromes can be defined in basically the same terms as for DS. Further progress in the knowledge of the brain and behavioural phenotypes of these other ID syndromes in ageing people will allow their problems with language and otherwise to be addressed.

The gains in longevity have motivated an increased interest in the ageing of DS people. About three decades ago, the possibility of a marked susceptibility of DS individuals to a degenerative condition known as Alzheimer disease (AD) was noted, as well as a tendency towards earlier anatomo-physiological and neuropsychological age-linked deterioration in comparison with ND and possibly ID people of other aetiologies. It was even suggested that beyond 35 to 40 years most if not all DS persons would develop a form of AD leading to major debility and the loss of most of the skills acquired earlier in life.

More recent work has somewhat improved this prognosis. It is now admitted (Wisniewski and Silverman, 1999) that DS does not necessarily mean progressive deterioration during middle age. There is no question, however, that there exists an elevated risk of AD or AD-like disease. AD actually is not a single but a complex of related diseases[1] in DS (between 25 and 45 per cent beyond 55 years – Zigman et al., 1997; Van Buggenhout et al., 2001). Neurological examination of the brains of DS persons who died over the age of 30 years reveal that pathological changes associated with AD (for example, brain atrophy, nerve cell loss, neurotransmitter changes, senile plaques, and neurofibrillary tangles – Mann, 1992) have taken place in the amygdala, hippocampus, and the frontal, temporal, and parietal cortices (Holland and Oliver, 1996, for a review). However, for these DS persons developing AD, there may be a 10- to 15-year latency period (as opposed to the typical 4 or 5 years in ND people) between the presence of important AD-type neuropathological changes, appearing at around 30 to 35 years, and clinical dementia that is undetectable in many DS adults until much later (Wisniewski and Silverman, 1996). Given the range of individual differences in both the neuropathological and clinical expression of AD in DS, it is possible that other genes (yet to be identified) located on chromosome 21 or other chromosomes (for example, the apo-E allele on chromosome 19) may influence the pathological process and be of equal or greater importance for the clinical manifestations of AD than is the triplication of the beta-amyloid precursor gene (also located on chromosome 21 and supplying one key factor to the AD neuropathology – see Zigman et al., 1996).

A limited number of studies have centred on cerebral metabolism in older DS individuals. Schapiro et al. (1987) measured the cerebral metabolic rate for glucose (CMRG) in cohorts of ND and DS individuals aged between 19 and 64 years. Mean hemispheric CMRG was lower in the older than in the younger DS subjects (and, as a rule, lower in DS than in ND subjects). Only some older DS subjects were clinically demented even if age reductions in neurological variables seemed to occur in most of them. In another cerebral study, however, Schapiro et al. (1992) found similar CMRG in non-demented DS persons over 35 years of age and ND controls. Another similar finding is supplied by Dani et al. (1996). In contrast, Deb et al. (1992) reported cerebral metabolic rates in seven older DS subjects comparable to those of younger DS subjects and slightly diminished rates (particularly in the posterior parieto-temporal and occipital zones) in nine other non-demented older DS subjects. Developments in the histopathological approach to dementia suggest, however, that age is probably not the sole cause, and may not even be the primary cause, of senile dementia (Brion and Plas, 1987). Moreover, DS people exposed to less stimulating environment later in life aged individuals, may suffer from (treatable) pseudodementias (often misdiagnosed as depressive states) (Campbell-Taylor, 1993; Florez, 2000).

The question remains, however, of a possible earlier onset of neuropsychological decline in DS adults unrelated to AD incipiens for most individuals (Brown, 1985), but more marked than in ID individuals with other aetiologies than DS (Thompson, 1999). Van Buggenhout et al. (2001) report a significant increase in the proportion of DS persons presenting additional health problems beyond 50 years (for example, hearing and sight losses, hypothyroidy). Although there are few data available on this topic, it would appear that the DS adults advancing in age are well aware of their increased functional limitations (such as lowering of cognitive and physical performance, loss of sensorial acuity, skin problems, additional dental and health problems; with men seemingly tending to resent these limitations more than women – Hannecart and Haelewyck, 2002).

Predispositions towards earlier ageing in DS may be associated with the overexpression of genes located on chromosome 21, distinct from the gene coding for amyloid preprotein. Similarly, the clinical phenotype of DS can be modulated by genes on chromosomes other than chromosome

21 (Royston et al., 1994) but these genes remain to be identified (Wisniewski and Silverman, 1996). Research is needed to assess the abilities of DS persons in their forties, and beyond, and to measure possible declines in neuropsychological functioning.

My co-workers and I have collected series of data relevant to the ageing question regarding language and other cognitive functions – particularly memory (Comblain, 1996; Rondal and Comblain, 1996; George et al., 1999, 2001).[2] The same instrument for analysing morphosyntactic aspects of language (BEMS; Batterie pour l'Évaluation de la Morpho-Syntaxe – Comblain, 1995) was used with three cohorts of DS subjects of different ages allowing fine cross-sectional comparisons (mean CAs approximately 16 years, 26 years, and 44 years respectively; mean MAs close to 4 years and 6 months in the three groups). The subjects were compared on the receptive subtests of the BEMS – nominal coreference in the case of personal pronouns, definite and indefinite articles, temporal morphological inflections, negative sentences, reversible and non-reversible passive sentences, sentences with coordinate clauses, sentences with temporal, causal, conditional, or consequential subordinate clauses, and sentences with relative subordinates in *qui* (grammatical subject) or *que* (direct grammatical object). None of the (minimal) differences registered in the receptive morphosyntactic functioning of the DS individuals in the three cohorts proved statistically significant at the conventional probability levels.

Regarding language production, no direct comparison of the younger and the older adults was possible because the same set of language productive measures was not used for comparing the adolescent and the younger adult groups (in what were actually two studies) (see below, in Comparison II, for the productive measures used). The paper by Rondal and Comblain (1996) contains the productive data resulting from the comparison of the same DS adolescents and younger adults as in the present report. Accordingly, no significant change was observed in mean length of utterance (MLU), or on an index of expressive morphosyntax and expressive referential lexicon (TVAP: Test de Vocabulaire Actif et Passif), or on a home-made test of lexical labelling (Test de Vocabulaire Productif – Comblain, 1996). Although I do not have specific data at hand to support my view, it is unlikely that marked changes in productive language would take place between 30 and 40 years in DS persons, particularly given that no significant change has been documented in the receptive abilities of the same DS persons and that no significant productive or receptive change has been revealed either by our analyses of the language of DS persons between 40 and 50 years (see below).

I argued some time ago upon reviewing the literature (cf. Rondal, 1995; Rondal and Comblain, 1996; Rondal and Edwards, 1997) that significant progress does not take place, at least in the phonological and the grammatical aspects of language, beyond roughly mid-adolescence. As I also indicated, progress may still be observed beyond that age in the conceptual and the pragmatic aspects of language (for example, vocabulary, semantics, conversational and more generally communicative abilities, and discourse organization). Hence the necessity to clearly distinguish between language components in these types of analyses. There are a few ambiguous suggestions and claims in the recent literature regarding the possibility of continuing language development in late adolescence and early adulthood in DS. Chapman (1999), for example, has documented progress over time (until 20 years CA; cross-sectional study design) in the discourse narratives of some DS subjects. She refuted the maturational hypothesis proposed by Lenneberg (1967) and Fowler (1990), according to which no marked language improvement is possible beyond early adolescence. I have suggested (Rondal and Edwards, 1997; Rondal and Comblain, 2002) that it makes more empirical sense to restrict maturational susceptibility to more formal components of language. Chapman's and other data, apparently contradicting the maturational hypothesis, are actually compatible with such a modified conception.

George et al. (1999; 2001) conducted a four-year longitudinal study with 12 DS subjects aged between 37 and 49 years (half women and half men). Their language functions (receptive as well as productive) were assessed at one-year intervals during the first two years. Four subjects did not maintain their participation beyond the second year. For the others, the study was continued for another two years using the same evaluation procedure. For eight subjects (four women and four men) a measure of cerebral metabolic rate (CMR) was made every year using the PET (positron emission tomography) scan technique. The cerebral imagery investigation was prolonged for two more years with seven of the eight subjects (one died in the meantime). The BEMS was used to assess receptive morphosyntax. A receptive lexical task (picture designation) adapted and modified after Bishop and Byng's (1984) test was given too. A task of verbal (semantic) fluency was applied. Subjects were requested to give verbally the largest possible number of category names in a period of one minute. The TVP was also administered. It counted 127 items divided into five semantic categories (fruits, clothes, vegetables, kitchen tools and objects, and animals). The phonetic length of the items was controlled (items of 1, 2, or 3 syllables long were presented), as well as the frequency of appearance of these items in the French language. Lastly, the test 'Récit sur images' (a narrative text about pictures; verbal recall, adapted from Chevrie-Müller, 1981) was given. This test takes into account the number of global ideas, words, and several formal and semantic characteristics of the narratives as the subjects freely recall them.

The statistical analyses carried out on the language measures (receptive as well as productive) failed to yield any significant result. Moreover, neither the syllabic length of the lexical items in the test nor their relative frequency in French actually influenced the lexical scores of the DS adults.

As to the CMR data, the left and right frontal, parietal, and temporal cortices of each subject were examined and the visual metabolic images from the associative cortical regions were evaluated in a semi-quantitative way on a scale from zero (normal metabolism) to two (severe metabolic reduction) (Hoffman et al., 1996). No CMR image proved normal in the strict acceptation in any DS subject and there was important interindividual variability. Metabolic reduction was more marked globally for the left hemisphere. Along the time dimension, there was a gradual decrease in global CMR for each of the two cerebral hemispheres and for the DS person. The average decreases, however, were largely due to three subjects in the cohort. Analysing the individual performances of these three subjects in the language tasks over the same interval of time, no clear indication of deterioration emerged that could be meaningfully related to the lowering CMR. It is possible, therefore, that global brain metabolism (particularly within the left cerebral hemisphere) can diminish subtantially in some DS persons without clear negative consequences – at least temporarily – on the language functions.

As our data show, no marked significant change seems to take place in the language of DS individuals between late adolescence and approximately 50 years. This is worth noting as functional modifications of language and memory have often been indicated as first signs of earlier ageing and degenerative diseases. Jodar (1992), for example, has suggested that in normal ageing, lexical and verbal comprehension are mostly preserved whereas verbal fluency, lexical labelling, and, more generally, the capacity for verbal production tend to decline. In cross-sectional work with 44 Italian DS individuals (25 males and 19 females) ranging in age from 14 to 43 years (average CA close to 26 years), centring on visual-perceptual abilities (using the Frostig Developmental Test of Visual Perception – DTVP – Frostig et al., 1963) and adaptive behaviour (using an Italian adaptation – Pedrabissi and Soresi, 1989 – of the Adaptive Behaviour Inventory of Brown and Leigh, 1986), Saviolo-Negrin et al. (1990) reported no significant age difference in their DS subjects regarding adaptive behaviour but a significant – if limited – decline in visual perception beyond 25 years of age, except in the visuomotor subtest of the DTVP.

What happens beyond 50 years or so in people with DS is not known at present for lack of systematic data. Hints may be derived from the limited literature in existence, pending verification in more extensive studies. Little to no change has been recorded in non-verbal reasoning, memory, receptive and expressive vocabulary, planning and attention, perceptual-motor, and adaptive skills until close to 60 years in a study by Das et al. (1995). However, the same authors signal that older DS subjects in their cohorts (slightly beyond 60 years) were actually performing worse than those in younger groups, particularly in tasks requiring planning and attention. This could tentatively be related to Ribes and Sanuy's (2000) observation of a slight decline in expressive language (particularly vocabulary) in some of their DS subjects beyond 38 years, with Prasher's (1996) suggestion regarding the existence of age-associated functional decline in short-term memory, speech, practical skills, activity, and general interests in approximately 20 per cent of individuals with DS aged 50 to 71 years, and with Moss et al.'s (2000) indication regarding a significant inverse relation of age to several aspects of auditory linguistic comprehension in a sample of DS adults between 32 and 65 years.

Cross-sectional studies are, of course, limited in their ability to demonstrate time changes as they compare different subjects at different ages, confounding interindividual and age-related variances. The problem is complicated by a possible cohort difference. Nowadays, younger ID subjects often participate in early cognitive intervention programmes (at least in the developed countries), whereas most older ones did not have such opportunities. Assuming that early intervention has the power of upgrading development in DS individuals (cf. the edited book by Rondal and Buckley, in press), the implication is that the comparisons with older cohorts of DS people may partially invalid.

A few longitudinal studies have been conducted. More, of course, are needed. Devenny et al. (1992) and Burt et al. (1995) did not observe significant changes in the cognitive functioning of DS individuals aged between 27 and 55 years and 22 and 56 years, in the two studies, respectively, over intervals of time ranging from three to five years. Devenny et al. (1996) signal only four cases of cognitive involution in 91 DS subjects followed for several years beyond the age of 50 years.

The above observations do not suggest rapid and marked age-related decline in cognitive and language functioning of DS even in subjects beyond 50 years, apart from episodic occurrences of progressive dementia.

For those people with DS who develop AD, the exact pattern of language involution has not been specified yet. In ND individuals, the language changes are most apparent first at the semantic level, particularly in the reduction of available vocabulary and breakdown of semantic associations (Martin, 1987). Difficulty in finding words is one of the most noticeable features of incipient AD. Auditory comprehension of words also presents deficits, as well as the processing of semantic complexity in sentences and paragraphs (Hart, 1988). Moreover, the quality of discourse, its cohesion and, in short, the whole pragmatics of language are gravely deteriorating (Maxim and Bryan, 1994).

It is repeatedly observed that the grammatical aspects of language seem to be largely spared in the early stages of AD, even if processing larger amounts of syntactic material is usually affected due to processing resource limitations (Appel et al., 1982; Kempler et al., 1987; Waters et al., 1995; Murillo Ruiz, 1999). Grammar is eventually disturbed to greater degrees together with the progressive breakdown of the language conceptual aspects and the complete collapse of pragmatic regulations (Maxim and Bryan, 1994).

There is no logical reason why the language prognosis of DS persons with AD should be any different from that of ID persons in similar conditions. Accordingly, predicted language profiles associated with AD persons with DS in the first stages of the disease would be characterized by major dissociations between morphosyntactic aspects, on the one hand, and language semantic and pragmatic aspects, on the other hand. The former aspects are underdeveloped in typical DS individuals. They could be affected a little as a direct result of incipient AD. The extent to which the latter language aspects deteriorate among individuals with DS will vary from person to person.

Individuals with DS seem to be susceptible to ageing (biologically as well as neuropsychologically) one or two decades prior to the norm (Vicari et al., 1994). Individuals with DS may experience the same involutions that occur in healthy ND people, but earlier in life. Regarding language, Table 3.3 lists frequent speech and language problems encountered in later life by ND individuals. It is possible that for DS individuals the effect of ageing (as well as that of incipient AD) could be particularly marked at first in those areas where greater weakness already exists (individually and/or syndromically).

Table 3.3 Frequent speech and language difficulties in ageing persons

1. Slower receptive and productive language processing.

2. Less efficient respiratory support for speech.

3. Aggravated hearing problems and reduced attention to auditory stimuli; difficulties in perceiving low-voiced and whispered speech, speech in noisy conditions, and in communicating on the telephone.

4. Additional difficulties in linguistic analysis, particularly with less frequent and/or more complex syntactic structures.

5. Additional difficulties in planning, producing or monitoring information in longer spoken discourse.

6. Augmented rates of dysfluencies (hesitation pauses, fillers, and interjections).

7. Reduced word fluency.

8. Increased difficulty in oral word discrimination and in retrieving infrequently used common and (even more) proper nouns.

Notes

1. Several works call for a differentiation between AD with early and late onset in ND people. Early onset AD seems to be characterized by shorter survival, more rapid cognitive deterioration, greater frequency of language disturbances (particularly regarding word comprehension and naming ability), more severe and widespread neurochemical

abnormalities, and a greater density of neurohistological lesions. The two variants of AD may also be genetically heterogeneous. Both chromosome 14 abnormalities and chromosome 21 amyloid precursor protein mutations appear to be restricted to the AD early onset variant (Roskind et al., 1995; Inamura et al., 1998).

2. Only the language data will be presented here. For other data, see the sources mentioned.

References

Abbeduto L, Hagerman R (1997) Language and communication in Fragile X syndrome. Mental Retardation and Developmental Disabilities Research Reviews 3: 313–22.

Abbeduto L, Keller-Bell Y (in press) Pragmatic and communication training. In J Rondal, S Buckley (eds) Language Intervention in Down Syndrome. London: Whurr.

Abrams M, Reiss A (1995) The neurobiology of fragile X syndrome. Mental Retardation and Developmental Disability Research Reviews 1: 269-75.

Akefeldt A, Akefeldt B, Gillberg C (1997) Voice speech and language characteristics of children with Prader-Willi syndrome. Journal of Intellectual Disability Research 41: 302–11.

Aman M, Singh N (1986) Aberrant Behavior Checklist: Manual. Aurora NY: Slosson Educational Publications.

Amir R, Van den Veyver I, Wan M, Tran C, Francke U, Zoghbi H (1998) Rett syndrome is caused by mutations in X–linked MECP2 encoding methyl-CpG-binding protein 2. Nature Genetics 23: 185–8.

Andersen W, Rasmussen R, Stromme P (2002) Levels of cognitive and linguistic development in Angelman syndrome: a study of 20 children. Logopedics and Phonology 26: 2–9.

Angelman H (1965) 'Puppet' children: a report on three cases. Developmental Medicine and Child Neurology 7: 681–8.

Appel J, Kertesz A, Fishman M (1982) A study of language functioning in Alzheimer's patients. Brain and Language 17: 73–91.

Atkinson J, King J, Braddick O, Nokes L, Anker S, Braddick F (1997) A specific deficit of dorsal stream function in Williams syndrome. Neuroreport 8: 1919–22.

Atkinson J, Anker S, Braddick O, Nokes L, Mason A, Braddick F (2001) Visual and visuospatial development in young children with Williams syndrome. Developmental Medicine and Child Neurology 43: 330–7.

Auranen M, Vanhala R, Vosman M, Levander M, Varilo T, Hietala M, Riikonen R, Peltonen L, Jarvela I (2001) MECP2 gene analysis in classical Rett syndrome and in patients with Rett-like features. Neurology 56: 611–17.

Baddeley A (1990) Human Memory. Hillsdale NJ: Erlbaum.

Bailey D, Hatton D, Tassone F, Skinner M, Taylor A (2001) Variability in FMRP and early development in males with Fragile X syndrome. American Journal on Mental Retardation 106: 16–27.

Baird P, Sadovnick A (1995) Life expectancy in Down syndrome. Lancet 2: 1354–6.

Barrett M, Diniz F (1989) Lexical development in mentally handicapped children. In M Beveridge, G Conti-Ramsden, Y Lendar (eds) Language and Communication in Mentally Handicapped People. London: Chapman & Hall, pp. 3–32.

Bellugi U, Marks S, Bihrle A, Sabo H (1988) Dissociation between language and cognitive functions in Williams syndrome. In D Bishop, K Mogford (eds) Language Development in Exceptional Circumstances. London: Churchill Livingstone, pp. 177–89.

Bellugi U, Bihrle A, Jernigan T, Trauner D, Doherty S (1990) Neuropsychological, neurological and neuroanatomical profile of Williams syndrome. American Journal of Medical Genetics Supplement 6: 115–25.

Bellugi U, Lichtenberger L, Mills D, Galaburda A, Korenberg J (1999) Bridging cognition, brain and molecular genetics: evidence from Williams syndrome. Trends in Neuroscience 22: 197–207.

Bellugi U, Lichtenberger L, Jones W, Lai Z, St George M (2000) The neurocognitive profile of Williams syndrome: a complex pattern of strengths and weaknesses. Journal of Cognitive Neuroscience 12: 7–29.

Belser R, Sudhalter V (2001) Conversational characteristics of children with Fragile X syndrome: repetitive speech. American Journal on Mental Retardation 106: 28–38.

Bender B, Puck M, Salbenblatt J, Robinson A (1984) Cognitive development of unselected girls with complete and partial monosomy. Pediatrics 73: 175–82.

Bever T (1970) The cognitive basis for linguistic structures. In J Hayes (ed.) Cognition and the Development of Language. New York: Wiley, pp. 279–362.

Bishop D (1983) Test of the Reception of Grammar. London: Medical Research Council.

Bishop D (1999) An innate basis for language? Science 286: 2283–4.

Bishop D, Byng S (1984) Accessing semantic comprehension: methodological considerations and a new clinical test. Cognitive Neuropsychology 1: 223–43.

Boehm A (1986) The Boehm Test of Basic Concepts. New York: Psychological Corporation.

Boer H, Clarke D (1999) Development and behaviour in genetic syndromes: Prader-Willi syndrome. Journal of Applied Research in Intellectual Disabilities 12: 296–301.

Boer H, Langton J, Clarke D (1999) Development and behaviour in genetic syndromes: Rubinstein-Taybi syndrome. Journal of Applied Research in Intellectual Disabilities 12: 302–7.

Borgraef M, Fryns J-P, Dielkens A, Pyck K, Van den Berghe H (1987) Fragile-X syndrome: a study of psychological profile in 23 prepubertal patients. Clinical Genetics 32: 179–86.

Boudreau D, Chapman R (2000) The relationship between event representation and linguistic skill in narratives of children and adolescents with Down syndrome. Journal of Speech Language and Hearing Research 43: 1146–59.

Bowey J (1996) On the association between phonological memory and receptive vocabulary in five-year-olds. Journal of Experimental Psychology 66: 44–78.

Bowey J (1997) What does nonword repetition measure? A reply to Gathercole and Baddeley. Journal of Experimental Child Psychology 67: 295–301.

Brauer Boone K, Swerdloff R, Miller B, Geschwind D, Razani J, Lee A, Gaw Gonzalo I, Haddal A, Rankin K, Lu P, Paul L (2001) Neuropsychological profiles of adults with Klinefelter syndrome. Journal of the International Neuropsychological Society 7: 446–56.

Bresson F (1991) Phylogeny and ontogeny of languages. In G Piérault le Bonniec, M Dolitsky (eds) Language Bases and Discourse Bases. Amsterdam: Benjamins, pp. 11–29.

Brion S, Plas J (1987) État actuel de l'approche histopathologique des démences. Psychologie Médicale 19: 1235–42.

Brown L, Leigh J (1986) Adaptive Behavior Inventory – ABI. Austin TX: Pro-Ed.

Brown W (1985) Genetics of aging. In M Janicki, H Wisniewski (eds) Aging and Developmental Disabilities: Issues and Approaches. Baltimore MD: Brookes, pp. 185–94.

Brun Gasca C, Conesa Perez M, Torres Gil M (2001) Retraso mental de base genetica: características de lenguaje. Revista de Logopedia Foniatria y Audiologia 21: 81–5.

Burt D, Loveland K, Chen Y-W, Chuang A, Lewis K, Cherry L (1995) Aging in adults with Down syndrome: report from a longitudinal study. American Journal on Mental Retardation 100: 262–70.

Butler M, Meaney F, Palmer C (1986) Clinical and cytogenetic survey of 39 individuals with Prader-Willi syndrome. American Journal of Medical Genetics 23: 793–809.

Cale W, Myers N (1978) Neurofibromatosis in childhood. Australian and New Zealand Journal of Surgery 48: 306–65.

Campbell-Taylor I (1993) Communication impairments in Alzheimer disease and Down syndrome. In J Berg, H Karlinsky, A Holland (eds) Alzheimer Disease, Down Syndrome and their Relationship. New York: Oxford University Press, pp. 175–93.

Capirci O, Sabbadini L, Volterra V (1996) Language development in Williams syndrome: a case study. Cognitive Neuropsychology 13: 1017–39.

Caplan D (1993) Language: Structure Processing and Disorders. Cambridge MA: MIT Press.

Capone G (2001) Down syndrome: advances in molecular biology and the neurosciences. Developmental and Behavioral Pediatrics 22: 40–59.

Cardoso-Martins C, Mervis CB, Mervis CA (1985) Early vocabulary acquisition by children with Down's syndrome. American Journal of Mental Deficiency 89: 451–8.

Carlin M (1988a) Longitudinal data show improved prognosis in cri-du-chat syndrome. American Journal of Human Genetics 41: A50.

Carlin M (1988b) The improved prognosis in cri-du-chat (5p-) syndrome. In W Fraser (ed.) Key Issues in Mental Retardation Research. London: Routledge, pp. 64–73.

Cassidy S (1997) Prader-Willi syndrome. Journal of Medical Genetics 34: 917–23.

Chapman R (1999) Language development in children and adolescents with Down syndrome. In J Miller, M Leddy, L Leavitt (eds) Improving the Communication of People with Down Syndrome. Baltimore MD: Brookes, pp. 41–60.

Chapman R, Schwartz S, Kay-Raining Bird E (1991) Fast-mapping in stories: Deficits in Down's syndrome. Communication at the Annual Meeting of the American Speech-Language-Hearing Association. Atlanta GA, November.

Chevrie-Müller C (1981) Epreuves pour l'Examen du Langage: Batterie Composite [Test of Language: Comprehensive Battery]. Paris: Editions du Centre.

Christian S, Robinson W, Huang B, Mutirangrera A, Liuc M, Nakao M, Surti U, Chakravati A, Ledbetter D (1995) Molecular characterization of two proximal deletion breakpoint regions in both Prader-Willi and Angelman syndrome patients. American Journal of Human Genetics 57: 40–8.

Clahsen H (1989) The grammatical characterization of developmental dysphasia. Linguistics 27: 897–920.

Clahsen H, Almazan M (1998) Syntax and morphology in Williams syndrome. Cognition 68: 167–98.

Clarke AM, Clarke AD, Berg J (1985) Mental Deficiency: The Changing Outlook. London: Methuen.

Clark C, Klonoff H, Hayden M (1990) Regional cerebral glucose metabolism in Turner syndrome. Canadian Journal of Neurological Sciences 17: 140–4.

Clarke D, Marston G (2000) Problem behaviors associated with 15q-Angelman syndrome. American Journal on Mental Retardation 105: 25–31.

Clayton-Smith J (1993) Clinical research in Angelman syndrome in the United Kingdom: observations on 82 affected individuals. American Journal of Medical Genetics 46: 12–15.

Coggins T, Carpenter R, Owings N (1983) Examining early intentional communication in Down's syndrome and nonretarded children. British Journal of Disorders of Communication 18: 99–107.

Coleman M, Brudbaker J, Hunter K, Smith G (1988) Rett syndrome: a survey of North American patients. Journal of Mental Deficiency Research 32: 117–24.

Comblain A (1995) Batterie pour l'Évaluation de la Morpho-syntaxe [Battery for the Assessment of Morpho-Syntax]. Laboratoire de Psycholinguistique de l'Université de Liège (unpublished).

Comblain A (1996) Mémoire de travail et langage dans le syndrome de Down [Working Memory and Language in Down Syndrome]. Doctoral dissertation in Psychology (Logopedics). Université de Liège (unpublished).

Cornish K, Munir F (1998) Receptive and expressive language skills in children with Cri-du-chat syndrome. Journal of Communication Disorders 31: 73–81.

Cornish K, Pigram J (1996) Developmental and behavioral characteristics of Cri du Chat syndrome. Archives of Diseases in Childhood 75: 448–50.

Courchesne E, Yeung-Courchesne R, Press G, Hesselink J, Jernigan T (1988) Hypophasia of cerebellar vermal lobules VI and II in autism. New England Journal of Medicine 318: 1349–54.

Cowan N (1992) Verbal memory span and the timing of spoken recall. Journal of Memory and Language 31: 668–84.

Craik F, Massani P (1969) Age and intelligence differences in coding and retrieval of word lists. British Journal of Psychology 63: 315–19.

Cromer R (1991) Language and Thought in Normal and Handicapped Children. Oxford: Blackwell.

Cromer R (1993) A case study of dissociations between language and cognition. In H Tager-Flusberg (ed.) Constraints on Language Acquisition: Studies of Atypical Children. Hillsdale NJ: Erlbaum, pp. 141–53.

Curfs L (1992) Psychological profile and behavioral characteristics in Prader-Willi syndrome. In S Cassidy (ed.) Prader-Willi Syndrome and Other 15q Deletion Disorders. Berlin: Springer-Verlag, pp. 221–2.

Curfs L, Schreppers-Tijdink G, Wiegers A, Borghraef M, Fryns JP (1990) The 49XXXXY syndrome: clinical and psychological findings in five patients. Journal of Mental Deficiency Research 34: 277–82.

Curtiss S (1989) Abnormal language acquisition and the modularity of language. In F Newmeyer (ed.) Linguistics: The Cambridge Survey. Cambridge UK: Cambridge University Press, Vol. 2, pp. 96–116.

Curtiss S, Yamada J (1992) The Curtiss-Yamada Comprehensive Language Evaluation (CYCLE). University of California at Los Angeles Department of Linguistics (unpublished).

Damasio A, Tranel D, Damasio H (1990) Face agnosia and the neural substrate of memory. Annual Review of Neuroscience 13: 89–109.

Damasio H, Damasio A (1989) Lesion Analysis in Neuropsychology. Oxford UK: Oxford University Press.

Dani A, Pietrini P, Furey M, McIntosh A, Grady C, Horwitz B, Freo U, Alexander G, Shapiro M (1996) Brain cognition in metabolism in Down syndrome adults in association with development of dementia. NeuroReport 7: 2933–6.

Daniel L, Gridley B (1998) Prader-Willi syndrome. In L Phelps (ed.) A Guidebook for Understanding and Educating Health-related Disorders in Children and Adolescents. A Compilation of 96 Rare and Common Disorders. Washington DC : American Psychological Association, pp. 534–40.

Das JP, Divis B, Alexander J, Parrila R, Naglieri J (1995) Cognitive decline due to aging among persons with Down syndrome. Research in Developmental Disabilities 16: 461–78.

De Renzi E, Faglioni P (1978) Normative data and screening power of a shortened version of the Token test. Cortex 14: 41–9.

De Renzi E, Vignolo L (1962) The Token test: a sensitive test to detect receptive disturbances in aphasics. Brain 85: 665–78.

Deb S, de Silva N, Gemmel H, Besson J, Smith F, Ebmeier K (1992) Alzheimer's disease in adults with Down syndrome: the relationship between the regional cerebral blood flow equivalents and dementia. Acta Psychiatrica Scandinavica 86: 340–5.

Defloor T, Van Borsel J, Curfs L (2000) Speech fluency in Prader-Willi syndrome. Journal of Fluency Disorders 25: 85–98.

Defloor T, Van Borsel J, Curfs L (2002) Articulation in Prader-Willi syndrome. Journal of Communication Disorders 35: 261–82.

Deltour JJ (1982) Test des Relations Topologiques [Test of Topological Relations]. Issy-les-Moulineaux, France: Editions Psychologiques.

Deltour JJ, Hupkens D (1980) Test de Vocabulaire Actif et Passif (TVAP) [Test of Expressive and Receptive Vocabulary]. Issy-les-Moulineaux, France: Editions Psychologiques.

Devenny D, Hill A, Patxot O, Silverman W, Wisniewski H (1992) Ageing in higher functioning adults with Down's syndrome: an interim report in a longitudinal study. Journal of Intellectual Disability Research 36: 241–50.

Devenny D, Silverman W, Hill A, Jenkins E, Sersen E, Wisniewski H (1996) Normal ageing in adults with Down's syndrome: a longitudinal study. Journal of Intellectual Disability Research 40: 208–21.

Dodd B, Leahy J (1989) Phonological disorders and mental handicap. In M Beveridge, G Conti-Ramsden, Y Lendar (eds) Language and Communication in Mentally Handicapped People. London: Chapman & Hall, pp. 33–56.

Dodd B, Thompson L (2001) Speech disorder in children with Down's syndrome. Journal of Intellectual Disability Research 45:(8) 316–25.

Dolk H, De Wals P, Gillerot Y, Lechat M, Aymé S, Beckers R, Bianchi F, Borlée I, Calabor A, Calzolari E, Cuschieri A, Galanti C, Goujard J, Hansen-Koening D, Harris F, Kargut G, Lillis D, Lungarotti M, Lye F, Marchi M, Nervin N, Radie A, Stool C, Syone D, Svel I, Ten Kate L, Zori R (1990) The prevalence at birth of Down's syndrome in 19 regions of Europe 1980–86. In W Fraser (ed.) Key Issues in Mental Retardation Research. London: Routledge, pp. 3–11.

Dunn H (2001) Importance of Rett syndrome in child neurology. Brain, Development 23: S38–S43.

Dunn L, Dunn P, Whetton C, Pintilie D (1982) British Picture Vocabulary Scales. Windsor, UK: NFER-Nelson.

Dykens E (1995) Measuring behavioral phenotypes: provocations from the 'new genetics'. American Journal on Mental Retardation 99: 522–32.

Dykens E, Cassidy S (1996) Prader-Willi syndrome: genetic, behavioral and treatment issues. Child and Adolescent Psychiatric Clinics of North America 5: 913–28.

Dykens E, Hodapp R (2001) Research in mental retardation: toward an etiologic approach. Journal of Child Psychology and Psychiatry 42: 49–71.

Dykens E, Kasari C (1997) Maladaptive behavior in children with Prader-Willi syndrome, Down syndrome and nonspecific mental retardation. American Journal on Mental Retardation 102: 228–237.

Dykens E, Hodapp R, Walsh K, Nash L (1992) Adaptive and maladaptative behavior in Prader-Willi syndrome. Journal of the American Academy of Child and Adolescent Psychiatry 31: 1131–6.

Dykens E, Leckerman J, Cassidy S (1996) Obsessions and compulsions in Prader-Willi syndrome. Journal of Child Psychology and Psychiatry 37: 995–1002.

Dykens E, Cassidy S, King B (1999) Maladaptive behavior differences in Prader-Willi syndrome due to paternal deletion versus maternal uniparental disomy. American Journal on Mental Retardation 104: 67–77.

Dykens E, Hodapp R, Finucane B (2000) Genetics and Mental Retardation Syndromes. Baltimore MD: Brookes.

Elliott T, Watkins J, Messa C, Lippe B, Chugani H (1996) Positron emission tomography and neuropsychological correlation in children with Turner's syndrome. Developmental Neuropsychology 12: 365–86.

Everman D, Cassidy S (2000) Genetics of childhood disorders: XII Genomic imprinting: breaking the rules. Journal of the American Academy of Child and Adolescent Psychiatry 39: 386–9.

Fabbro F, Moretti R, Bava A (2000) Language impairments in patients with cerebellar lesions. Journal of Neurolinguistics 13: 173–88.

Fishler K, Koch R (1991) Mental development in Down syndrome mosaicism. American Journal on Mental Retardation 96: 345–51.

Florez J (2000) El envejecimiento de las personas con sindrome de Down. Revista Sindrome de Down 17: 16–24.

Fowler A (1990) Language abilities in children with Down's syndrome: evidence for a specific syntactic delay. In D Cicchetti, M Beeghly (eds) Children with Down Syndrome: A Developmental Perspective. New York: Cambridge University Press, pp. 302–28.

Fowler A, Gelman R, Gleitman L (1994) The course of language learning in children with Down's syndrome. In H Tager-Flusberg (ed.) Constraints on Language Acquisition: Studies of Atypical Children. Hillsdale NJ: Erlbaum, pp. 91–140.

Frangistakis J, Ewart A, Morris C, Mervis C, Bertrand J, Robinson B, Klein B, Ensing G, Everett L, Green E, Proschel C, Gutowski N, Noble M, Atkinson D, Odelberg S, Keating M (1996) Lim-kinase 1 hemizygosity implicated in impaired visuospatial constructive cognition. Cell 86: 59–69.

Friefeld S, MacGregor D (1993) Sensory-motor coordination in boys with fragile X syndrome. In JA Holden and B Cameron (eds) Proceeedings of the First Canadian Fragile X Conference. Kingston Ontario: Oudwanda Resource Center, pp. 59–65.

Frostig M, Maslow P, Lefever D, Whittlesy J (1963) The Marianne Frostig Developmental Test of Visual Perception. Palo Alto CA: Consulting Psychologist Press.

Galaburda A, Wang P, Bellugi U, Rosen M (1994) Cytoarchitectonic anomalies in a genetically based disorder: Williams syndrome. Cognitive Neuroscience and Neuropsychology 5: 753–7.

Gathercole S, Baddeley A (1990) Monological memory deficits in language disordered children: is there a causal connection? Journal of Memory Language 29: 336–60.

Gathercole S, Baddeley A (1993) Working Memory and Language. Hillsdale NJ: Erlbaum.

Gathercole S, Willis C, Emslie H, Baddeley A (1992) Phonological memory and vocabulary development during the early school years. A longitudinal study. Developmental Psychology 28: 887–98.

George M, Thewis B, Van der Linden M, Salmon E, Rondal JA (1999) Langage et mémoire chez les sujets vieillissants porteurs d'un syndrome de Down: Étude longitudinale. Rapport final d'activité. Université de Liège: Laboratoire de Psycholinguistique (unpublished).

George M, Thewis B, Van der Linden M, Salmon E, Rondal JA (2002) Elaboration d'une batterie d'évaluation des fonctions cognitives de sujets âgés avec syndrome de Down. Revue de Neuropsychologie 11: 549–79.

Gérard CL, Guillotte E, Servel E, Barbeau M (1997) Évaluation et rééducation des troubles de la communication chez les enfants porteurs d'un syndrome de l'X fragile. Approches Neuropsychologiques des Apprentissages de l'Enfant 45: 224–6.

Gersch M, Goodart S, Pasztor L, Harris D, Weiss L, Overhauser J (1995) Evidence for a distinct region causing a cat-like cry in patients with 5p deletions. American Journal of Human Genetics 56: 1404–10.

Geschwind D, Boone K, Miller B, Swerdloft R (2000) Neurobehavioral phenotype of Klinefelter syndrome. Mental Retardation and Developmental Disability Research Review 6: 107–16.

Ginther D, Fullwood H (1998) Turner's syndrome. In L Phelps (ed.) A Guidebook for Understanding and Educating Health-related Disorders in Children and Adolescents. A Compilation of 96 Rare and Common Disorders. Washington DC: American Psychological Association, pp. 691–5.

Gratchev V, Bashina V, Klushnik Ulas V, Gorbachaskaya N, Vorsanova S (2001) Clinical neurophysiological and immunological correlations in classical Rett syndrome. Brain, Development 23: S108–S112.

Greenwald C, Leonard L (1979) Communicative and sensorimotor development of Down's syndrome children. American Journal of Mental Deficiency 84: 296–303.

Guideri F, Acampa M, DiPerri T, Zappella M, Hayek Y (2001) Progressive cardiac dysautonomia observed in patients affected by classic Rett syndrome and not in the preserved speech variant. Journal of Child Neurology 16: 370–3.

Gunn P, Berry P, Andrews R (1982) Looking behavior of Down's syndrome infants. American Journal of Mental Deficiency 87: 344–7.

Gutman A, Rondal JA (1979) Verbal operants in mother's speech to nonretarded and Down's syndrome children matched for linguistic level. American Journal of Mental Deficiency 83: 446–52.

Hagerman R (1995) Molecular and clinical correlations in fragile X syndrome. Mental Retardation and Developmental Disabilities Research Review 1: 276–80.

Hagerman R (1996) Biomedical advances in developmental psychology: the case of fragile X syndrome. Developmental Psychology 32: 416–24.

Halliday M (1985) An Introduction to Functional Grammar. London: Arnold.

Hannecart M, Haelewyck MC (2002) Le vieillissement commence par la vie: approche exploratoire de la perception du vieillissement et de la qualité de vie chez les personnes présentant un handicap mental. Journal de la Trisomie 21 5: 17–23.

Hart A (1988) Language and dementia: a review. Psychological Medicine 18: 99–112.

Hennekam R, Boogaard V, Doorne V (1991) A cephalometric study in Rubinstein-Taybi syndrome. Journal of Craniofacial Genetics and Developmental Biology 20: 33–40.

Hennekam R, Baselier A, Beyaert E, Bos A, Block J, Jansma H, Nilsen-Thorbecke V, Veerman H (1992) Psychological and speech studies in Rubinstein-Taybi syndrome. American Journal on Mental Retardation 96: 645–60.

Hoffman J, Hamson M, Welsh K, Earl N, Raine S, Delong D, Coleman R (1996) Interpretation variability of 18FDG-positron emission tomography studies in dementia. Investigation in Radiology 31: 316–22.

Holland A, Oliver C (1996) Down's syndrome and the links with Alzheimer's disease. Journal of Neurology, Neurosurgery and Psychiatry 59: 111–14.

Hopper P, Thompson S (1980) Transitivity in grammar and discourse. Language 56: 251–99.

Inamura J, Takatsuki T, Fujimori M, Hirono N, Ikejiri Y, Shimomura T, Hashimoto M, Yamashita S, Mori E (1998) Age at onset and language disturbances in Alzheimer's disease. Neuropsychologia 36: 945–9.

Inhelder B (1968) The Diagnosis of Reasoning in the Mentally Retarded. New York: Day.

Jancar J, Jancar P (1996) Longevity in Down syndrome: a twelve year survey (1984–1995). Italian Journal of Intellectual Impairment 9: 27–30.

Jarrold C, Baddeley A (1997) Short-term memory for verbal and visuospatial information in Down's syndrome. Cognitive Neuropsychiatry 2: 101–22.

Jarrold C, Baddeley A, Phillips C (1999) Down syndrome and the phonological loop: the evidence for and importance of a specific verbal short-term memory deficit. Down Syndrome 6: 61–75.

Jarrold C, Baddeley A, Hewes A (2000) Verbal short-term memory deficits in Down syndrome: a consequence of problems in rehearsal? Journal of Child Psychology and Psychiatry 40: 233–44.

Jernigan T, Bellugi U, Sowell E, Doherty S, Hesselink J (1993) Cerebral morphologic distinctions between Williams and Down's syndromes. Archives of Neurology 50: 186–91.

Jodar M (1992) Envejecimiento normal versus demencia de Alzheimer: Valor del lenguaje en el diagnóstico diferencial. Revista de Logopedia Foniatria y Audiologia 12: 171–9.

Jolleff N, Ryan M (1993) Communication development in Angelman's syndrome. Archives of Childhood Disabilities 69: 148–50.

Jones W, Bellugi U, Lai Z, Chiles M, Reilly J, Lincoln A, Adolphs R (2000) Hypersociability in Williams syndrome. Journal of Cognitive Neuroscience 12(supplement): 30–46.

Karmiloff-Smith A, Grant J, Berthoud I, Davies M, Howlin P, Udwin O (1997) Language and Williams syndrome. How intact is intact? Child Development 68: 274–90.

Karmiloff-Smith A, Tyler L, Voice K, Sims K, Udwin O, Howlin P, Davies M (1998) Linguistic dissociations in Williams syndrome: evaluating receptive syntax in on-line and off-line tasks. Neuropsychologia 36: 343–51.

Kempler D, Curtiss S, Jackson C (1987) Syntactic preservation in Alzheimer's disease. Journal of Speech and Hearing Research 30: 343–50.

Kernan K (1990) Comprehension of syntactically indicated sequences by Down's syndrome and other mentally retarded adults. Journal of Mental Deficiency Research 34: 169–78.

Kerr A, Corbitt J (1994) Rett syndrome: from gene to gesture. Journal of the Royal Society of Medicine 87: 562–6.

Kerr A, Montague J, Mils B, Ther D, Stephenson J (1987) The hands and the mind pre- and post-regression in Rett syndrome. Brain and Development 9: 487–90.

Kerr A, Belichenko P, Woodcock J, Woodcock M (2001) Mind and brain in Rett disorder. Brain Development 23: S44–S49.

Kinsbourne M, Hiscock M (1983) Asymmetrics of dual task performance. In J Hellige (ed.) Cerebral Hemisphere Asymmetry: Method, Theory and Application. Hillsdale NJ: Erlbaum, pp. 114–29.

Kishino T, Lalande M, Wagstaff J (1997) UBE3A/E6–AP mutations cause Angelman syndrome. Nature Genetics 15: 70–3.

Kleppe S, Katayama K, Shipley K, Foushee D (1990) The speech and language characteristics of children with Prader-Willi syndrome. Journal of Speech and Hearing Disorders 55: 300–9.

Korenberg J, Chen X, Schipper R, Sun Z, Gonsky R, Gerwehr S, Carpenter N, Daumer C, Dignan P, Distche C, Graham J, Hugdins L, McGillivray B, Miyazaki K, Ogasawara N, Park J, Pegon R, Pueschel S, Sack G, Fay B, Schuffenhauer S, Soukup S, Yamanaka T (1994) Down syndrome phenotypes. The consequences of chromosomal imbalance. Proceedings of the United States National Academy of Sciences 91: 4997–5001.

Korenberg J, Chen X, Hirota H, Lai Z, Bellugi U, Burian D, Roe B, Matsuoka R (2000) Genome structure and cognitive map of Williams syndrome. Journal of Cognitive Neuroscience 12: 89–107.

Kumin L (2001) Speech intelligibility in individuals with Down syndrome: a framework for targeting specific factors for assessment and treatment. Down Syndrome Quarterly 6: 1–8.

Kumin L, Adams J (2000) Developmental apraxia of speech and intelligibility in children with Down syndrome. Down Syndrome Quarterly 5: 1–7.

Kytterman M (1995) On the prevalence of Angelman syndrome. American Journal of Medical Genetics 59: 405.

Lacombe D, Sabra R, Taint L, Batten T (1992) Confirmation of an assignment of a locus for Rubinstein-Taybi syndrome gene to 16p133. American Journal of Medical Genetics 44: 126–8.

Laws G (1998) The use of nonword repetition as a test of phonological memory in children with Down syndrome. Journal of Child Psychology and Psychiatry 39: 1119–30.

Legins E, Descheemacker M, Spaepen A, Casaer P, Fryns J-P (1994) Neurofibromatosis Type 1 in childhood: a study of the neuropsychological profile in 45 children. Genetic Counseling 5: 51–60.

Leiner C, Leiner A, Dow R (1991) The human cerebro-cerebellar system: its computing cognitive and language skills. Behavioral Brain Research 44: 113–28.

Leiner C, Leiner A, Dow R (1993) Cognitive and language functions of the human cerebellum. Trends in Neurosciences 16: 444–7.

Lejeune J, Gautier M, Turpin R (1959) Études des chromosomes somatiques de neuf enfants mongoliens. Comptes Rendus de l'Académie des Sciences de Paris 248: 1721–2.

Lejeune J, Lafourcade J, Berger R (1963) Trois cas de délétion partielle du bras court d'un chromosome 5. Compte Rendus de l'Académie des Science de Paris 257: 3098–102.

Lenneberg E (1967) Biological Foundations of Language. New York: Wiley.

Lenneberg E, Nichols I, Rosenberger E (1964) Primitive stages of language development in mongolism. In D McRock, E Weinstein (eds) Disorders of Communication Proceedings of the Association for Research in Nervous and Mental Disease. Baltimore MD: Williams & Wilkins, Vol. 17, pp. 119–37.

Leonard L (1992) The use of morphology by children with specific language impairment. Evidence from three languages. In R Chapman (ed.) Processes in Language Acquisition and Disorders. Chicago: Mosby, pp. 40–67.

Leonard M, Schowalter JE, Landy G, Ruddle FH, Lubs HA (1979) Chromosomal abnormalities in the New Haven newborn study: a prospective study of development of children with sex chromosome anomalies. In A Robinson, HA Lubs, D Bergsma (eds) Birth Defects. New York: Alan R Liss, pp. 115–59.

Lewandowski L, Costenbader V, Richman R (1985) Neuropsychological aspects of Turner syndrome. International Journal of Clinical Neuropsychology 7: 144–7.

Lombroso P (2000) Genetics of childhood disorders: XVI Angelman syndrome: a failure to process. Journal of the American Academy of Child and Adolescent Psychiatry 39: 931–3.

Lomelino C, Reiss A (1991) 49XXXXY syndrome: behavioural and developmental profiles. Journal of Medical Genetics 28: 609–12.

Losh M, Bellugi U, Reilly J, Anderson D (2000) Narrative as a social engagement tool: the excessive use of evaluation in narratives from children with Williams syndrome. Narrative Inquiry 10: 265–90.

Luria A (1961) The Role of Speech in the Regulation of Normal and Abnormal Behaviour. London: Pergamon.

Luria A, Vinogradova O (1959) An objective investigation of the dynamics of semantic systems. British Journal of Psychology 50: 89–105.

Mackenzie S, Hulme C (1987) Memory span development in Down's syndrome severely subnormal and normal subjects. Cognitive Neuropsychology 4: 303–19.

Madison L, George C, Moeschler J (1986) Cognitive functioning in the Fragile-X syndrome: a study of intellectual memory and communication skills. Journal of Mental Deficiency Research 30: 129–48.

Maes B, Fryns JP, Van Walleghem M, Van den Berghe H (1994) Cognitive functioning and information processing of adult mentally retarded with fragile X syndrome. American Journal of Medical Genetics 50: 190–200.

Mandoki M, Summer G, Hoffman R, Riconda D (1991) A review of Klinefelter's syndrome in children and adolescents. Journal of American Academy of Child and Adolescent Psychiatry 30: 167–72.

Mann D (1992) The neuropathology of the amygdala in ageing and in dementia. In J Aggleton (ed.) The Amygdala: Neurobiological Aspects of Emotion, Memory and Mental Dysfunction. New York: Wiley-Liss, pp. 575–93.

Marcell M, Armstrong V (1982) Auditory and visual sequential memory of Down syndrome and nonretarded children. American Journal of Mental Deficiency 87: 86–95.

Marcell M, Weeks S (1988) Short-term memory difficulties and Down's syndrome. Journal of Mental Deficiency Research 32: 153–62.

Markman E (1990) Constraints children place on word meanings. Cognitive Science 14: 57–77.

Martin A (1987) Representations of semantic and spatial knowledge in Alzheimer's patients: implications for models of preserved learning and amnesia. Journal of Clinical and Experimental Neuropsychology 9: 121–4.

Martin N, Snodgrass G, Cohen R (1984) Idiopathic infantile hypercalcaemia – a continuing enigma. Archives of Diseases in Childhood 59: 605–13.

Masataka N (2001) Why early linguistic milestones are delayed in children with Williams syndrome: late onset of hand banging as a possible rate limiting constraint on the emergence of canonical babbling. Developmental Science 4: 158–64.

Matalainen R, Airaksinen E, Mononen T, Launiala K, Kaariainen R (1995) A population-based study on the causes of severe and profound mental retardation. Acta Pediatrica 84: 261–6.

Maxim J, Bryan K (1994) Language of the Elderly: A Clinical Perspective. London: Whurr.

Mazzocco M, Turner J, Denckla M, Hoffman K, Scanlon D, Vellutino F (1995) Language and reading deficits associated with neurofibromatosis type I. Evidence for a not-so-non verbal learning disability. Developmental Neuropsychology 11: 503–22.

Michele G, Presta M, Di Salle F, Serra L (1993) Cerebellar vermis hypoplosia in a case of cri-du-chat syndrome. Acta Neurologica 15: 92–6.

Miles S, Chapman R (2002) Narrative content as described by individuals with Down syndrome and typically developing children. Journal of Speech Language and Hearing Research 45: 175–89.

Miller J (1999) Profiles of language development in children with Down syndrome. In J Miller, M Leddy, L Leavitt (eds) Improving the Communication of People with Down Syndrome. Baltimore MD: Brookes, pp. 11–39.

Mills D, Alvarez T, St George M, Appelbaum L, Bellugi U, Neville H (2000) Electrophysiological studies of face processing in Williams syndrome. Journal of Cognitive Neuroscience 12(supplement): 47–64.

Money J, Alexander D (1986) Turner's syndrome: further demonstration of the presence of specific cognitional deficiencies. Journal of Medical Genetics 3: 47–8.

Moric-Petrovic S, Laca Z, Markovic S, Markovic V (1973) 49XXXXY karyotype in a mentally retarded boy. Journal of Mental Deficiency Research 17: 73–80.

Moser H (1992) Prevention of mental retardation (genetics). In L Rowitz (ed.) Mental Retardation in the Year 2000. New York: Springer-Verlag, pp. 66–82.

Moss S, Tomoeda C, Bayles K (2000) Comparison of the cognitive-linguistic profiles of Down syndrome adults with and without dementia to individuals with Alzheimer's disease. Journal of Medical Speech–Language Pathology 8: 69–81.

Mostofsky S, Mazzocco M, Aakalu G, Warsofsky I, Denkla M, Reiss A (1998) Decreased cerebellar posterior vermis size in Fragile X syndrome: correlation with neurocognitive performance. Neurology 50: 121–30.

Murillo Ruiz B (1999) Estudio de la evolución del lenguaje en la demencia Alzeimer [A Study of Language Evaluation in Alzheimer Disease]. Barcelona: ISEP Editorial.

Murphy D, Allen G, Haxby J, Largay K, Daly E, White B, Powell C, Schapiro M (1994) The effects of sex steroids and the X chromosome on female brain function: a study of the neuropsychology of adult Turner syndrome. Neuropsychologia 32: 1309–23.

Murphy D, Mentis M, Pietrini P, Grady C, Daly E, Haxby J, De La Granja M, Allen G, Largay K, White B, Powell C, Horwitz B, Rapoport S, Schapiro M (1997) A PET study of Turner's syndrome: effects of sex steroids and the X chromosome on brain. Biological Psychiatry 41: 285–98.

Netley C, Rovet J (1982) Verbal deficits in children with 47XXY and 47XXX karyotypes: a descriptive and experimental study. Brain and Language 17: 58–72.

Newell K, Sandborn B, Hagerman R (1983) Speech and language dysfunction in the fragile X syndrome. In R Hagerman, P McBogg (eds) The Fragile X Syndrome: Diagnosis. Biochemistry and Intervention. Dillon CO: Spectra, pp. 175–200.

Nicholls R, Knoll J, Buther M, Karam S, Lalander M (1989) Genetic imprinting suggested by maternal heterodisomy in nondeletion Prader-Willi syndrome. Nature 342: 281–5.

Nicholls R, Pai G, Gottlieb W, Cantu E (1992) Paternal uniparental disomy of chromosome 15 in a child with Angelman syndrome. Annals of Neurology 32: 512–18.

Niebuhr E (1978) The cri-du-chat syndrome. Human Genetics 42: 143–56.

Nielsen J, Ravn K, Schwartz M (2001) A 77-year-old woman and a preserved speech variant among the Danish Rett patients with mutations in MECP2. Brain and Development 23: S230–S232.

Noonan J, Ehmke D (1963) Associated noncardiac malformations in children with congenital heart disease. Journal of Pediatrics 63: 468–70.

Nora J, Nora D, Sinha H, Spangler W, Lubs J (1974) The Ullrich-Noonan syndrome. American Journal of Diseases in Children 127: 48–55.

Nyhan W (1972) Behavioral phenotypes in organic genetic disease. Pediatric Research 6: 1–9.

O'Connor N, Hermelin B (1963) Speech and Thought in Severe Subnormality. London: Macmillan.

O'Connor N, Hermelin B (1991) A specific linguistic ability. American Journal on Mental Retardation: 95: 673–80.

Overhauser J, Huang X, Gersch M, Wilson W, McMahon J, Bengtsson U, Rojas K, Meyer M, Wasmuth J (1994) Molecular and phenotypic mapping of the short arm of chromosome 5: sublocalization of the critical region for the cri-du-chat syndrome. Human Molecular Genetics 34: 247–52.

Owens R, MacDonald J (1982) Communicative uses of the early speech of non-delayed and Down syndrome children. American Journal of Mental Deficiency 86: 503–10.

Palmer C, Reichmann A (1976) Chromosomal and clinical findings in 110 females with Turner syndrome. Human Genetics 35: 35–49.

Park E, Bailey J, Cowell C (1983) Growth and maturation of patients with Turner syndrome. Pediatric Research 17: 1–7.

Patwardhan A, Eliez S, Bender B, Linden M, Reiss A (2000) Brain morphology in Klinefelter syndrome. Neurology 54: 2218–23.

Pedrabissi R, Soresi S (1989) Adattamento dell'ABI con oggetti RM di diversa gravità ed eziologia. Trento, Italy: Erickson.

Penner K, Johnston J, Faircloth B, Irish P, Williams C (1993) Communication cognition and social interaction in Angelman syndrome. American Journal of Medical Genetics 46: 34–9.

Pennington B (1995) Genetics of learning disabilities. Journal of Child Neurology 10: S69–S78.

Pennington B, Puck M, Robinson A (1980) Language and cognitive development in 47 XXX females followed since birth. Behavior Genetics 10: 31–41.

Pezzini G, Vicari S, Volterra V, Milani L, Ossella M (1999) Children with Williams syndrome. Is there a single neuropsychological profile? Developmental Neuropsychology 15: 141–55.

Phelps L (ed.) (1998) A Guidebook for Understanding and Educating Health-related Disorders in Children and Adolescents. A Compilation of 96 Rare and Common Disorders. Washington DC: American Psychological Association.

Pinter J, Eliez S, Schmitt J, Capone G, Reiss A (2001) Neuroanatomy of Down's syndrome: a high-resolution MRI study. American Journal of Psychiatry 158: 1659–65.

Prasher V (1996) Age-associated functional decline in adults with Down's syndrome. European Journal of Psychiatry 10: 129–35.

Prouty L, Royers R, Stevenson R, Dean J, Palmer K, Simensen R, Coston G, Schwartz C (1988) Fragile X syndrome: growth development and intellectual function. American Journal of Medical Genetics 30: 123–42.

Pueschel S, Thuline H (1991) Chromosome disorders. In J Matson, J Mulick (eds) Handbook of Mental Retardation. Elmsford NY: Pergamon, pp. 115–38.

Reilly J, Klima E, Bellugi U (1990) Once more with feeling: affect and language in atypical populations. Development and Psychopathology 2: 367–91.

Reiss A, Abrams M, Greenlaw R, Freund L, Denkla M (1995) Neurodevelopmental effects of the FMR-1 full mutations in humans. Nature Medicine 1: 159–67.

Reiss A, Eliez J, Schmitt E, Straus E, Lai Z, Jones W, Bellugi U (2000) Neuroanatomy of Williams syndrome: a high-resolution MRI study. Journal of Cognitive Neuroscience 12: 65–73.

Reynell J (1985) Reynell Developmental Language Scales. Windsor UK: NFER-Nelson.

Ribes R, Sanuy J (2000) Declive cognitivo en memoria y lenguaje: indicadores del proceso de envejecimiento psicologico en la persona con sindrome de Down. Revista Sindrome de Down 17: 54–9.

Roberts J, Mirrett P, Burchinal M (2001) Receptive and expressive communication development of young males with Fragile X syndrome. American Journal on Mental Retardation 106: 216–30.

Rondal JA (1975) Développement du langage et retart mental: une revue critique de la littérature en langue anglaise. L'Année Psychologique 75: 513–47.

Rondal JA (1978) Maternal speech to normal and Down's syndrome children matched for mean length of utterance. In C Meyers (ed.) Quality of Life in Severely and Profoundly Retarded People: Research Foundations for Improvement. Washington DC: American Association on Mental Deficiency, pp. 193–265.

Rondal JA (1985) Langage et communication chez les handicapés mentaux [Language and Communication in Mental Handicap]. Brussels: Mardaga.

Rondal JA (1995) Exceptional language development in Down syndrome: implications for the cognition-language relationship. Cambridge MA: Cambridge University Press.

Rondal JA (1998) Cases of exceptional language in mental retardation and Down syndrome: explanatory perspectives. Down Syndrome 5: 1–15.

Rondal JA (in press) Atypical language development in mental retardation. Theoretical implications. In L Abbeduto (ed.) Language and Communication. International Review of Research in Mental Retardation. New York: Academic Press.

Rondal JA, Buckley S (eds) (in press) Language Intervention in Down Syndrome. London: Whurr.

Rondal JA, Comblain A (1996) Language in adults with Down syndrome. Down Syndrome 4: 3–14.

Rondal JA, Comblain A (1999) Current perspectives on developmental dysphasias. Journal of Neurolinguistics 12: 181–212.

Rondal JA, Comblain A (2002) Language in ageing persons with Down syndrome. Down Syndrome 8: 1–9.

Rondal JA, Edwards S (1997) Language in Mental Retardation. London: Whurr.

Rondal JA, Cession A, Vincent E (1988) Compréhension des phrases déclaratives selon la voix et l'actionnalité du verbe chez un groupe d'adultes trisomiques 21. Université de Liège Laboratoire de Psycholinguistique (unpublished).

Rosen M, Jones W, Wang P, Klima E (1995) Face processing: remarkable sparing in Williams syndrome. Genetic Counseling 6: 138–40.

Rosenberg S, Abbeduto L (1993) Language and Communication in Mental Retardation Development Processes and Intervention. Hillsdale NJ: Erlbaum.

Roskind M, Carta A, Bravi D (1995) Is early onset Alzheimer disease a distinct group within the Alzheimer disease population? Alzheimer Disease and Associated Disorders 9 (supplement 1): 2–6.

Ross J, Stefanatos G, Roeltgen D, Kushner H, Cutler G (1995) Ulrich-Turner syndrome: neurodevelopmental charges from childhood through adolescence. American Journal of Medical Genetics 58: 74–82.

Ross J, Roeltgen D, Feuillan P, Kushner H, Cutler G (2000) Use of estrogen in young girls with Turner syndrome. Neurology 54: 164–70.

Rovet J, Netley C, Keenan M, Bailey J, Stewart J (1996) The psychoeducational profile of boys with Klinefelter syndrome. Journal of Learning Disabilities 29: 180–96.

Royston M, Mann D, Pickering-Brown S, Owen F (1994) Apolipoprotein E e2 allele promotes longevity and protects patients with Down's syndrome from dementia. Neuroreport 5: 2583–5.

Rubinstein J, Taybi H (1963) Brood thumbs and toes and facial abnormalities: a possible mental retardation syndrome. American Journal of Diseases in Children 105: 88–108.

Saint-Arroman F, Alozy C (1998) Neurofibromatoses: troubles cognitifs et prise en charge orthophonique. Actes des entretiens de Bichat d'Orthophonie. Paris: Expansion Scientifique Française, pp. 146–53.

Salbenblatt J, Meyers D, Bender B, Linden M, Robinson A (1989) Gross and fine motor development in 45X and 47XXX girls. Pediatrics 84: 678–82.

Samango-Sprouse C (2001) Mental development in polysomy X Klinefelter syndrome (47XXY; 48XXXY): effects of incomplete activation. Seminars in Reproductive Medicine 19: 193–202.

Sandberg A, Ehlers S, Hogberg B, Gillberg C (2000) The Rett syndrome complex. Autism 4: 249–67.

Saviolo-Negrin N, Soresi S, Baccichetti C, Pozzan G, Trevisan E (1990) Observations on the visual perceptual abilities and adaptive behavior in adults with Down syndrome. American Journal of Medical Genetics Supplement 7: 309–13.

Schapiro M, Haxby J, Grady C, Duara R, Schlageter N, White B, Moore A, Sunadaram M, Larson S, Rapoport S (1987) Decline in cerebral glucose utilization and cognitive function with aging in Down's syndrome. Journal of Neurology, Neurosurgery and Psychiatry 50: 766–74.

Schapiro M, Haxby J, Grady C (1992) Nature of mental retardation and dementia in Down syndrome: study with PET CL and neuropsychology. Neurobiology of Aging 13: 723–34.

Schmitt J, Eliez S, Warsofsky I, Bellugi U, Reiss A (2001a) Enlarged cerebellar vermis in Williams syndrome. Journal of Psychiatric Research 35: 225–9.

Schmitt J, Eliez S, Warsofsky I, Bellugi U, Reiss A (2001b) Corpus callosum morphology of Williams syndrome: relation to genetics and behavior. Developmental Medicine, Child Neurology 43: 155–9.

Segawa M (2001) Pathophysiology of Rett syndrome from the standpoint of clinical characteristics. Brain, Development 23: S94–S98.

Seung H, Chapman R (2000) Digit span in individuals with Down syndrome and in typically developing children: temporal aspects. Journal of Speech, Language and Hearing Research 43: 609–20.

Shallice T (1988) From Neuropsychology to Mental Structure. New York: Cambridge University Press.

Sheldon L, Turk J (2000) Monozygotic boys with Fragile X syndrome. Developmental Medicine, Child Neurology 42: 768–74.

Shprintzen R (1997) Genetics, Syndrome and Communication Disorders. San Diego CA: Singular.

Simon J, Keenan J, Pennington B, Taylor A, Hagerman R (2001) Discourse processing in women with Fragile X syndrome: evidence for a deficit establishing coherence. Cognitive Neuropsychology 18: 1–18.

Sinclair H (1971) Sensorimotor action patterns as a condition for the acquisition of syntax. In R Huxley, E Ingram (eds) Language Acquisition: Models and Methods. New York: Academic, pp. 121–35.

Sinclair H (1987) Language: a gift of nature or a homemade tool? In S Modgil, C Modgil (eds) Noam Chomsky: Consensus and Controversy. New York: Falmer, pp. 112–29.

Singer N, Bellugi U, Bates E, Jones W, Rossen M (1994) Contrasting Profiles of Language Development in Children with Williams and Down Syndromes (Tech Rep N°9403). San Diego CA: University of California Department of Psychology and Cognitive Science.

Slobin D (1973) Cognitive prerequisites for the development of grammar. In C Ferguson, D Slobin (eds) Studies of Child Language Development. New York: Holt, Rinehart & Winston, pp. 607–19.

Smith BL, Oller K (1981) A comparative study of pre-meaningful vocalizations produced by normally developing and Down's syndrome infants. Journal of Speech and Hearing Disorders 46: 46–51.

Smith N, Tsimpli I (1995) The Mind of a Savant. Language Learning and Modularity. London: Blackwell.

Smith S, Pennington B, DeFries J (1996) Linkage analysis with complex behavioral traits. In M Rice (ed.) Toward a Genetics of Language. Mahwah NJ: Erlbaum, pp. 29–44.

Smith A, Robson L, Buckholz B (1998) Normal growth in Angelman syndrome due to paternal UPD. Clinical Genetics 53: 223–5.

Sohner L, Mitchell P (1991) Phonatory and phonetic characteristics of prelinguistic vocal development in cri du chat syndrome. Journal of Communication Disorders 24: 10–13.

Sokolov J (1992) Linguistic imitation in children with Down syndrome. American Journal on Mental Retardation 97: 209–21.

Solot C, Zackai E, Obringer A, Konkle D, Handler S, Meadows A (1990) Communication disorders in children with neurofibromatosis Type 1. In A Rubinstein, B Korf (eds) Neurofibromatosis: A Handbook for Patients, Families and Healthcare Professionals. New York: Thieme Medical Publishers, pp. 67–92.

Spinelli M, Oliveira Rocha A, Giacheti C, Richieri-Costa A (1995) Word-finding difficulties, verbal paraphasias and verbal dyspraxia in ten individuals with fragile X syndrome. American Journal of Medical Genetics 60: 39–43.

Stedman's Medical Dictionary (1990) Baltimore MD: Williams & Wilkins.

Stevens C, Carey J, Blackburn B (1990) Rubinstein-Taybi syndrome: a natural history study. American Journal of Medical Genetics Supplement 6: 30–7.

Stevens T, Karmiloff-Smith A (1997) Word learning in a special population: do individuals with Williams syndrome obey lexical constraints? Journal of Child Language 24: 737–65.

Stewart D, Bailey J, Netley C (1986) Growth and development from early to midadolescence of children with X and Y chromosomal aneuploidy. In S Ratcliffe, V Paul (eds) Prospective Studies on Children with Sex Chromosome Aneuploidy. New York: Liss, pp. 119–82.

Stiles J, Sabbadini L, Capirci D, Volterra V (2000) Drawing abilities in Williams syndrome: a case study. Developmental Neuropsychology 18: 213–35.

Stoel-Gammon C (1980) Phonological analysis of four Down's syndrome children. Applied Psycholinguistics 1: 31–48.

Stoel-Gammon C (in press) Speech acquisition and approaches to intervention. In JA Rondal, S Buckley (eds) Language Intervention in Down Syndrome. London: Whurr.

Stojanovik V, Perkins M, Howard S (2001) Language and conversational abilities in Williams syndrome. Research Report, University of Sheffield, Department of Human Communication Sciences (unpublished).

Strauss D, Eyman R (1996) Mortality of people with mental retardation in California with and without Down syndrome 1986–1991. American Journal on Mental Retardation 100: 643–51.

Stumpof D, Alkesne J, Amiegers J (1988) Neurofibromatis conference statement. Archives of Neurology 45: 575–8.

Sudhalter V, Scarborough H, Cohen I (1991) Syntactic delay and pragmatic deviance in the language of males with fragile X syndrome. American Journal of Medical Genetics 43: 65–71.

Summers J, Feldman M (1999) Distinctive pattern of behavioral functioning in Angelman syndrome. American Journal on Mental Retardation 104: 376–84.

Summers J, Allison D, Lynch P, Sandler L (1995) Behaviour problems in Angelman syndrome. Journal of Intellectual Disability Research 39: 97–106.

Swaab D, Purba J, Hofman M (1995) Alterations in the hypothalamic paraventricular nucleus and its oxytocin neurons in Prader-Willi syndrome: a study of five cases. Journal of Clinical Endocrinology and Metabolism 80: 573–9.

Taine L, Goizet C, Wen Z, Petrij F, Breuning M, Aymé S, Sanra R, Arveiler B, Lacombe D (1998) Submicroscopic deletion of chromosome 16p133 in patients with Rubinstein-Taybi syndrome. American Journal of Medical Genetics 78: 267–70.

Tassabehji M, Metcalfe K, Karmiloff-Smith A, Carette M, Grant J, Dennis N, Reardon W, Splitt M, Read A, Donnai D (1999) Williams syndrome: use of chromosomal microdeletions as a tool to dissect cognitive and physical characteristics. American Journal of Human Genetics 64: 118–25.

Thomas M, Grant J, Barham Z, Gsödl M, Laing E, Lakusta L, Tyler L, Grice S, Peterson S, Karmiloff-Smith A (2001) Past tense formation in Williams syndrome. Language and Cognitive Processes 16: 143–76.

Thompson S (1999) Examining dementia in Down's syndrome. Decline in social abilities in DS compared with other learning disabilities. Clinical Gerontologist 20: 23–44.

Tomasello M (1995) Language is not an instinct. Cognitive Development 10: 131–56.

Trevathan E, Moser H (1988) Diagnostic criteria for Rett syndrome. Annals of Neurology 23: 425–8.

Turner G, Webb T, Wake S, Robinson H (1996) Prevalence of the fragile X syndrome. American Journal of Medical Genetics 64: 196–7.

Tyler L, Karmiloff-Smith A, Voice J, Stevens T, Grant J, Udwin O, Davies M, Howlin P (1997) Do individuals with Williams syndrome have bizarre semantics? Evidence from lexical organization using an on-line task. Cortex 33: 515–27.

Uchino J, Suzuki M, Hoshino K, Nomura Y, Segawa M (2001) Development of language in Rett syndrome. Brain, Development 23: S233–S235.

Vallar G, Papagno C (1993) Preserved vocabulary acquisition in Down's syndrome: the role of phenological short-term memory. Cortex 29: 467–83.

Van Borsel J, Dhooge I, Verhoye K, Derde K, Curfs L (1999) Communication problems in Turner syndrome: a sample survey. Journal of Communication Disorders 32: 435–46.

Van Buggenhout G, Lukusa T, Trommelen J, De Bal C, Hamel B, Fryns J-P (2001) Une étude pluridisciplinaire du syndrome de Down dans une population résidentielle d'arriérés mentaux d'âge avancé: implications pour le suivi médical. Journal de la Trisomie 21 2: 7–13.

Verger K, Junque C (2000) Recuperacion de las lesiones cerebrales en la infancia: polemica entorno a la plasticidad cerebral. Revista de Logopedia Foniatria y Audiologia 20: 151–7.

Verkerk A, Pieretti M, Sutcliffe J, Fu Y, Kuhi D, Pizzuti A, Reiner O, Richards S, Victoria M, Zhang F, Eussen B, Van Ommen G, Blonden L, Riggens G, Chastain J, Kunst C, Galjaard H, Caskey C, Nelson D, Dostra B, Warren S (1991) Identification of a gene (FMR-1) containing a CHGG repeat coincident with a breakpoint cluster region exhibiting right variation in Fragile X syndrome and length variation in fragile X syndrome. Cell 65: 905–14.

Vicari S, Nocentini U, Caltagirone C (1994) Neuropsychological diagnosis of aging in adults with Down syndrome. Developmental Brain Dysfunction 7: 340–8.

Vilkman E, Niemi J, Ikonen U (1988) fragile-X speech in Finnish. Brain and Language 34: 203–21.

Volterra V, Capirci O, Pezzini G, Sabbadini L, Vicari S (1994) Linguistic Abilities in Italian children with Williams Syndrome. Paper presented at the Sixth International Professional Conference, San Diego CA, July.

Wallerstein R, Anderson C, Hay B, Gupta P, Gibas L, Ansari K, Cowchock F, Weinblatt V, Reid C, Levitas A, Jackson L (1997) Submicroscopic deletions at 16p131 in Rubinstein-Taybi syndrome: frequency and clinical manifestations in a North–American population. Journal of Medical Genetics 34: 203–6.

Walzer S (1985) X chromosome abnormalities and cognitive development: implications for understanding normal human development. Journal of Child Psychology and Psychiatry 26: 177–84.

Walzer S, Bashir A, Silber A (1991) Cognitive and behavioural factors in the learning disabilites of 47XXY and 47XYY boys. Birth Defects 26: 45–58.

Wang P, Bellugi U (1994) Evidence from two genetic syndromes for a dissociation between verbal and visual-spatial short-term memory. Journal of Clinical and Experimental Neuropsychology 16: 317–22.

Wang P, Doherty S, Hesselink J, Bellugi U (1992) Callosal morphology concurs with neuropathological findings in two neurodevelopmental disorders. Archives of Neurology 49: 407–11.

Waters G, Caplan D, Rochon E (1995) Processing capacity and sentence comprehension in a patient with Alzheimer's disease. Cognitive Neuropsychology 12: 1–30.

Webb T, Bundey S, Thake A, Todd J (1986) Population incidence and segregation ratios in Martin-Bell syndrome. American Journal of Medical Genetics 23: 573–80.

Wechsler D (1958) The Measurement and Appraisal of Adult Intelligence. New York: Baillière Tindall & Cox.

Willard H (1995) The sex chromosomes and X chromosome inactivation. In C Schiver, A Beaudet, W Sly, D Valli (eds) The Metabolic and Molecular Basis of Inherited Disease. New York: McGraw-Hill, pp. 719–35.

Williams C, Zori R, Hendrickson J, Stalker H, Marum T, Whidden E, Driscoll D (1995) Angelman syndrome. Current Problems in Pediatrics 25: 216–31.

Wilson M, Dyson A (1982) Noonan syndrome: speech and language characteristics. Journal of Communication Disorders 15: 347–52.

Wishart J (1988) Early learning in infants and young children with Down syndrome. In L Nadel (ed.) The Psychobiology of Down Syndrome. Cambridge MA: MIT Press, pp. 7–50.

Wisniewski K, Kida E (1994) Abnormal neurogenesis and synaptogenesis in Down syndrome brain. Developmental Brain Dysfunction 17: 1–12.

Wisniewski H, Silverman W (1996) Alzheimer disease neuropathology and dementia in Down syndrome. In JA Rondal, J Perera, L Nadel, A Comblain (eds) Down Syndrome: Psychological Psychobiological and Socio-educational Perspectives. London: Whurr, pp. 43–52.

Wisniewski H, Silverman W (1999) Down syndrome and Alzheimer disease: variability in individual vulnerability. In JA Rondal, J Perera, L Nadel (eds) Down Syndrome: A Review of Current Knowledge. London: Whurr, pp. 178–94.

Witt-Engerstrom I (1987) Rett syndrome: a retrospective pilot study on potential early predictive symptomatology. Brain and Development 9: 481–6.

Wolf-Schein E, Sudhalter V, Cohen I, Fisch G, Hanson D, Pfadt A, Hagerman R, Jenkins E, Brown W (1987) Speech-language and the fragile X syndrome. Journal of the American Speech-Language-Hearing Association 29: 35–8.

Xiang F, Buervenich S, Nicolao P, Bailey M, Zhang Z, Anvret M (2000) Mutation screening in Rett syndrome patients. Journal of Medical Genetics 37: 250–5.

Yamada J (1990) Laura: A Case for the Modularity of Language. Cambridge MA: MIT Press.

Yamashita Y, Kondo I, Fukuda T, Morishima R, Kusaga A, Iwanaga R, Matsuisi T (2001) Mutation analysis of the methyl-CpG-binding protein 2 gene (MECP2) in Rett patients with preserved speech. Brain and Development 23: S157–S160.

Zappella M (1997) The preserved speech variant of the Rett complex: a report of eight cases. European Child and Adolescent Psychiatry 6: 23–5.

Zappella M, Meloni I, Lango I, Hayek G, Renieri A (2001) Preserved speech variants of the Rett syndrome: molecular and clinical analysis. American Journal of Medical Genetics 104: 14–22.

Zigler E (1969) Developmental versus difference theories of mental retardation and the problem of motivation. American Journal of Mental Deficiency 73: 536–56.

Zigman W, Silverman W, Wisniewski H (1996) Aging and Alzheimer's disease in Down syndrome: clinical and pathological changes. Mental Retardation and Developmental Disabilities Research Reviews 2: 73–9.

Zigman W, Schup N, Haaveman M, Silverman W (1997) The epidemiology of Alzheimer disease in intellectual disability: results and recommendations from an international conference. Journal of Intellectual Disability Research 41: 76–80.

Zisk P, Bialer I (1967) Speech and language problems in mongolism: a review of the literature. Journal of Speech and Hearing Disorders 32: 228–41.

Chapter 4
School inclusion

SALVATORE SORESI, LAURA NOTA

For too long the treatment of individuals with disabilities was influenced by prejudices, sometimes held by the very people who were responsible for their care. This brought about the notion that it was necessary to isolate individuals with impairments and disabilities[1] – especially particularly 'visible' ones – to protect oneself against them and to deny them numerous rights such as the right to vote, to emigrate, to marry, procreate, or have possessions. Those same individuals were, at best, the object of 'pity' and 'charity' – especially on the part of religious organizations, which considered it utopian and naïve to try to ease their difficulties or to increase the likelihood of their actively participating in community life.

Recently a new ideological and social awareness, supported by progress in medical, psychological and educational disciplines, has reduced these prejudices and has convinced specialists and others that, under certain conditions, improvement and inclusion would also be possible for individuals showing clear forms of impairment and disability.

Since the 1960s, however, international laws and regulations have granted these 'different' individuals the same rights and dignity that they grant to everyone. We are convinced that, today, any debate on how to formulate methods for habilitation and rehabilitation must respect the individuals who benefit from them and never offend their dignity.

In these final two chapters we will consider the 'conditions' that might be assumed to be necessary to make inclusion possible. To this end, we will recall the experiences of several countries and illustrate the Italian stance on integration, which is considered by many as particularly enlightened and advanced.

From institutionalization to integration

The first 'scientific' documentation on the treatment of individuals with disabilities dates back to the nineteenth century when, in France, Itard attempted to treat the so-called 'savages' of Aveyron and, in Switzerland, Guggenbuehl became interested in individuals with clear cognitive deficits. These 'pioneers' focused the attention of the scientific community on the possibility of facilitating an improvement even in individuals who were traditionally considered impossible to cure and educate. As they were individuals needing systematic treatment and care, the setting up of special 'nursing homes' was then thought the most appropriate response to their needs.

The first nursing home for individuals with mental disabilities was built near Berne in Switzerland in 1839 and was directed by Guggenbuehl. As reported by Thompson (1977), in the US it was Wilbur who established the first institutions in the first half of the 1800s in Massachusetts. He started by giving shelter in his own home to children with mental disabilities. In 1855 his 'experimental school' moved to Boston and soon became the prototype of the institutions that were opened in the nineteenth century.

In Europe, the contribution of Montessori (1870–1952) was particularly important as she was the first to show that even children with severe mental problems could make achievements in reading, writing and manual abilities. She began to spread the idea that the way of conceiving and treating disabilities could be very different from the methods that were popular in her times (Befring, 1994). As reported by Babini and Lama (2000), Montessori's most famous book *Il mètodo della psicologìa scientìfica* [*The Method of Scientific Psychology*], translated in the US in 1912, three years after its Italian publication, soon found a strong international reception – so much so that, with the support of Harvard University's Education Department, it was reprinted six times within a few months. When, in 1913, Montessori was in New York for a conference on Italian Education, she was introduced to the audience by John Dewey; she was welcomed with great ceremony and her concept of special education, which was rooted in the paradigms typical of experimental psychology, was recognized as a 'social medicine' that soon became the steady reference point for many institutions and individuals involved in the treatment of people with disabilities.

In Italy during the nineteenth century the first institutions were opened and the first special schools set up, thanks to municipal initiatives (in Rome, Milan, Naples, Turin, Genoa, Florence, Venice and Palermo) that arose from the recognition that schools could not offer adequate treatment to children with mental disabilities. These institutions opened with the encouragement of some great pioneers of special education (including not only Montessori, but also De Sanctis, Montesano, Bonfigli, and others). Interestingly, as Soresi (1981) underlined, they were set up by local initiatives in a type of administrative 'devolution' and, economically speaking, in the most advantaged nations.

The main function of these institutions and schools, in the US and in Europe alike, was recognized to be that of protecting society from individuals who could not be treated at home and who did not draw any benefit from attending school but rather created problems for the school itself. However, despite the good intentions initially underlying the establishment of these institutions, as time went by they turned into actual detention areas for individuals whom society considered to be undesirable (Thompson, 1977).

The first research studies on the analysis of the effects of institutionalization began to appear in the mid-twentieth century: Goldfarb (1944, 1947), for instance, compared children brought up in adoptive families with institutionalized children and observed that the latter had poorer language, showed more deviant behaviours and usually gained lower scores on psychological development tests. Provence and Lipton (1962) reported similar results when they studied 72 institutionalized children and concluded that life in institutions could actually cause, promote or worsen mental retardation itself. In this connection, Thormalen (1965) highlighted the fact that in these institutions operators devoted very little time (1.9 per cent) to educational activities and a lot (37 per cent) to carrying out activities that individuals with disabilities could have done themselves. They were thus consolidating dependence. Klaber (1969) underlined how individuals in these institutions spent between 33 per cent and 50 per cent of their time in total passivity and between 15 per cent and 20 per cent showing autistic behaviours.

Although several researchers and scholars started to have doubts about institutionalization and special schools, the move from exclusion to integration in the ordinary context of schoolchildren with disabilities was actually started in the US thanks to the brave initiatives of enlightened parents and family members who took their case to court (see Diana vs. Pennsylvania, 1971). This led to the spreading of the 'Rights to Equal Educational Opportunities' charter, which was actually extended to all individuals with disabilities regardless of severity and development level. It also led to the first inclusion attempts which found support in the normalization movement, which spread the conviction that educational curricula can and must be enjoyed by everyone in the least restricted way possible. This was the beginning of so-called mainstreaming, which had the effect of promoting and encouraging the appreciation and acceptance of individuals with disabilities by stimulating awareness about ongoing difficulties and discomfort in their lives (Keller and Sterling-Honig, 1993; Jenkins et al., 1985).

In Italy, at the end of the 1970s, the movement toward deinstitutionalization was accelerated by heated debates on the social causes of deviance. For the first time, at least in Italy, political forces and health and social workers who traditionally did not interact began to work together, inspired by the writings of Goffman (1968), Laing (1968), Cooper (1972) and Basaglia (1967). Their led to the closure of mental homes and the setting up of community psychiatric care. These debates soon began to examine the role of schools and accused them of being the result of a system that was mainly based on the principles of capitalism, productivity and conformism. The special school was accused of simply, at best, managing and controlling those forms of deviance that the common school often produced. The discussion started to include the relationships between schoolchildren's socio-cultural levels and their school achievement, between characteristics of the social classes and the likely appearance of psychological problems – so much so that the capitalistic socio-economic system itself was regarded by some as the 'cause' of the onset of marginalization and deviance (Soresi, 1981). In a spontaneous and uncoordinated way, experimentation with inclusion 'models' began, which envisaged, on the one hand, the dismantling of the special school and the setting up of class-groups of individuals with disabilities in normal schools and, on the other, significant changes in the basic curricula that would allow schoolchildren with mental disabilities to participate in some shared educational activities.

The Italian law

Following the debates mentioned above, 'integration' and the dismantling of special schools started in a spontaneous way and without special resources and support. This drew the attention of the establishment and the legislators to the problems of individuals with disabilities, and they felt the need to regulate what was occurring spontaneously in several Italian regions. Several laws were approved, which were carefully studied by foreign governments and workers in the field. Without a doubt, the most important and famous was law 118 of 30 March 1971, which not only defined the different 'protected categories' of citizens and ratified the closure of mental homes but, in Article 28, also regularized the existing attempts at integration of children with disabilities into the school system by stating that 'compulsory education was to take place in the regular classes of the state school'.

The clear choice of school inclusion and the need for a democratic school open to everyone was further confirmed a few years later in law 517/1977. It was considered as particularly innovative because it:

- abolished different and special classes;
- established the principle that the school had to include and provide support for children with disabilities, in both the elementary school and the middle school;

- introduced the role of the special education teacher who was to work alongside the regular class;
- stated that teaching and learning had to be rooted in joint responsibility and in an educational programming respectful of children's different needs and that educational efforts had to be directed not only toward individuals with disabilities who were considered 'teachable' but to everyone regardless of the degree of severity of their disabilities.

After some 20 years of school integration experiences, in 1992 law 104 gave firm rules on the community and work inclusion of individuals with disabilities, underlining the need to aim at their maximum autonomy by establishing preventive, curative, rehabilitative, juridical, economic and social services. Article 2 refers to the importance of prevention (health information and education, and the detection and removal in the work environment of risk factors that might cause congenital malformations and pathologies), the requirement for early diagnosis and a prevention programme that safeguards children from birth. In order to promote the right to education and instruction it requires a functional-dynamic profile to be drawn up, describing the individual's strengths and weaknesses as well as ambits of intervention. The profile is drawn up by class teachers together with special education teachers, health and social operators and parents. This law reiterates the concept of school inclusion of individuals with disabilities in all schools, that is to say also in high schools and universities, and calls for greater linkage between school and extra-school activities. Besides supplying rules about teachers' pre-school and in-service training, Article 14 addresses organizational flexibility and educational and teaching stability. In particular, it envisages the implementation of open classes, which can be formed in accordance with students' needs, and compulsory consultation between teachers of different classes. Lastly, among other things, it also envisages specific examination modalities, allowing the partial replacement of the subject matter curriculum in accordance with the actual teaching carried out in compulsory schools, the utilization of equivalent tests, longer time allocation and forms of support in high schools, and the necessary aids for university examinations.

In 1994 law 104 was subsequently regulated by a Decree of the President of the Republic, known as the Act of Guidance and Coordination, on the tasks of the local health and social security offices as regards schoolchildren with disabilities, which gave a series of important requirements for inclusion, specifying the criteria to be followed as:

- The *identification of schoolchildren with disabilities* (Article 2), which must be done by 'the specialist after notification from the services or the head of the school involved, or by the developmental psychologist working at the local health services . . . within ten days from the day of notification'.

- The drawing up of the so-called *functional diagnosis* (Article 13) understood as an analysis of the functional damage to the child. The functional diagnosis is carried out by a multidisciplinary unit, which is made up of a specialist in the appropriate pathology, a child neuro-psychiatrist, a rehabilitation therapist, and social workers at the local health service. The functional diagnosis combines clinical, psychological and social elements. The clinical elements are derived from a medical examination and from the acquisition of previous medical records, if any. The psychosocial elements are derived from a specific report that includes the child's personal data and data about the characteristics of the family.

It is also stated that the functional diagnosis must necessarily comprise:

- the schoolchild's physiological and pathological medical history, with particular reference to conditions at birth and neuropsychological development from 0 to 16 years of age, vaccinations, illnesses, hospitalizations, possible therapeutic programmes under way, surgical operations, previous rehabilitation experiences;
- a clinical diagnosis, drawn up by a specialist in the pathology in question, referring to the aetiology and the functional consequences of the disability and predicting its natural evolution.

The functional diagnosis must take into particular consideration:

- cognitive ability (level of development actually achieved);
- relational-affective ability (level of self-esteem and relationships with others);
- linguistic ability (comprehension, production and alternative languages);
- sensory ability (degree and type of deficit with particular reference to eyesight, hearing and touch);
- motor ability (gross and fine motor movements);
- neuropsychological ability (memory, attention, time-space organization);
- personal and social autonomy.

Furthermore, the Act of Guidance suggests the drafting of the 'functional dynamic profile' that follows the functional diagnosis and indicates the foreseeable level of development that the child should acquire in the short (6 month) and medium (2 year) term. The dynamic functional profile is drawn up by the multidisciplinary unit, the class teachers and the special education teachers of the school, who make their report on the basis of their experience of similar situations, with the collaboration of the child's parents. Article 4 goes on to indicate what must be included in the profile (functional descriptions of the difficulties, analysis of cognitive, relational-affective, communication, linguistic, sensory, motor abilities, neuropsychological development and development of autonomy and learning) and the frequency with which the profile should be updated.

Important steps toward the inclusion of students with disabilities have recently been made in other official documents. For instance, the Regulation on Autonomy approved by the government on 25 September 1999 explicitly mentions school inclusion (in Article 4). It requires education, training, and instruction appropriate for the characteristics of the students involved. It states that a correct approach to school inclusion should involve:

- timetable flexibility;
- personalized teaching in accordance with the general principle of schoolchildren's class inclusion;
- modular organization of groups of schoolchildren coming from the same class or from different classes or from different grades;
- the bringing together of disciplines into wider disciplinary fields;
- the use of teachers in ways that can be modified in different classes or sections of classes in accordance with possible differences in the methodological and organizational choices required by the instructional programme;
- the exchange of teachers between schools;
- the integration of training curricula with disciplines chosen by the school institutions;
- the availability of options to students and their families, taking into account schoolchildren's different needs.

From the above it is apparent that responsibility for what is done to promote inclusion rests with the individual school, which is called upon to show planning and decisional abilities, organizational flexibility, ability to get involved, and professionalism without the alibi that current legislation does not allow or plan for the personalization of teaching and learning experiences.

The principles of inclusion have also been reiterated in other recent official documents:

- Decree 249 of the President of the Republic of 24 June 1998 (Ruling on the Statute of Secondary School Students), regarding high schools, states in Article 1, that the school community must work to guarantee its citizens training, the right to study, development of each individual's potentialities, and recovery from disadvantages that they might have experienced. Students' rights include the right to benefit from curricula that take into consideration their learning rhythms and their life needs. Among the duties is the requirement to respect all fellow students. Students with disabilities are also granted the right to education appropriate to their abilities and potential. In any case, they too 'have some duties' – so much so that disciplinary measures can be applied to students with disabilities, even mental disabilities, whenever they break the rules. It is also said that nobody can be considered 'irrecoverable' and that students with disabilities also have a sense of responsibility for their own actions and can therefore benefit from disciplinary sanctions, which are educational rather than corrective.

- Decree 331 of the Minister for Education of 24 July 1998 (regulations on re-planning of school networks, class structures and school person-nel organizations) provides important information about organizational matters for those engaged in activities of inclusion planning. In particular, besides establishing the number of students in each class, Article 45 envisages the 'possibility of planning didactic activities for small groups of students or for larger groups enrolled in different classes'. However, this method of organization does not lead to fixed groups of students with disabilities in such a way that they may lose contact with their reference class.

- Decree 323 of the President of the Republic of 23 July 1998 (which rules on state examinations for high school, in accordance with Article 1, law 425 of 10 December 1997) addresses another important aspect: learning assessment. It recalls the principles established in law 427/97 on the setting up of tasks that must take into consideration students' impairments and disabilities, and provide assistance. Article 13 states that, in case of failure, 'the student must receive a certificate' of 'acquired competencies, knowledge and abilities, even professional ones if applicable, and the credits allotted in the examination'.

- Law 449 of 18 February 1997 requires that there must be a post for a special education teacher for every 138 students attending state district schools.

- Finally, all teachers, as a part of their regular training, must attend courses that enable them to acquire attitudes and competencies relevant to the inclusion at school of children with disabilities (Decree of 26 June 1998 of the Ministry for University and Scientific Research).

Study plans for the degree course in primary school education (for nursery and elementary school teachers) and in postgraduate schools for secondary school teachers must include at least 400 hours relevant to the inclusion at school of students with disabilities, as well as 100 hours of practical training with the aim of acquiring experience in special education teaching.

These laws sanction the right to school inclusion and public education of every individual with disabilities, from elementary school to university, independently of disability level. It can be said that this is an innovative law, attentively scrutinized by legislators of other nations. In the US, school inclusion is regulated by the Americans with Disability Act (ADA) (PL 101-336) of 1990, which aims, on the one hand, to forbid segregation in public and private sectors and, on the other, to anticipate the assistance that an individual with particular needs might require.

This Act is not equivalent to the Italian law. In fact it states the right of individuals with disabilities to be included in an environment as little restricted as possible; that is to say, 'inclusion refers to giving public and free schooling to all students with disabilities in an environment that is as near as possible to normal schooling' (Zionts, 1997: 4). This statement can be interpreted in different ways: Osborne and DiMattia (1994) say that there are those who have thought that it applied to individuals with mild disabilities, and Zionts (1997) maintains that it is the concept of the least restricted environment that has been differently understood. As regards schooling, it is a duty to include children in common contexts as long as the nature and severity of their disabilities are not so great as to stop them from gaining satisfactory benefit from the school system. Unlike the situation under Italian law, there are conditions imposed on inclusion – so much so that students with severe and multiple disabilities can actually be denied this 'right' (Stowe and Turnbull, 2001).

The advantages of inclusion for the children

In our opinion, quite apart from the advantage of promoting respect for human rights, Italian laws have also promoted an acceptance in society of what the scientific research has emphasized for years. Inclusion, if correctly implemented (in contrast with what happens when individuals with disabilities simply join a class without proper preparative steps), seems to have cognitive, scholastic, and social advantages not only for students with disabilities but also for normal ones.

The advantages of inclusion for children with disabilities

Inclusion seems to guarantee the best school performance, as has now been well documented. The reviews carried out between the end of the 1970s and the beginning of the 1980s (Semmel et al., 1979; Strain and Kerr, 1981; Wang and Baker, 1985) clearly demonstrate that individuals with disabilities placed in normal contexts show higher ability than those in special classes. In the former there is a climate that encourages competition and emphasizes the learning of at least the basic scholastic abilities. Lipsky and Gartner (1991: 43) maintain that 'special education must be changed for one simple reason: it doesn't work'. Normal environments, in fact, are highly stimulating and provide more opportunities for 'incidental' learning (Bricker, 1978). Even though inclusion can lead to fewer massive rehabilitation interventions, this does not provoke a slowing down of cognitive, linguistic, motor and social growth (Peck and Cooke, 1983; Odom and McEvoy, 1988; Buyesse and Bailey, 1993; Lamorey and Bricker, 1993), and this is the case even when special support procedures are not used (Jenkins et al., 1985). As far as *social development* is concerned, Jenkins et al. (1985) have compared the performances of students with disabilities included in normal schools and of those attending special schools. When the two groups of individuals (included versus non-included) were compared, those in the first group showed significantly fewer motor behaviours and more social interactions. Children with disabilities who are included tend to use better developed forms of play if they interact with normal children (Guralnick and Groom, 1987; Bailey et al., 1993), activate more social initiative behaviours (Hunt et al., 1994), and show higher rates of awareness and responsibility (Giangreco et al., 1993). A normal environment causes a major sense of satisfaction with relationships when compared to conditions of total segregation and it also produces a more realistic awareness of the child's own social possibilities (Heiman and Margalit, 1998).

Children included in regular classes show greater confidence in themselves, more positive attitudes toward the school and higher health levels than those in special classes; Peetsma and Roeleveld (1998) went as far as to say that inclusion does not negatively influence their self-image either. Further, in a longitudinal study, Peetsma et al. (2001) were able to verify that attending regular classes, in addition to producing better school achievement, did not negatively affect school motivation.

Advantages of inclusion for children without disabilities

In school environments where specific activities are carried out to aid inclusion and to make it a real opportunity for everyone involved, effects on classmates as regards both social and cognitive development can be observed. For instance, the children become more aware of their classmates' difficulties and accept differences to a greater degree (Peck et al., 1992; Giangreco et al. 1993); they have a more positive attitude toward disabilities and a better knowledge of their rights (Beh-Pajooh, 1991); they develop friendly relationships that stimulate a sense of responsibility toward the classmate with difficulties (Grenot-Scheyer, 1994; Staub et al., 1994). From a social point of view classmates can learn to interact with different types of people and have the opportunity to widen their social behaviours. Evans et al. (1994) affirm that experiencing inclusion can increase the probability of having to deal with problem situations in which individuals can be called upon to exercise their problem-solving and social-reasoning abilities. This stimulates the ability to give the correct importance to the differences and behaviour of classmates with disabilities, to make comparisons between feelings that can be experienced in different situations, to understand the value of others and to accept individual differences. Diamond (2001) has measured the level of social acceptance the help strategies achieved and the ability to know emotions in preschool children who attended inclusive classes. The data collected by this researcher confirm the positive influence that such an experience can provide for children who have had the opportunity of playing with children with disabilities and of integrating with them in school activities. Such children show higher acceptance levels of diversities, greater understanding of emotions and produce a greater number of ideas on ways of helping other people.

Results obtained with high school students are also interesting. For example, Murray-Segert (1989) reports that normal students say that inclusion allows greater knowledge of the phenomenon of disability, provides the opportunity to learn how to help other people and in general prepares them to deal with difficulties. This led this researcher to state that such experiences must be considered particularly important in the Western world, in which there are few opportunities to experience the social roles that require one to assume responsibility for the wellbeing of other individuals. Peck et al. (1990), interviewing high school students who had developed friendly relationships with some severely disabled youths, report the adolescents as saying that thanks to these experiences they had a better understanding of other people, they had developed a higher self-concept and, above all, thanks to the help they had given, they were less afraid of unusual or inadequate behaviours and gave less importance to appearance. Helmstetter et al. (1994) found the following in a group of students who had had the opportunity to attend inclusive classes: responsiveness toward the needs of others, a positive view of relationships with individuals with disabilities, a sense of personal maturity and a tendency toward tolerance, attention to personal values and the values of others, and an appreciation of diversity.

Besides positively influencing socio-cognitive development, experiencing inclusion seems to have a positive effect on cognitive development. In this regard, Cushing and Kennedy (1997) wanted to verify the effect that mediation strategies could have on normal individuals. Some students, chosen according to specific criteria, had to give correct support to their schoolmates at particular points during school activities and, in particular, had to adapt the given schoolwork after having carefully listened to and taken note of what to do and give them further explanations and help their participation in class activities. The authors reported an improvement in efficiency and school competence in the normal students involved; they recorded increased attention, a better homework level, and greater participation in class life. Moreover, the analyses conducted in a follow-up situation showed that these benefits tended to last.

There are also some interesting studies that underline how the possibility of attending inclusive classes as early as the nursery school favours the growth of a specific knowledge of impairments, of disabilities and of their consequences (Diamond, 1993; Diamond and Hestenes, 1996). In this regard, Smith and Williams (2001) examined the comprehension that children from 4 to 12 years had of the physical, cognitive and social abilities of children with various disabilities. They found that, according to the impairment considered, the children's evaluation differed as to the ability of each individual. In inclusive schools even the younger children were able to indicate the consequences of different impairments, in particular the physical and sensory ones. The authors also observed that most of the participants were able to indicate the negative consequences on social behaviour of emotional-behavioural problems such as those associated with attention disorders and hyperactivity.

Integration alone is not enough

The integration of students with disabilities in normal schools necessarily produces significant effects on the climate of the class and puts the psycho-pedagogical preparation of teachers under a severe strain. It is clear that it is not realistic to expect the simple integration of children to produce in itself personalized teaching abilities in teachers who have not received specific training, nor satisfactory interaction abilities in classmates who find themselves dealing with peers who, because of their disability, do not facilitate the activation and maintenance of gratifying relationships.

There are a few 'critical points' that must still be resolved about the kind of acceptance experienced by individuals with disabilities in an inclusive school. In our opinion, those who deal with school inclusion should consider the following areas, in particular, which should form the subjects of specific intervention projects:

- Classmates tend not to interact 'spontaneously' with students with disabilities: research studies such as those by Guralnick (1980) and Diamond (1993), to mention only the better known, clearly indicate that normal students do not generally choose as playmates students with disabilities, who are rather less accepted than their normal classmates.
- Students with disabilities are generally less accepted than their 'normal' classmates and experience a social status that is decidedly lower (Tampieri et al., 1988; Larrivee and Horne, 1991).
- The period of inclusion does not appear to facilitate the onset of satisfactory relationships between normal students and students with disabilities – on the contrary, the level of acceptance often seems to diminish as time goes on, and, in any case, remains low even after long periods of inclusion (Brewer and Smith, 1989).
- The quality and quantity of integration that occurs seems to be significantly influenced by teachers' attitudes, by the parents of students both with and without disabilities, and by choices of social health workers (Tampieri et al., 1988). The conviction that peer acceptance is, at least in part, mediated by the teacher is supported also by Dodge et al. (1982). They showed that evaluations of students' social adjustment supplied by the teachers correlated with the school evaluation and with the acceptance levels found in the classrooms.

- Other research studies underline specific relationships between teachers' behaviour and students' acceptance: educational styles centred on punishment whereby teachers frequently resort to rebukes, criticism and disciplinary reprimands seem to correlate negatively with the acceptance levels that students show toward their classmates, whether included or not, while, on the other hand, the frequent use of feedback, educational methods characterized by teacher presence and relationships which reinforce help behaviours and solidarity seem to improve the atmosphere in class as well as increasing acceptance (Larrivee, 1985; Soresi and Nota, 2001).

Moreover, although opinions vary among teachers, perplexity on inclusion tends to increase in the presence of severe disability and marked forms of poor adjustment. They often complain of not having the necessary competence and/or longer 'teaching times', as well as lacking a variety of resources and supports that are rarely available (Horne, 1985; Scruggs and Mastropieri, 1996). Teachers' attitudes become more negative as inclusion situations require curriculum changes and actually interfere with the learning of others; they show greater acceptance of situations that require little extra work, such as the inclusion of socially difficult children, but they have a negative approach toward the inclusion of children with behavioural and learning disabilities (Wilczenski, 1997).

Moreover, on the one hand there seems to be a management that is generally little prepared in the matter of inclusion, which pays more attention to bureaucratic and administrative aspects and to satisfying the demands of the community (Evans et al., 1992; Weiner and Norton, 1993), and on the other hand there are parents who seem to accept the principle of inclusion only to complain if children with disabilities are placed in their own children's classes (Hayes and Gunn, 1988).

Setting up an inclusive environment: training the people involved

As Groppo (1983: 44) maintained, inclusion refers

> to results, at the end of a process of school and social inclusion, which implies on the one hand the overcoming of socio-cultural prejudices, which cause the creation of marginalizing social barriers, and, on the other, the solution of technical organizational, rehabilitation and training problems, which allows attention to be given to the current structural and instrumental deficiencies of the school and of the Local Councils and to the lack of professional training of the social, educational and school operators.

The 'determinants' of the quality and quantity of inclusion must therefore be sought 'outside' the individual with disabilities, in the quality of the social health services provided, in the characteristics of the school and work environments and in the inclination of the social groups to accept or marginalize situations of clear difference.

The quality of inclusion must therefore be considered to be dependent on the context in which inclusion takes place and as the result of the capacity of those involved to intervene appropriately. This requires sophisticated observational abilities to highlight the 'differences' from existing students with the aim of making decisions about different 'treatments'.

Teaching ability, parents' educational sensitivity and the professionalism of those involved in assistance, care and rehabilitation, as well as their 'inclusive' abilities, could be measured by defining the amount of attention devoted to individual differences and the ability to differentiate intervention ways for different students. If this had been the normal way to deal with education and teaching problems, then the need to resort to 'personalized' approaches would not have seemed remarkable (Soresi, 1998; World Health Organization, 1997).

In order to realize a truly inclusive environment it is therefore necessary to plan for the specific training of the people with a significant role in this environment and who have the power to characterize it. Those who should be involved are:

- regular teachers;
- social workers and health workers who are involved in various ways in the inclusion processes of individuals looked after by the local health services;
- parents of normal children;
- classmates of children with disabilities.

Specific experiments were carried out in Italy with the aim of promoting good environments for integration. They were characterized by:

a) active participation of the individuals considered each time;
b) strong realism;
c) rigorous planning;
d) gradual teaching/learning processes.

With regard to point a), learning theorists agree that the active participation of individuals in the training activities should be facilitated in order to enable, maintain and generalize learning. As Fontana Tommasucci (1983: 50) recalls 'a purely receptive or "responding" student does not learn new behaviors . . . he or she must "build" his or her repertory through a continual non-generic work which corresponds to activities aiming at achieving the preset goal'. Ways were therefore found to make the intervention as active as possible: training in goal setting, which emphasizes the definition of directly observable performances, frequent use of 'models' to be observed and imitated, constant use of feedback, analysis of the effects exercised on participants by the different proposals.

With regard to point b), criticism is often directed to the educational services about the 'distance' between their proposals and real, everyday situations. In order to diminish the gap between the 'artificial' situation presented in the training and the 'family' reality that parents and teachers experience daily, some 'homework' was given that had a threefold aim:

- To allow an efficient assessment of the interventions carried out in the training sessions (quantifying learning in view of a teaching evaluation).
- To facilitate recall and use of what is learned in the training in places and with times other than the training situations. From this point of view, a number of teachers, social workers, health workers and parents have often reported that they continued to discuss the 'homework' and the proposals put forward even during the week in between sessions.
- To allow analysis of modifications arising from suggestions that were brought up by the parents and operators themselves. For this reason in each meeting and in each training unit, most of the available time was devoted to the analysis of the homework with all types of participants.

Lastly, as concerns rigorous planning, we have taken into account the need to proceed with an intentional and rigorous programme. In fact efficacious management of learning cannot avoid a series of decisions aiming, on the one hand, to create environmental conditions facilitating learning and, on the other hand, to reduce the likelihood of extemporaneous, chance and occasional interventions. The most important decisions made in the intervention planning concerned:

- goal setting and modality to define goals in order to allow an intersubjective verification of their achievement;
- the choice of assessment procedures in the presence of the prerequisites necessary for the activation of the various training units;
- the choice of a planning modality for the training unit, aiming at facilitating learning;
- the choice of procedures to verify the efficiency of the proposed interventions.

In particular, as regards goal setting, in accordance with Mager (1967), we decided to define clearly: conditions of goal evaluation, directly observable performances that proved goal achievement, expected mastery criteria in order to avoid subjective evaluations by the various operators. As far as the assessment of the prerequisites is concerned, reaching the mastery criterion of the previous unit was considered sufficient. To facilitate goal attainment for each training unit, a specific learning guide was devised and the teaching techniques listed below were used. Finally, as regards the assessment of efficacy of intervention and of the programme as a whole, it was decided to examine, for each training unit, how the participants fared in reaching the mastery criteria set for them. For some interventions perceived satisfaction levels as well as normative procedures were used.

Teaching techniques used

As already mentioned, each training unit planned the verbal and non-verbal behaviours that the trainer should show in the training situation to facilitate achievement of each goal. In particular, it gave instructions on how to recall the abilities learned in the previous sessions, how to communicate the goal of the current session, how to use the teaching techniques envisaged in an appropriate way, and how to verify achievement of criteria. The intervention planned for the use of the following teaching techniques: instructions – used when it was necessary to give definitions, description of knowledge and abilities and the advantages associated with improving them (Schumaker et al., 1988); modelling – used when it was considered necessary to 'show' the abilities and behaviours that were to be learned (Carter and Sugai, 1988; Kerr and Nelson, 1989); and role-play – considered necessary to train participants on how to deal with difficult situations and produce assertive solutions in such contexts (Gaylord-Ross and Haring, 1987). In addition, social reinforcements and feedback of information (Ladd, 1981; Soresi and Nota, 2000) were frequently used, as were other teaching techniques of a more cognitive type, such as self-observation, self-evaluation of one's own performances and the 'cognitive' anticipation of the various situations (Schumaker et al., 1988). Each training unit was articulated in the following way:

* prerequisite recall – that is to say, the analysis of the knowledge and abilities examined in the previous training unit, of each participant's homework and of the activities carried out to further maintenance and generalization;
* introduction of the new knowledge and abilities through the presentation of specific definitions and research data, drawn from the most up-to-date literature, and discussion of what is proposed;
* simulations and/or exercises aiming to facilitate better understanding and easier learning of what is proposed;
* analysis and discussion of the simulation activities and of the exercises carried out, as well as a summary of what has been considered;
* homework assignment.

At the end of the activity, reinforcing information about the work done by participants and feedback about their performance were provided. In addition, everyone was given a handout that reported the issues dealt with together with bibliographic notes, the criterion task and the homework allotted.

We would like to emphasize that there was an agreement between ourselves and the participants, who were all volunteers: on the one hand, we promised to carry out a training activity that would improve participants' abilities, cover specific material and supervise the activities done in class and family contexts; on the other hand, they promised to attend the training, to bring the required material and to do what they were asked. Meeting dates, schedules, and type of participation required were specified beforehand. In accordance with Tams and Eyberg (1976), it was stated at the outset that if any participant missed two consecutive sessions, he or she would have to go back to the 'waiting list' and wait for the next training activity to be started before resuming his or her training.

The places where the training would take place were prearranged. Some places are more suitable than others. It is important to use welcoming environments (with desks and chairs suitable for adults, in contexts that actually allow simulations, role-plays, and so forth, to take place). It is important to pay careful attention even to such 'decorative' factors as the quality of the paper material handed out, and to check the actual usability of the training materials and supports (blackboards, videorecorders, notice boards, and so forth). This encourages people to think that their training is considered 'important' and 'serious' and makes them understand that the activities offered are not impromptu and superficial but are deserving of their attention.

The teachers' involvement programme

The teachers' involvement programme included 46 nursery, elementary and middle-school teachers from a north Italian district. In choosing them it was decided to select the 'regular' teachers, as the success of inclusion seems to depend on them rather than on specialist teachers. As already stated, in fact, inclusion requires adjustments and changes to the programme and to the usual teaching modalities in order to meet the needs and necessities of heterogeneous groups of participants (Garvar-Pinhas and Schmelkin, 1989). The programme was carried out in two phases.

The first, based on what had been proposed to parents and social health workers, aimed at facilitating inclusion and personalization of learning.

The issues dealt with in the first phase are summarized below:

- *First training unit:* conditions of teaching and learning.
- *Second training unit:* defining the aims.
- *Third training unit:* personalizing the aims.
- *Fourth training unit:* choosing the aims.
- *Fifth training unit:* systematic observation.
- *Sixth training unit:* direct and indirect observation.
- *Seventh training unit:* learning disabilities.
- *Eighth training unit:* personalized teaching.
- *Ninth training unit:* how to personalize teaching.
- *Tenth training unit:* how to teach acceptance of disabilities.

The second phase was arranged in three modules which dealt with the following issues:

First module

1. The functional diagnosis.
2. Instruments for the analysis of cognitive processes (first part).
3. Instruments for the analysis of cognitive processes (second part).
4. Instruments for the analysis of reading abilities.
5. Instruments for the analysis of writing abilities.
6. Instruments for the analysis of logical-mathematical abilities.

Second module

7. Personalized educational plan.
8. Deficit-centred training.
9. Programming personalized teaching.
10. Increasing and stimulating cognitive abilities.
11. How to increase reading abilities.
12. How to increase writing abilities.
13. How to increase logical-mathematical abilities.
14. How to improve the study method (first part).
15. How to improve the study method (second part).
16. How to improve social abilities.

Third module

Twelve group meetings every two weeks with the aim of defining and verifying the personalized education projects.

The first four training units aimed to obtain a shared view of the concepts of learning and teaching. In accordance with Deci and Chandler (1986), learning was considered essentially as the set of the *cognitive and non-cognitive processes through which the human being acquires, uses and maintains his own and others' knowledge and experience.* This was intended to convince teachers that sustaining and facilitating learning (teaching) cannot limit itself only to emphasizing cognitive aspects (memory, attention, perception) and school abilities (reading, writing, arithmetic), but that it is at least as important to consider the non-cognitive aspects – motivational, behavioural, relational, and so forth.

Our concern was to ensure that teachers could describe themselves essentially in terms of learning facilitators and facilitators of school inclusion. Our aim was that they should be able to remain aware of the need for attentiveness in inclusion programmes on the understanding that, in the school context, a variety of difficult 'cases' exist with which they must deal. For instance, teachers should be able to choose and

implement teaching modalities that are effective for different students
and, in particular, for those who:

- are successful in all learning sectors;
- do not yet have the necessary prerequisites to successfully begin dealing with the programme arranged by the school;
- present specific learning difficulties, despite possessing normal or
  higher than normal intelligence;
- have adequately developed a series of basic abilities, but are unable to
  adequately apply them because they have not had the opportunity to
  practise them and have very few opportunities to do so in their daily
  life;
- are unable to benefit in a satisfactory way from the normal curricula
  because of mental difficulties and require substantial personalized
  teaching programmes;
- present emotional and relational problems that inhibit them from
  using the teaching found in normal schools;
- may not share all the values or follow the rules of the rest of the class,
  being of a different culture and race, in addition to having linguistic
  and communication problems;
- have specific impairments (visual, hearing, motor, and so forth) and
  despite benefiting from the use of supports and prostheses see their
  likelihood of participating in school life diminished.

It can be very difficult to choose educational procedures because the
behaviour and performance of students is not always evident beforehand, so our aim was to strengthen teachers' abilities to define and set
objectives by making reference to a markedly experimental psycho-edu-
cational literature (for example, Mager, 1967; Gagnè, 1965; De
Landsheere, 1971). They were expected to be able to describe attainable
goals using an operational and intersubjectively justifiable language,
indicating:

- the performance or performances that students or groups would have
  to be able to show indicating with precision what they would be taught
  'to say and do';
- the situations in which performances were expected to be shown;
- mastery criterion – the quality and/or amount of desired performance
  that had to be established in order to be able to claim that the intervention was successful.

As far as goals were concerned, the teachers had to be able to ascertain
their relevance and suitability. Relevance means being able to justify why
an objective is chosen. Teachers were then prepared to single out criteria
related to specific legal norms, or suggestions in the literature, or to the
frequency of use of particular abilities in school and extra-school
environments, or, lastly, to the 'enjoyment' and pleasantness level associated with teaching and learning.

Suitability means controlling whether and to what extent the aims singled out are suitable to the characteristics of the participants they had been devised for, or whether it would have been more appropriate, before dealing with them, to single out some others that, if attained, would make a good starting point for the continuation of the teaching activity. Teachers were trained to use specific task analysis procedures to establish these and to observe the abilities considered necessary to proceed with the teaching.

The fifth and sixth training units aimed at increasing the teachers' ability to discriminate between occasional and systematic observation, to note the negative consequences of certain procedures, and to indicate the procedures that would allow the realization of activities of systematic observation (stating the observation ambit, devising and using procedures for coding and recording the collected information, choosing times and methods, checking reliability and validity). Teachers had to be able to differentiate between direct and indirect observation; direct observation refers to data collection operations in which the observer records and measures the observed events and whose aim is only to record the 'manifest levels', as Fox (1969) defined them, that is to say, what an individual says and does, where, when and in whose presence he or she behaves in this or that way. *Indirect observation*, refers to recording the reactions individuals show in the presence of more-or-less structured and ambiguous stimuli intentionally devised and proposed by the observers – for example, reactions during an interview, during the administration of questionnaires, evaluation scales, tests, and so forth. The teachers had to be able to devise simple instruments for direct observation of behaviours facilitating school inclusion, to choose between a number of instruments, and to use them correctly. In this connection, special emphasis was given to evaluation and nomination sociometric measures that were useful to the analysis of levels of social acceptance within the class (Coie et al., 1990).

The goal of the seventh training unit was to increase teachers' ability to distinguish between the various difficult situations found in the class – individuals with mental disabilities, with learning difficulties, with sociocultural disadvantages – and to take into consideration specific indicators suggesting such differences. The eighth and ninth training dealt with the personalization of goals and to the planning of training units allowing personalization of teaching. By considering the characteristics of students and groups, teachers could assist attainment of the mastery criteria specified in the preset goals. Setting up the training unit enabled teachers to reflect and decide on which materials and intervention strategies could turn out to be more advantageous and useful.

These abilities were considered important as they would allow teachers to choose which interventions to carry out with which students, without 'forcing' the more able ones to do the 'same things' that had been planned for the less able ones, and to privilege, as far as possible, teaching and learning areas that allow for goal differentiations. Moreover, these abilities would also allow advantages to be drawn from almost any curriculum arranged in such a way as to leave room for improving and studying in depth. This is certainly so for history, geography and natural sciences, but also for mathematics and linguistics – disciplines that, from a psychological, educational and training viewpoint, allow students 'to go back and study more in depth', but also 'to stop a little to verify something' and to anticipate developments and consequences. Lastly, it was emphasized that there are areas of teaching, such as those dealing with autonomy, personal and social adjustment, vocational guidance, and so on, which, although particularly important for students with disabilities, are also relevant for students without particular difficulties.

The last training unit aimed at strengthening teachers' abilities to go further into the concept of inclusion to promote it in the classroom by using specific curricula that might encourage students to hold positive attitudes toward diversity, as well as enabling them to develop adequate pro-social abilities of helping and collaborating with their classmates in difficulty (Soresi and Nota, 2001).

The training session lasted for two hours and took place once a week. The whole first phase of the course lasted for about three months. Each meeting involved a restricted group of teachers (no more than 25) so as to allow everyone's active participation, discussions and role-plays, and analysis of the 'homework' — specific activities aiming at maintaining and generalizing what was proposed in the training. As an example, the objective chosen for training unit 7 is reported in Table 4.1. To check whether the goal had been attained, at the end of the sixth training unit the criterial task shown in Table 4.2 was used.

Table 4.1 Example of an objective teachers' programme

Conditions:
In the presence of:
a. a 12-item multiple choice criterion task requiring the definition of learning difficulties, hypotheses about the factors that might have caused them, the criteria to utilize to define them and the type of relational and motivational problems that such individuals could show;
b. request to describe the learning difficulties of one of his/her students.

Performances:
The teacher:
a. supplies correct answers to the criterion task items;
b. describes the learning difficulties of one of his/her students.

Mastery criterion:
The aim is attained when the teacher:
a. answers correctly at least 10 of 12 items in the criterion task;
b. describes at least one situation of learning difficulty, differentiating it from situations of mental disability and socio-cultural disadvantage.

Table 4.2 Example of a criterion task, teachers' programme

Criterion task of training unit 6, Mastery criterion: 10/12

1. The learning difficulties concern:
-   deficits in the global development of intellectual processes
-   deficits in one or more of the processes involved in the understanding and use of written and spoken language
-   deficits in perceptual and sensory processes

2. When individuals deal with new unexpected tasks typically:
-   they may experience discomfort and difficulties while learning, without however being diagnosed as individuals with learning disabilities
-   they deal with them and resolve them without any difficulties
-   if they experience difficulties they have certain impairments and disability

3. If a student shows difficulties in learning it means that:
-   in such a situation he or she 'cannot learn'
-   in such a situation he or she 'does not want to learn'
-   in such a situation he or she 'refuses to learn'

4. As it concerns the 'causes of learning difficulties', the 'intrinsic unidimensional' hypothesis refers to:
-   difficulties that can be found in teaching processes
-   emotional-behavioural problems existing in the student's family
-   deficits in cognitive processes not necessarily implied in that specific learning

5. As it concerns the 'causes of learning difficulties', the 'extrinsic unidimensional' hypothesis refers to:
-   difficulties that can be found in teaching processes
-   emotional-behavioural problems existing in the student's family
-   deficits in cognitive processes not necessarily implied in that specific learning

6. As it concerns the 'causes of learning difficulties', the 'multidimensional or interactive' hypothesis refers to:
-   difficulties that can be found in teaching processes
-   contextual and personal causes
-   deficits in cognitive processes not necessarily implied in that specific learning

7. Indicate, among the following, the criteria that must be followed to correctly describe a learning difficulty:
-   coming from socio-culturally disadvantaged environments
-   absence of dysfunctions at cerebral structure level
-   presence of specific rather than generalized deficits
-   non-systematic school attendance
-   a lower-than-average intelligence quotient (IQ)
-   absence of neurological disabilities
-   discrepancy between cognitive potential and school achievement
-   presence of brain and/or sensory lesions since birth

Table 4.2 Example of a criterion task, teachers' programme (contd)

8. Individuals with learning difficulties differentiate from those with mental retardation in as much as:
*   the former have a normal IQ
*   the former have a lower than average IQ
*   the former show clear genetic damage

9. Emotional and relational problems of individuals with learning difficulties:
*   are due above all to their character and disposition
*   are connected especially to the teaching-learning context
*   are the cause of their learning difficulties

10. In relation to learning, motivation:
*   determines the extent and quality of school achievement
*   increases with the increase of learning
*   depends on the intellectual level of the learner

11. Individuals with learning difficulties:
*   seem to have better social abilities than their peers
*   seem to have the same social abilities as their peers
*   seem to have significant differences in social abilities compared with their peers

12. According to recent research, teachers:
*   have a lower number of positive relationships with students with learning difficulties
*   have a higher number of positive relationships with students with learning difficulties
*   treat students with learning difficulties the same way as they treat all the others

In the second and third phase of the training activities the same method was followed; however, attention was directed in particular toward increasing abilities necessary to assess cognitive and school abilities, reading, writing and logical-mathematical skills. In particular, instruments were presented that were standardized for the Italian context and addressed the analysis of competencies of students with greater difficulties. The teachers had to show their knowledge of the theoretical models to which the instruments made reference and their competence in their application and in the analysis and interpretation of results.

As concerns the second phase, our aim was to increase teachers' abilities to devise specific individualized interventions for students with difficulties within the class context and in collaboration with the special education teachers and social and health workers.

Besides being asked to apply training techniques (with the appropriate modifications) to strengthen different abilities, teachers were also required to devise teaching pathways in view of what we have defined as the 'core curriculum', that is to say the essential aspects of the different disciplines, including also the 'more important' ones such as mathematics, history, science and languages. They had to carry out 'adjustment' and modification tasks. The former were tasks that did not alter the preset goals in terms of performance or mastery criteria, but rather that changed their conditions and those of the proposed materials (size of character, images describing action sequences typically given verbally, presence of colours that allowed discrimination between different concepts, and so forth). Modification, on the other hand, could concern:

- revision of goal mastery criteria (fewer items in the criterion task or establishing items considered particularly representative of learning);
- choice of specific activities to be given special attention in the different curricula (comprehension rather than speediness in reading, for instance);
- choice of important goals that could be achieved with the cooperation of teachers in different disciplinary areas (for example, writing words in a foreign language on the computer).

The teachers had to be aware that if these changes are devised only for the disabled students included in a class, 'exclusion' and marginalization dynamics were likely to occur and significantly decrease levels of class participation. To avoid that, the tasks to be carried out – not all of which were easy – required the active participation of the class teachers, especially the most competent ones from a training-disciplinary point of view, in the organization of training activities personalized for different learners and not only for the disabled students (Montgomery, 1987). Proposing 'normal' school activities increased the students' likelihood of having many experiences, allowed frequent interactions with their peers without disabilities thanks to their shared learning experiences, and decreased the risk of falling into what Visser (1993) called 'educational segregation'. Where such tasks had actually been carried out, remarkable improvements in the proposed training activities had been obtained and a more fruitful collaboration had been established between the students themselves (Koegel et al., 2001). Harrower and Dunlap (2001) suggested specific operations to be carried out as 'antecedents' of school activities and as 'consequences' of the same. The former try to anticipate in an individualized way the carrying out of the most difficult and complex tasks to be done in class, so that the student can be prepared to deal with them with less discomfort. If, for instance, it is planned that a student should read and comment upon a passage, it is appropriate for this activity to be presented to the student a few days beforehand by trying to get him or her ready to answer questions that he or she might be asked in class and in the presence of other students. As regards contingencies, the aim was for teachers to be able to pass from continual reinforcing procedures to intermittent reinforcing procedures in order to favour generalization and maintenance of the abilities learned.

To encourage the teachers involved in the inclusion experience to maximize learning opportunities for all students, particular attention was paid to issues associated with study strategies and social abilities. Particular attention was paid to strengthening the class group's abilities to self-manage their own behaviour by always bearing in mind the type of task that was assigned in class during the lessons. Training units were also set up with the aim of increasing ability to take notes in a concise and effective way, to analyse the text to be read and studied, to verify comprehension levels, and to plan one's own study activities both in class and at home. Class study would give teachers greater opportunities to focus in a more individualized way on students with bigger difficulties.

These training units (perhaps with adjustments) can also be used to the advantage of all the students in the class, as well as to increase their self-regulation abilities (Dunlap et al., 1991; Agran et al., 2001; Harrower and Dunlap, 2001).

Strengthening social abilities within the class context not only allows the implementation of activities favouring adjustment processes in all students (Nota and Soresi, 1997) but also enables the improvement of abilities that allow peer mediation and teaching strategies planning for classmates' involvement (how to communicate desires and objectives, how to involve and please classmates, how to share tasks and responsibilities, and so on). Without this preliminary training, for students with and without disabilities alike, group work and play are very likely to transform into a scenario in which the easiest and most common behaviours, which are not necessarily the most adequate and positive, become consolidated. Within educational contexts that have always stimulated competition and ignored the need to teach collaboration and solidarity, it is likely that, when situations are difficult and performances inadequate, threats, punishments and denigration appear among the 'spontaneous' teacher behaviours. In addition to not favouring the onset of positive interactions, they actually reinforce stereotypes, prejudices, and negative attitudes toward situations and individuals who are weaker and in greater difficulty (Odom et al., 1993; Nota and Soresi, 1997). Paying attention to such matters allows the realization of what has recently been defined by Ochs and collaborators (2001) as 'positive inclusion', in which classmates can actually involve the student with disabilities in school tasks.

The third phase included supervision meetings, which took place every two weeks. They allowed teachers' implementation of the programmed interventions and individualized activities to be checked. Support and feedback were provided together with reinforcement of what had been done. This facilitated generalization and maintenance of the abilities learned.

Social and health workers (usually an educational psychologist, a child neuropsychiatrist, a speech therapist, an educator and a social worker) who had benefited from specific training activities on school inclusion (see the programme for the involvement of social and health operators) also participated in these activities. Specific training units, centred on assertive behaviours and teamwork, were then given to strengthen their collaboration abilities. In particular, the aim was to teach:

- how to express desires and opinions;
- how to ask for help and collaboration;
- how to show disappointment and that one is encountering difficulties;
- how to deal with pressure and aggressiveness from others;
- how to collaborate in setting goals and planning training units;
- how to collaborate in the realization of the training units;
- how to support colleagues' work.

A focus on increasing the assertive abilities of teachers and social and health workers has also allowed collaboration in planning training units and other joint school interventions. Teachers capable of recognizing their own and others' social abilities, and who can appreciate the social competence of colleagues and of students in reinforcing them and who can be models of adequate social behaviour, would create the sort of environment advocated by researchers such as Maag (1990) that is able to increase social abilities, particularly of individuals most at risk.

Checking the effectiveness of the teacher training activity

Criterion verification of preset goal attainment showed that the mastery criterion was reached by 90 per cent of participants in almost all the training units (except for the fourth, which required additional time for the content analysis) and that the amount of learning observed at the end of each training unit could be considered satisfactory.

Two months after the end of the course, questionnaires were distributed in which, among other things, participants were asked to give anonymously their evaluation of the activity.

In particular, over 90 per cent of participants considered the assigned homework important and useful, 87.78 per cent said that they used the course contents in planning their professional activity, and 82.60 per cent said that they were able to plan personalized interventions in a team. We think these results underline the fact that the experience was evaluated rather positively on the whole and it has brought significant changes to the usual teaching processes (Soresi and Nota, 2001).

The involvement programme for social and health workers

Obviously, a project on facilitating inclusion should involve disability professionals. In order to allow effective collaboration between health services, schools and families, a training programme was started in the first year of experimentation entitled 'course for inclusion facilitators' just to underline the role that, in our opinion, social and health workers and services should have in this specific field.

The programme was arranged over 10 units that dealt with some important issues of the inclusion process, along the guidelines of what had been proposed for teachers. Here are the titles of the units:

- *First training unit:* professionalism and rehabilitation.
- *Second training unit:* the objectives of rehabilitation.
- *Third training unit:* choice of objectives.
- *Fourth training unit:* how to observe behaviours.
- *Fifth training unit:* group observation.
- *Sixth training unit:* instruments for the analysis of inclusion.
- *Seventh training unit:* how to intervene to address inadequate behaviours.
- *Eighth training unit:* increasing social abilities: principles.
- *Ninth training unit:* increasing social abilities: how to teach them.
- *Tenth training unit:* increasing help and prosocial behaviours.

These meetings were followed by another 12, one every two weeks, with the aim of defining and verifying the personalized educational programmes, together with teachers and parents..

The activity focused on abilities necessary for the definition and choice of objectives and for the management of maladaptive behaviours. Moreover, these workers were encouraged to collaborate with the class teachers to improve class climate and quality of interpersonal relationships (Keenan, 1997). A specific example of an objective that we sought to achieve is presented in Table 4.3 and refers to training unit 8. Table 4.4 shows an example of a criterial task.

Table 4.3 Example of an objective: staff programme

Objective of the eighth training unit

Conditions:
in the presence of:
a. a structured 10-item multiple-choice criterial task, to define social abilities, the reasons why it is important to improve such abilities, formulate examples of social deficits in individuals with learning difficulties and the consequences associated with such difficulties;
b. to describe some objectives to achieve with a student.

Performance:
the staff member:
a. supplies answers to the criterial task;
b. describes three objectives connected to the social abilities to achieve with a student.

Mastery criterion:
the objective is considered reached if the staff member:
a. answers correctly at least 8 of 10 items in the criterial task;
b. describes at least one objective connected to the social abilities to achieve with a student.

Table 4.4 Example of a criterial task: staff programme

Social abilities, Mastery criterion: 8/10

1. To favour an individual's global development it is necessary to:
   * increase cognitive abilities especially
   * increase relational abilities especially
   * increase both cognitive and relational abilities
   * wait until the individual reaches maturity

2. Social abilities:
   * refer to verbal and non-verbal behaviours which affect responses of one's own interpersonal context
   * are verbal behaviours that allow us to establish good relationships with others
   * are behaviours involving individuals' feelings
   * are the behaviours we have when we wish to be good toward others

3. The frequent use of social abilities:
   * allows us to better manipulate others
   * allows us to convince others
   * allows us to do what we wish
   * helps us to establish relationships which are positive and gratifying to ourselves and to others

4. Social abilities are:
   * learned and improvable
   * innate and stable
   * determined by the individual's disposition
   * determined by the individual's character

5. Social ability deficits usually entail (tick all the answers you consider to be correct):
   * presence of shy and/or aggressive behaviours
   * severe forms of maladjustment
   * difficulties in understanding others
   * difficulties in behaving like others would wish

6. Verbal social abilities concern (tick all the answers you consider correct):
   * the expression of one's wishes
   * the expression of the positive aspects concerning oneself and others
   * doing what others wish
   * stopping others from being aggressive toward oneself
   * defending oneself from undue pressures and interferences
   * being able to make everybody happy
   * being considerate with everyone

7. Individuals with learning difficulties:
   * do not usually show particular social ability difficulties
   * are typically very agreeable in relationships with others
   * typically show social difficulties higher than their peers
   * are usually insensitive from an affective point of view

Table 4.4 Example of a criterial task: staff programme (contd)

8. Social abilities deficits present in individuals with learning difficulties (tick all the answers you consider to be correct):
- stop others from establishing positive relationships with them
- make adjustment and social inclusion more difficult
- make others implement greater help behaviours toward them
- cannot be brought under control because of their cognitive difficulties

9. The increase of social abilities proposes:
- to make individuals more compliant
- to recognize and evaluate one's interpersonal relationships
- to satisfy first of all one's own needs
- to satisfy first of all the needs of people who are near us

10. The development of social abilities facilitates especially:
- school inclusion
- school learning
- teachers' benevolence
- implementation of rehabilitation interventions

Checking the effectiveness of the operator training activity

The effectiveness of the training programme for social and health workers was considered satisfactory in terms of achievement of the objectives set for each training unit, the levels of participant satisfaction (checked through an especially devised questionnaire) and the number of personalized training programmes the students were able to complete with the collaboration of teachers and parents of the children with disabilities (Soresi and Nota, 2001).

The parent involvement programme

The programme aiming to stimulate family involvement belongs to a category of parent training (PT) interventions suggested in Soresi (1992). This initiative could not involve a large number of parents because, as is well known, PT programmes can only be implemented within small-group contexts. It was therefore thought appropriate to begin by proposing it to those who held leadership roles within the school and could be considered particularly important in spreading a view on educational issues within the community. In the first experimental year the programme, which was proposed first to 26 parents and then to another 20, was presented in 10 training units, which allowed the in-depth presentation of some issues important to education and to parent participation in school life. The titles are presented below:

- *First training unit:* what are behaviours?
- *Second training unit:* how behaviours are learned.
- *Third training unit:* behaviour observation.
- *Fourth training unit:* analysis of problem behaviours.
- *Fifth training unit:* punishment.
- *Sixth training unit:* alternatives to punishment.
- *Seventh training unit:* educational bargaining.
- *Eighth training unit:* couple conflicts and educational inconsistency.
- *Ninth training unit:* communication styles within the family.
- *Tenth training unit:* participation in school life.

The meetings followed the same methodology used in the teacher training activity expounded above. In this case too, the training took place once a week and each training unit lasted two hours. As an example, Table 4.5 shows the objective envisaged in the third training unit. The criterion task used to verify whether the objective was reached is illustrated in Table 4.6.

Checking the effectiveness of intervention

To verify the effectiveness of the programme a task was planned to check learning by setting a mastery criterion task that was reported satisfactory. It was also possible to check maintenance of learning through a criterion task and the administration of a questionnaire to collect information on the generalization of what was learned in the family context. The follow-up group was made up of 18 parents. Nine of them had completed the

Table 4.5 Example of an objective: parents' programme

Objective of the Third Training Unit

Conditions:
in presence of:
a. a 10-item multiple-choice structured criterial task requiring parents to indicate which indices should be privileged in an observation activity and the reasons why it is important to do such activity;
b. a request to set up a direct observation card on a behaviour shown by a son/daughter.

Performance:
the parent:
a. supplies answers to the criterial task;
b. sets up an observation schedule on which to record frequency and length of behaviour.

Mastery criterion:
the objective is considered reached if the parent:
a. answers correctly at least 8 out of 10 items in the criterial task;
b. sets up a behaviour observation card, at least as frequency.

Table 4.6 Example of criterial task: parents' programme

Training Unit 3: How to observe, Mastery criterion: 8/10

1   The two main recording types that can be used during an activity of observation refer to:
*   quantity and speed (How often? How fast?)
*   quality and length (How well? For how long?)
*   length and frequency (For how long? How many times?)
*   easiness and speed (How easy? How fast?)

   Indicate the type of recording you would use to verify the reaching of each of the following objectives. Write the letter 'F' to indicate frequency (how many times) and the letter 'L' to indicate length (for how long):

2. You want to teach Martino to perform the request 'Come here!' At present he does not always come when he is called.

3. You want to improve Michela's way of working. At present she often stops because she either chats or daydreams.

3. You want to teach Carlo to catch the ball when it is thrown to him. At present he often lets it drop.

4. You want to teach Lisa to spend more time with others. At present she spends only a little time with others.

5. You want to teach Marcello to make his bed every morning. At present he hardly ever does it.

6. You want to teach Paola to wash her hands after she has been to the toilet. At present she hardly ever does it.

8. You want Giacomo to get back home from school more quickly.

9. It is appropriate to observe and accurately record:
*   all children's behaviours
*   behaviours needing educational interventions
*   children's adequate behaviours
*   behaviours shown very rarely by children

10. It is appropriate to record accurately because:
*   in this way our son/daughter realizes we are interested in him/her
*   in this way improvements can be checked
*   in this way one learns to observe
*   in this way the partner will at last believe what he/she is told

course 10 months earlier; the others over 2 years earlier. Data collected on the criterion task allow us to say that most parents of both groups remember at least 81.25 per cent of the concepts dealt with in the parent training activity (that is to say, they answered 13 out of 16 questions correctly). Between the two groups of parents no significant differences were recorded on the 'amount' of recall shown. As regards the questionnaire on the generalization and evaluation of the experience, the parents showed good levels of satisfaction and they almost unanimously stated that the course had been useful and important (Soresi and Nota, 2001).

The involvement programme for first and sixth graders

In the literature there are several programmes whose aim is to facilitate inclusion by adequately preparing the class group to welcome the child with disabilities. In many of these programmes a simulation activity was used in which individuals without disabilities were made to experience different difficult situations like, for example, walking blindfolded, moving around in a wheelchair, performing tasks without hearing the instructions very clearly, and so on. The idea is that knowing and experiencing a condition of disability would make help, solidarity and acceptance behaviours more likely.

In order to be able to check the effectiveness of these interventions some experimental and control groups were established. Participants attending their first year at elementary school were given the following training units:

- *First training unit:* nobody is the same as I am: we are all different.
- *Second training unit:* everybody has difficulties and can make mistakes.
- *Third training unit:* visual disabilities.
- *Fourth training unit:* hearing disabilities.
- *Fifth training unit:* motor disabilities.
- *Sixth training unit:* learning disabilities.
- *Seventh training unit:* a classmate to help.
- *Eighth training unit:* how to interview a mother or a teacher.
- *Ninth training unit:* interviewing a mother and a teacher.
- *Tenth training unit:* how to help a classmate in difficulty.

The contents of the programme for the middle-school children were very similar to those of the programme for elementary school children. With the middle-school children, however, greater stress was laid on the analysis of the differences characterizing 'normal' individuals, definitions of impairment and disability were introduced, and films were shown to highlight the difficulties these individuals can meet in their everyday life.

It was also emphasized that there was a need to avoid giving help to class-mates with difficulties unless it was really necessary, as excessive help can make them think that they are unable to do anything. This sense of low self-esteem can actually produce further demotivation or, even worse, cause deterioration in their performance of tasks. This could then cause more frequent help interventions and trigger off a vicious circle that is often decidedly counterproductive (Graham and Baker, 1990). Lastly, the following were examined: maladaptive behaviour, criteria that can be used to define behaviour as inadequate and techniques that can be used to manage such behaviour should a classmate show it.

Much time was devoted to the fact that inadequate class behaviours were not confined to classmates with disabilities and that knowing what to do in such situations would certainly contribute to a better class atmosphere.

An example of an objective that we sought to achieve is presented in Table 4.7 and refers to the ninth training unit, which was for middle-school students and referred to how to react in presence of inadequate behaviours.

Table 4.7 Example of an objective: children's programme

Objective of the Ninth Training Unit

Conditions:
a) During role-play, where there is the simulation of inadequate behaviours that either the student with disabilities or another classmate might show;
b) During role-play, where there is the simulation of alternative adequate behaviours that either the student with disabilities or another classmate might show.

Performances:
the student:
a) Has not paid attention to the classmate's performances;
b) Reinforces the adequate behaviours.

Mastery criterion:
the objective can be considered achieved if the student:
a) Moves away and keeps a serious face;
b) Smiles and says he/she is happy about what the other is doing.

In order to ascertain the effectiveness of the programme, two types of evaluation were used: criterion and normative. With regard to the first, Table 4.8 shows the percentages of participants who, at the end of each training unit, had reached the mastery criterion.

As regards the other type of evaluation, it was considered appropriate to use a sociometric measure with two direct observation sessions carried out at three and four months respectively after the beginning of inclusion. The analyses are reported below.

Table 4.8 Involvement programme for first and sixth graders: criterion evaluation of learning

Training units	Percentages of M.C. achievement (first graders)	Percentages of M.C. achievement (sixth graders)
1	100	100
2	100	100
3	100	100
4	100	87.50
5	85.71	100
6	100	100
7	100	87.50
8	85.71	100
9	100	100
10	100	100

Sociometric analyses

To find out the acceptance level of the students with disability, at first we used Moreno's sociometric test, asking all the students of the classes involved to indicate which classmates they would or would not like to have with them when doing some activities. The following indices were considered: CR: number of choices received from each member of the class group; RR: number of refusals received from each member of the class group. As can be observed from Table 4.9, the group that had benefited from the elementary school intervention (the experimental group) expressed a higher mean number of choices than the control group. Considering the class as a whole, it could be observed that the students

Table 4.9 Involvement programme for first graders: sociometric indices

First graders

Indices	Experimental group		Control group		t	p
	M	SD	M	SD		
CR	5.66	1.96	4.33	2.16	0.23	0.81
RR	3.71	2.05	4.66	1.96	0.04	0.96

Indices	Class trend		Indications received from the student with disability
	M	SD	
CR	4.28	2.16	5
RR	3.42	2.10	0

included in the first grade had received a number of choices higher than the class mean and a remarkably smaller number of refusals (CR 4.28, SD 2.16; RR 3.42, SD 2.10).

These positive findings, however, can only be seen as suggestive because there were very few participants in the experiment and the statistical significance levels reached do not allow us to draw particularly 'strong' and generalizable conclusions.

As regards the activity with the sixth graders, the sociometric investigation revealed that the mean number of choices made in the experimental class was higher than that recorded in the control class and that this relationship becomes inverted when we consider the number of refusals. Furthermore, this tendency was also confirmed in the experimental class itself (see Tables 4.10 and 4.11).

Table 4.10 Involvement programme for sixth graders: sociometric differences between experimental and control group

Sociometric data: differences between experimental Group A vs control group made up of students from another class

Indices	Experimental group		Control group		t	p
	M	SD	M	SD		
SR	8.89	2.58	7.00	3.09	2.07	0.04
RR	5.10	2.42	6.75	3.90	1.56	0.12

Sociometric data: differences between experimental group B vs control group made up of students from the same class where intervention took place

Indices	Experimental group		Control group		t	p
	M	SD	M	SD		
SR	9.37	3.20	8.54	2.11	0.68	0.5
RR	5.00	2.25	5.18	2.44	0.15	0.87

Table 4.11 Involvement programme for sixth graders: sociometric indices of included students with disabilities and class trends

| | Classes (Group A) in which intervention was carried out | | | | Classes in which intervention was not carried out | |
| | Class trend | | Indications received from student with disability | | Class trend | Indications received from student with disability |
Indices	M	SD	M	SD		
SR	8.89	2.58	11	7.00	3.09	8
RR	5.10	2.42	2	6.75	3.90	3

Direct observation of class inclusion

In order to support the sociometric data with other data, a time-sampling observation activity at fixed 2-minute intervals was carried out, considering 27 behaviour categories that could be grouped in three different areas:

- teacher-included student relationships;
- classmates-included student relationships;
- isolation and passive behaviours.

Analyses carried out on the records of two observation sessions, one at two and one at three months after the beginning of the school year, allow us to state that:

- As regards the class interaction observed in first graders it is the special education teacher above all who interacts with the included student with behaviours of a 'guide to learning' and with physical and gestural help. Interactions initiated toward classmates are present for 22 per cent of the time and they were activated 72 per cent of the time by children of the experimental group. During the interaction, however, isolation and passiveness is considerable (60 per cent of the time).
- As regards class interaction observed in the middle school, it is possible to highlight the interaction observed in the experimental and in the control class. In the experimental class, relationships class teachers initiated toward the included student occurred 25 per cent of the time, while they were almost non-existent in the control class. The special education teacher, in the case of the experimental class, interacted with the included student for 26 per cent of the time, whereas in the other class this was observed for over 50 per cent of the time.
- Relationships that classmates initiated toward disabled students occurred 10 per cent of the time in the experimental class and were almost non-existent in the control class.
- Isolation and passiveness, for the disabled student, seemed to occur 35 per cent of the time in the control class and 26 per cent in the experimental class.

Taking the above into account, in the second year of experimentation it was thought appropriate to supply teachers and social and health operators with indications and instruments on how to increase positive relational behaviours and on how to go about detecting the interactions present in the class.

The advantages of inclusion for teachers and the school

A school that can create inclusive environments improves its quality considerably because it puts together two viewpoints: one grounded in the recognition that students with disabilities have the same rights as their classmates, and another that accepts that differences exist and have to be carefully examined. This implies planning and creating advantageous circumstances for individuals with difficulties, because having the same rights does not necessarily mean having to benefit from the same interventions, which could obviously turn out to be inappropriate when students with marked difficulties are involved (Minnow, 1990). The combination of these two viewpoints, equal rights but different treatments, requires – as we have tried to highlight in the previous pages – competent and trained personnel and careful planning. Besides creating advantages for students with disabilities, this will be important for all those students who find themselves interacting in a school context that pays greater attention to individual needs and to the quality of educational and social interactions that occur within it.

Effective management of inclusion is, we believe, an important opportunity to implement teaching and learning experiences from which everyone should benefit because, as Sailor recalls (1991), it facilitates:

- educational and training activities in several environments, even 'nonscholastic' ones (extension of the class space) by a variety of 'teachers and teachings';
- collaboration between peers and adults (be they professional or not) who are truly interested in achieving shared objectives;
- insertion in a common curriculum of the teaching of abilities that are functional to community adjustment (social abilities and interpersonal problem solving) from which all the students will be able to benefit.

This will have a greater probability of occurring if:

- the planning of any educational activity is totally organized by the school community, thus avoiding the 'growth' of special groups and offices;
- all students are guaranteed the possibility of receiving the attention they need and the support of all teachers regardless of their specializations and roles;
- all students can actually benefit from personalized interventions, school supports and resources;
- all students can record improvements in learning and be assessed not only according to preset standard performances, but in the light of the progress that it was possible to make;
- all students, but also teachers, have some form of learning and teaching support available (tutoring, teaching groups, cooperative learning, supervisions, and so forth);
- particular importance is attributed to prevention of maladjustment disabilities but also to marginalization and institutionalization;
- the quality of school inclusion is the object of systematic monitoring and evaluation (Soresi and Nota, 2001).

This will contribute – at least this is our wish – to an end to grouping students on the basis of supposed homogeneous competence levels and entrusting them to a single teacher, even if he or she is specialized in teaching individuals with a particular type of disability. All teachers should be acquainted with the problems associated with teaching individuals with disabilities, as the need to resort to personalized teaching does not only concern the presence of students with a particular impairment. The model of an inclusive school relies on the use of several resources, including teachers, students and other adults not necessarily employed by the school organization.

What is sure is that inclusion requires competent specialists who are specially trained. It is necessary for education and social and health service providers not only to master the techniques necessary to promote effective educational activities but also to be capable of transforming the school environment into an environment capable of integrating the different circumstances that can arise in a class, and setting up efficient and effective peer collaboration there that could provide students with the support necessary for successful inclusion (Guralnick, 2001). This different school organization cannot but guarantee more learning opport- unities and be useful and advantageous for other students at risk in the school. There are actually many studies that highlight how about 50 per cent of the school population can be considered at risk for many different reasons (for a review see Soresi and Nota, 2001): individuals experiencing financial problems, linguistic problems – immigrants, for instance – family troubles. An inclusive environment can guarantee all students equal access to knowledge, as well as equal opportunities to learn and develop critical thinking (Zionts and Baker, 1997). It would not be at all surprising to find that what is proposed for disabled students can also produce significant advantages for those who do not find themselves in this unfortunate situation.

Note

1. We use the terms 'impairment' and 'disability' as defined by the World Health Organization (WHO, 2001).

References

Agran M, Blanchard C, Wehmeyer M, Hughes C (2001) Teaching students to self-regulate their behavior: the differential effects of students- vs Teacher-delivered reinforcement. Research in Developmental Disabilities 22: 319–32.

Babini VP, Lama L (2000) Una donna nuova: Il femminismo scientifico di Maria Montessori [The New Woman: The scientific feminism of Maria Montessori]. Milan: Franco Angeli.

Bailey DB, McWilliam RA, Ware WB, Burchinal MR (1993) Social interactions of toddlers and preschoolers in same-aged and mixed-age play groups. Journal of Applied Developmental Psychology 14: 161–76.

Basaglia F (1967) L'istituzione Negata [The Denied Institution]. Turin: Einaudi.

Befring E (1994) Laering og skole: Vilkar for eit verdig liv [Learning and School: Conditions for a Dignified Life]. Oslo Norway: Det Norske Samlaget.

Beh-Pajooh A (1991) The effect of social contact on college students' attitudes toward severely handicapped students and their educational integration. Journal of Mental Deficiency Research 35: 339–52.

Brewer N, Smith JM (1989) Social acceptance of mentally retarded children in regular schools in relation to years mainstreamed. Psychological Reports 64: 375–80.

Bricker D (1978) Rationale for the integration of handicapped and nonhandicapped preschool children. In M Guralnick (ed.) Early intervention and the integration of handicapped and nonhandicapped preschool children. Baltimore: University Park Press, pp. 3–26.

Buyesse V, Bailey DB (1993) Behavioral and developmental outcomes in young children with disabilities in integrated and segregated settings: a review of comparative studies. Journal of Special Education 26: 434–61.

Carter J, Sugai G (1988) Teaching social skills. Teaching Exceptional Children 20: 68–71.

Coie JD, Dodge KA, Kupersmidt J (1990) Group behavior and social status. In SR Asher, JD Coie (eds) Peer Rejection in Childhood. Cambridge: Cambridge University Press, pp. 17–59.

Cooper D (1972) La morte della famiglia [The Death of the Family]. Turin: Einaudi.

Cushing L, Kennedy CH (1997) Academic effects of providing peer support in general education classrooms on students without disabilities. Journal of Applied Behavior Analysis 30: 139–51.

De Landsheere G (1971) Evaluation continue et exames, prècis de docimimologie. Brussels: Labor.

Deci EL, Chandler CL (1986) The importance of motivation for the future of the LD. Journal of Learning Disabilities 19: 581–94.

Diamond KE (1993) Pre-school children's conceptions of disability in their peers. Early Education and Development 4: 123–9.

Diamond KE (2001) Relationships among young children's ideas, emotional understanding and social contact with classmates with disabilities. Topics in Early Childhood Special Education 21: 104–13.

Diamond KE, Hestenes LL (1996) Preschool children's conceptions of disabilities: the salience of disability in children's ideas about others. Topics in Early Childhood and Special Education 16: 458–75.

Dodge KA, Coie JD, Brakke NP (1982) Behavior patterns of socially rejected and neglected preadolescents: the roles of social approach and aggression. Journal of Abnormal Child Psychology 10: 398–410.

Dunlap LK, Dunlap G, Koegel LK, Koegel RL (1991) Using self-monitoring to increase independence. Teaching Exceptional Children 23: 17–22.

Evans JH, Bird KM, Ford LA, Green JL, Bischoff RA (1992) Strategies for overcoming the resistance to the integration of students with special needs into neighborhood schools: a case study. CASE in Point 7: 1–16.

Evans IM, Salisbury CL, Palombaro MM, Goldberg JS (1994) Children's perceptions of fairness in classroom and interpersonal situations involving peers with severe disabilities. Journal of the Association for Persons with Severe Handicaps 19: 326–32.

Fontana Tommasucci L (1983) Presupposti psicopedagogici e applicazióni dell'istruzióne programmata [Psychopedagogic considerations and applications]. In S Soresi (ed.) Territòrio e comunità educativa dei handicappati [Territory and Educational Community for Handicapped People]. Pordenone: ERIP Editrice.

Fox DJ (1969) The Research in Education. New York: Holt Rinehart & Winston.

Gagnè M (1965) The Conditions of Learning and Theory of Instruction. New York: Holt, Rinehart & Winston.

Garvar-Pinhas A, Schmelkin LP (1989) Administrators' and teachers' attitude toward mainstreaming. Remedial and Special Education 10: 38–43.

Gaylord-Ross R, Haring T (1987) Social interaction research for adolescents with severe handicaps. Behavioral Disorders 12: 264–75.

Giangreco MF, Dennis R, Cloninger C, Edelman S, Schattman R (1993) 'I've counted Jon': transformational experiences of teachers educating students with disabilities. Exceptional Children 59: 359–72.

Goffman E (1968) Asylunus. Turin: Einaudi.

Goldfarb W (1944) The effects of early institutional care on adolescent personality. American Journal of Orthopsychiatric 14: 441–7.

Goldfarb W (1947) Variations in adolescent adjustment of institutionally-reared children. American Journal of Orthopsychiatric 17: 449–57.

Graham S, Baker GP (1990) The down side of help: an attributional developmental analysis of helping behavior as a low-ability cue. Journal of Educational Psychology 82: 1–15.

Grenot-Scheyer M (1994) The nature of interactions between students with severe disabilities and their friends and acquaintances without disabilities. Journal of the Association for Persons with Severe Handicaps 19: 253–62.

Groppo M (1983) Anàlisi crìtica dell'integrazióne scolastica degli handicappati [A critical analysis of handicapped children's inclusion]. In L Silvestrelli, Psicologia ed Handicap [Psychology and Handicap]. Rome: Bulzoni Editore.

Guralnick MJ (1980) Social interactions among pre-school children. Exceptional Children 46: 48–253.

Guralnick MJ (2001) A framework for change in early childhood inclusion. In MJ Guralnick, Early Childhood Inclusion: Focus on Change. Baltimore MD: Paul H Brookes, pp. 3–35.

Guralnick MJ, Groom JM (1987) The peer relations of mildly delayed and non-handicapped preschool children in mainstreamed playgroups. Child Development 58: 1556–72.

Harrower JK, Dunlap G (2001) Including children with autism in general education classrooms. Behavior Modification 25: 762–84.

Hayes K, Gunn P (1988) Attitude of parents and teacher toward mainstreaming. Exceptional Child 35: 31–8.

Heiman T, Margalit M (1998) Loneliness depression and social skills among students with mild mental retardation in different educational settings. Journal of Special Education 32: 154–63.

Helmstetter E, Peck CA, Giangreco MF (1994) Outcomes of interactions with peers with moderate or severe disabilities: a statewide survey of high school students. Journal of the Association for Persons with Severe Handicaps 19: 263–76.

Horne MD (1985) Attitudes towards Handicapped Students: Professional Peer and Parent Reactions. Hillsdale NJ: Erlbaum.

Hunt P, Staub D, Alwell M, Goetz L (1994) Achievement by all students within the context of cooperative learning groups. Journal of the Association for Persons with Severe Handicaps 19: 290–301.

Jenkins J, Speltz M, Odom S (1985) Integrating students with moderate and severe disabilities into general education classes. Exceptional Children 61: 425–39.

Jenkins JR, Odom SL, Speltz ML (1989) Effects of integration and structured play on the development of handicapped children. Exceptional Children 55: 420–8.

Keenan SM (1997) Program elements that support teachers and students with learning and behavior problems. In P Zionts (ed.) Inclusion Strategies. Austin TX: Pro-Ed, pp. 117–38.

Keller D, Sterling-Honig A (1993) Curriculum to promote positive interactions of preschoolers with a disabled peer introduced into the classroom. Early Child Development and Care 96: 27–34.

Kerr MM, Nelson CM (1989) Strategies for Managing Behavior Problems in the Classroom. Columbus OH: Merrill.

Klaber MM (1969) The retarded and institutions for the retarded – a preliminary report. In SB Sarason, J Doris (eds) Psychological Problems in Mental Deficiency. New York: Harper & Row.

Koegel LK, Koegel RL, Frea WD, Fredeen R M (2001) Identifying early intervention targets for children with autism in inclusive school settings. Behavior Modification 25: 745–61.

Ladd GW (1981) Effectiveness of a social learning method for enhancing children's social interaction and peer acceptance. Child Development 52: 171–8.

Laing R (1968) La polìtica dell'esperiènza [The Politics of Experience]. Milan: Feltrinelli.

Lamorey S, Bricker DD (1993) Integrated programs: effects on young children and their parents. In C Peck, S Odom, D Bricker (eds) Integrating Young Children with Disabilities into Community-based Programs: From Research to Implementation. Baltimore MD: Paul H Brookes, pp. 249–69.

Larrivee B (1985) Effective Teaching for Successful Mainstreaming. New York: Longman.

Larrivee B, Horne MD (1991) Social status: a comparison of mainstreamed students with peers of different ability levels. Journal of Special Education 25: 90–101.

Lipsky DK, Gartner A (1991) Restructuring for quality. In JW Lloyd, NN Singh, AC Repp (eds) The Regular Education Initiative: Alternative Perspectives on Concepts, Issues and Models. Sycamore IL: Sycamore, pp. 43–56.

Maag JW (1990) Social skills training in schools. Special Services in the Schools 6: 1–19.

Mager F (1967) Goal Analysis. Belmont CA: Fearon Publishers Lear Siegler.

Mager F (1990) Preparing Instructional Objectives. Belmont CA: Lake.

Minnow M (1990) Making all the Difference: Inclusion, Exclusion and American Law. Ithaca NY: Cornell University Press.

Montgomery JK (1987) Mainstreaming orthopedically handicapped students in a regular public school. In MS Berres, P Knoblock (eds) Program Models for Mainstreaming. Rockvill MD: Aspen, pp. 169–89.

Murray-Segert C (1989) Nasty Girls, Thugs and Humans Like Us: Social Relations between Severely Disabled and Non-disabled Students in High School. Baltimore MD: Paul H Brookes.

Nota L, Soresi S (1997) I comportamenti sociali: dall'anàlisi all'intervènto [Social Abilities: Assessment and Treatment]. Pordenone: ERIP Editrice.

Ochs E, Kremer-Sadlik T, Solomon O, Sirota KG (2001) Inclusion as social practice: views of children with autism. Social Development 10: 399–419.

Odom SL, McEvoy MA (1988) Integration of young children with handicaps and normally developing children. In S Odom, M Karnes (eds) Early Intervention for Infants and Children with Handicaps: An Empirical Base. Baltimore MD: Paul H Brookes, pp. 241–68.

Odom SL, McConnell SR, Chandler LK (1993) Acceptability and flexibility of classroom-based social interaction interventions for young children with disabilities. Exceptional Children 60: 226–36.

Osborne AG, DiMattia P (1994) The IDEA's least restrictive environment mandate: legal implication. Exceptional Children 61: 6–14.

Peck CA, Cooke TP (1983) Benefits of mainstreaming at the early childhood level: how much can we expect? Analysis and Intervention in Development Disabilities 3: 1–22.

Peck C A, Donaldson J, Pezzoli M (1990) Some benefits nonhandicapped adolescents perceive for themselves from their social relationship with peers who have severe handicaps. Journal of the Association for Persons with Severe Handicaps 15: 241–9.

Peck CA, Carlson P, Helmstetter F (1992) Parent and teacher perceptions of outcomes for typically developing children enrolled in early childhood programs: a statewide survey. Journal of Early Intervention 16: 53–63.

Peetsma T, Roeleveld J (1998) Relatie tussen cognitief en psychosocial functioneren van leerlingen uit special – en basisonderwijs. Amsterdam: SCO-Kohnstamm Institut van de Universiteit van Amsterdam.

Peetsma T, Vergeer M, Roeleveld J, Karsten S (2001) Inclusion in education: comparing pupils' development in special and regular education. Educational Review 53: 125–35.

Provence S, Lipton RC (1962) Infants in Institutions. New York: International Universities Press.

Sailor W (1991) Special education in the restructured school. Remedial and Special Education 12: 8–22.

Schumaker J, Hazel J, Pederson C (1988) Social Skills for Daily Living: Program Basics. Circle Pines MN: American Guidance Service.

Scruggs TE, Mastropieri MA (1996) Teacher perceptions of mainstreaming/inclusion 1958–1995: a research synthesis. Exceptional Children 63: 59–74.

Semmel MI, Gottlieb J, Robinson NM (1979) Mainstreaming: perspectives on educating handicapped children in the public school. In Berliner DC (ed.) Review of Research in Education. Washington DC: American Educational Research Association, pp. 223–79.

Smith LA, Williams JM (2001) Children's understanding of the physical, cognitive and social consequences of impairments. Child: Care, Health and Development 27: 603–17.

Soresi S (1981) Problemi ed Esperiènze di Integrazióne Scolàstica e Sociale degli Handicappati [Problems and Experiences in School and Social Inclusion of Persons with Handicaps]. Pordenone: ERIP Editrice.

Soresi S (1992) Sperimentazióne di un programma di parent training con genitóri di adolescènti handicappati. In R Juliani (ed.) Apprendiménto ed Abilità Sociali [Learning and Social Abilities]. Pordenone: ERIP Editrice, pp. 25–48.

Soresi S (1998) Psicològia dell'handicap e della riabilitazióne [Psychology of Handicap and Rehabilitation]. Bologna: Il Mulino.

Soresi S, Nota L (2000) A social skill training for persons with Down's syndrome. European Psychologist 5: 34–43.

Soresi S, Nota L (2001) La facilitazióne dell'integrazióne scolàstica [The Facilitation of School Inclusion]. Pordenone: ERIP Editrice.

Staub D, Schwartz IS, Gallucci C, Peck CA (1994) Four portraits of friendship at an inclusive school. Journal of the Association for Persons with Severe Handicaps 19: 314–25.

Stowe M, Turnbull HR (2001) Legal considerations of inclusion for infants and toddlers and for preschool-age children. In MJ Guralnick (ed.) Early Childhood Inclusion: Focus on Change. Baltimore MD: Paul H Brookes, pp. 69–100.

Strain PS, Kerr MM (1981) Mainstreaming of Children in Schools: Research and programmatic issues. New York: Academic Press.

Tampieri G, Soresi S, Vianello R (1988) Ritardo Mentale: Rassegna di Ricerche [Mental Retardation: A Review of Research]. Pordenone: ERIP Editrice.

Tams V, Eyberg S (1976) A group treatment program for parents. In EJ Mash, LC Handy, LA Hamerlynk (eds) Behavior Modification Approach to Parenting. New York: Brunner/Mazel.

Thompson T (1977) History of treatment and misconceptions concerning the mentally retarded. In T Thompson, J Grabowski (eds) Behavior Modification of the Mentally Retarded. Oxford: Oxford University Press, pp. 3–15.

Thormalen PW (1965) A study of on-the-ward training of trainable mentally retarded children in a state institution. California Mental Health Research Monograph, vol. 4 (whole issue).

Visser J (1993) A broad, balanced, relevant and differentiated curriculum. In J Visser, G Upton (eds) Special Education in Britain after Warnock. London: Fulton, pp. 10–12.

Wang M C, Baker ET (1985) Mainstreaming programs: designs, features and effects. Journal of Special Education 19: 503–21.

Weiner R, Norton M (1993) Inclusion: a study of administrative perspectives. Journal of School Administrators Association of New York State 23: 6–10.

Wilczenski FL (1997) Development of a scale to measure attitudes toward inclusive education. Educational and Psychological Measurement 55: 291–9.

World Health Organization (1997) ICIDH-2: International Classification of Functioning and Disability. Geneva: WHO.

World Health Organization (2001) New Guidelines to Measure Health. Geneva: WHO.

Zionts P (1997) Inclusion: chasing the impossible dream? Maybe. In P Zionts (ed.) Inclusion Strategies. Austin TX: Pro-Ed, pp. 3–26.

Zionts P, Baker P (1997) Inclusion and diversity: powerful words with powerful meaning. In P Zionts (ed.) Inclusion Strategies. Austin TX: Pro-Ed, pp. 339–67.

Chapter 5
Social and community inclusion

Laura Nota, Salvatore Soresi

A fairly large number of scientific research works has focused on the analysis of the relationship between institutionalization, deinstitutionalization and adaptive behaviour. Cohen et al. (1977) used the Adaptive Behavior Scale to assess changes in the adaptive behaviour of 92 individuals with severe mental disabilities transferred from large institutions to smaller residential structures. They found sudden and significant adaptive functioning changes in domestic activities, self-determination, assuming responsibilities, as well as an improvement in antisocial and stereotyped behaviours. They concluded that adults with severe cognitive disabilities typically respond to deinstitutionalization with an increase in the range and number of behaviours they initiate, although some of these behaviours may turn out to be undesirable.

Thompson and Carey (1980) studied a group of women with mental disabilities and found that, after deinstitutionalization, they showed improvements in language development, domestic activities and social abilities. Hemming et al. (1981) analysed the progress of individuals with severe learning disabilities two years after they had been transferred from a large institution to small bungalows. Improvements were observed in autonomy, health, mathematical abilities, domestic activities, self-determination and responsibilities. Most improvements were still observed 9 months after the move, but only improvements associated with housekeeping were still present after 2 years. Kleinberg and Galligan (1983) also examined the effects of deinstitutionalization on adaptive behaviour, studying 20 individuals aged between 18 and 75 with IQs from 10 to 51, with a period of institutionalization varying from 5 to 59 years, who had been transferred from a large institution to small residential structures housing eight to 10 individuals. In order to evaluate adaptive behaviour, the Adaptive Behavior Scale (ABS et al., 1974) and the Minnesota Scales were used with evaluations carried out at 0, 4, 8 and 12 months from the move. Antisocial behaviours of individuals with an IQ greater than 20 decreased significantly between the first and the second evaluation, whereas this was not observed in individuals with an IQ below 20. For both groups antisocial behaviours were actually more frequent between the third and fourth evaluation, that is to say after 4 to 8 months from deinstitutionalization. The improvement in housekeeping abilities begins to show up immediately after the move and seemed to remain fairly stable, albeit with different results according to severity of disability. Kleinberg and Galligan (1983) concluded their work by saying that new placements typically increase antisocial behaviours in individuals with a higher degree of disability, whereas they cause a decrease in such behaviours in individuals with higher cognitive abilities. Similar results have also been highlighted by other studies, such as those by Fine et al. (1990), Hemming et al. (1981), Kleinberg and Galligan (1983).

However, the adaptive behaviour changes following deinstitutionalization found by different researchers are not consistent and this is probably due to the fact that individuals with different characteristics, in terms of both severity of disability and place they were moved to, were not taken into consideration. Improvements seem to affect language, domestic activity and socialization. This could be associated with the fact that the new arrangements asked for greater commitment in house management, more frequent verbal interactions, and more opportunities to be involved in a number of social activities. These improvements would take place immediately after deinstitutionalization and might make one think, as suggested by Kleinberg and Galligan (1983), that these abilities already existed in their repertory, but that the institutionalized environment had not allowed them to emerge. The new environments not only allowed it but also reinforced it, thus showing that deinstitutionalization should also be accompanied by a series of systematic interventions and effective training sessions, especially with regard to adaptive abilities. Mere 'relocation', in fact, would not seem to produce significant long-term effects because maladaptive behaviours would also tend to increase.

Social participation, self-determination and quality of life

Social and community inclusion brings to mind some related concepts, such as social participation, empowerment, self-determination and quality of life. The social participation construct is proposed by the World Health Organization, which in 2001 published the International Classification of Functioning, Disability and Health – ICF, accepted by 191 countries. The ICF stimulates a change of focus that was traditionally based on the mortality rates found in the populations, the analyses of individuals' lives, 'of the way they find themselves living with their pathologies and try to improve their life conditions in view of a productive and enriching existence' (WHO 2001: 1). Other WHO documents (World Health Organization, 1997; Soresi, 1998, 2001; Nota et al., 2002) indicate that disability is no longer considered as a problem associated with a minority group of individuals and the ICF proposes a modality to evaluate the social and physical impact on the functioning of an individual. For example when an individual finds it very difficult to get to his place of work in a building not equipped with an appropriate access ramp or lift, the ICF suggests carrying out wide-ranging interventions aimed at installing whatever is needed to overcome environmental barriers, rather than considering the individual unable to carry out his/her job.

The ICF considers all illnesses on the same plane, regardless of their causes, and places mental and cognitive disorders on the same level as physical and sensory pathologies. While carrying out evaluation two dimensions should be considered:

• organic functioning and anatomical structure
• activities carried out and participation levels.

Activities are the behaviours individuals carry out in order to execute tasks, errands, and actions. Disabilities, which in the first edition were referred to as differences by defect or by excess from what is usually done in everyday life, are now presented in terms of 'activity limitations'. They concern the difficulties an individual may have in executing activities.

Participation refers to an individual's involvement level in life situations in relation to his or her health, conditions and bodily functions, in activities that he/she can actually carry out. What in the previous editions was presented in terms of handicap is now presented as 'participation restrictions'. In considering participation, the WHO emphasizes that this concerns personal care, motility, information exchange, social relationships, domestic life, education, work, economic life, and social, civil and community life. At the international level, numerous are the international efforts striving to better define the life situations of individuals who might need habilitation and rehabilitation interventions and/or to increase their levels of community life participation (Soresi and Nota, 2000).

The concept of self-determination is linked to those of empowerment and self-regulation, which should be borne in mind by those who are concerned with individuals with activity and participation level limitations. 'Empowerment' means giving power or authority to an individual and requires habilitation and rehabilitation to maximize autonomy and participation levels in such a way as to allow even individuals with activity limitations to exercise power and control on the choices they make about their own life conditions. It implies that everyone must be given great value and dignity and that all individuals are free to make their own decisions about how to lead their lives (Emener, 1993). Social and health interventions should therefore aim at strengthening the individuals they deal with, favouring an increase in autonomy, levels of participation and social inclusion.

Self-determination was first introduced toward the end of the 1970s when some movements, both in the US and in Europe, were fighting for deinstitutionalization and for rights to be recognized and guaranteed to individuals with impairments and disabilities. This term, which was used politically and ideologically in order to underline the right of nations and peoples to self-government in contrast to any attempt at ideological, political, and economic 'colonization' and interference, was soon considered appropriate to indicate the right of individuals with disabilities to autonomously exercise control over their own existence (Wehmeyer and Schwartz, 1998).

From a purely psychological viewpoint, there are three different perspectives for the analysis of self-determination. The first is derived from the learning theories; the second is clearly behaviouristic, taking direct inspiration from Skinner (1973); the third is sociocognitive and continues to have its main reference in Bandura (1977).

Apart from the emphasis given to the different components of self-regulation by the various approaches, it is indeed a particularly complex and diversified construct as it implies:

- ability to make choices;
- ability to implement decisions that are considered advantageous;
- ability to solve problems;
- ability to single out and pursue personal objectives;
- ability to manage one's own needs autonomously;
- ability to read events by resorting to an internal locus of control;
- sufficiently high levels of self-efficacy;
- ability to evaluate one's own situation.

At first sight, and probably in a superficial way, the construct of self-determination appears drastically opposed to the idea that there may be other, especially environmental factors, which determine an individual's behaviour. That it is 'context-dependent', even in particularly independent and autonomous individuals, is certainly undeniable, as it always shows up within a social context: 'This focus on the social nature of the concept directs our attention to the interaction between a person's capacity to choose and act and the social environment that mediates opportunities for those choices and action' (Mithaug, 1998: 42).

The construct of self-determination is particularly important where individuals with disabilities are concerned, because the reference to massively clinical, health and rehabilitation treatment models may reinforce the idea that individuals with disabilities, especially those with severe disabilities, cannot make choices or decisions (Lipsky and Gartner, 1989). As a consequence, they may be considered as lacking autonomy and as being unable to make adequate choices – they are not even allowed to express any wishes or preferences where choices would not be particularly risky or dangerous for their health and safety. For instance, they are not allowed choices (within a range of options) about what to eat, what to wear, what to do in their free time, which people to stay with, when to wake up in the morning, when to go to bed at night, and so on.

This would strengthen that sense of learned helplessness, dear to the learning theories, which besides producing negative feelings and low expectations, brings about inaccurate self-evaluation and often also unrealistic expectations. The data existing in the literature are clear about that: Wehmeyer and Schwartz (1998) highlighted that among youths with mental disabilities attending the final years at high school, those with the highest levels of self-determination were those who stated that their aspiration was to live by themselves, to have a certain amount of money at their disposal, and to have greater opportunities to enter the world of work. The same authors maintained that individuals with mental disabilities with high levels of self-determination experience better quality of life and make a higher number of choices than controls with the same IQ, but lower levels of self-determination. Wehmeyer and Bolding (2001) observed that shifting to less restrictive life conditions (from institution to group home, from group home to independent life, from supported employment to competitive work) produces higher levels of self-determination and adaptive functioning. As regards the relationship between life environment and self-determination, it is clear that:

- individuals living by themselves or in the family are more self-determined than individuals living in wider contexts or group homes (Wehmeyer et al., 1995);
- self-determination is higher when individuals live in environments with no more than five people and is lower when individuals live in environments comprising six to 16 people (Tossebro, 1995; Stancliffe et al., 2000);
- individuals with mental disabilities have higher levels of self-determination when the environment is *not very restrictive* (Stancliffe and Wehmeyer, 1995); adequately trained teachers are able to increase self-determination even in individuals with severe mental retardation (Stancliffe, 1997).

With a group of 40 individuals with mental disability, Soresi and Nota (2000) have highlighted the existence of a significant correlation between self-determination measures and estimated levels of satisfaction that these individuals are supposed to experience according to the staff, and with regard to maladjustment problems, that it is the individuals with low levels of self-determination who show higher isolation, mood changes, difficulty in interpersonal relationships and forms of slowing of psychomotor activity. By examining the role of environmental characteristics on self-determination and comparing individuals with slight and moderate disability who are included in different work contexts, the same authors observed the presence of a significant interaction between level of difficulty and work situation. Whereas individuals with slight mental disability, in particular those moving from a sheltered workshop to competitive employment, showed an improvement in going from a non-work situation to a work situation, those with greater difficulties did not seem to benefit from such a move and, rather, presented a drop in self-determination when they were included in a sheltered workshop.

This also seems to affect significantly the quality of life experienced by these individuals. As Cowen (1994) suggests, quality of life, besides lack of illness and satisfaction of basic needs, involves psychological and relational aspects that have never been taken into consideration when talking about 'health' – for example, to what extent the individual feels at ease in his or her professional and family environments (school and work), the extent of satisfaction experienced in interpersonal relationships, the likelihood of carrying out various activities and errands in accordance with age and abilities. Some psychological factors (recognizing one's own objectives, experiencing a sense of belonging, being able to control one's destiny and that of significant others) and sufficient levels of satisfaction contribute to determining the level of wellbeing actually enjoyed (Shedler et al., 1993).

Felce and Perry (1995) pointed out that many definitions of quality of life (QoL) exist in the literature: Borthwick-Duffy (1992), for instance, maintains that it is determined by life conditions, satisfaction about one's conditions and the individual's aspirations, values and expectations. Landesman (1986) underlined the measurable aspects of life conditions, related to physical health, life environment, social relationships, working activity and financial possibilities, and defined personal satisfaction as the subjective answer to such conditions. Edgerton (1990) included the opportunity individuals have of maintaining or changing their own life conditions. In addition to the definitions so far considered and as proof of the interest in QoL on the part of health and rehabilitation researchers, Hughes et al. (1995) have examined 87 studies on QoL and found as many as 44 definitions of it and 1,243 different measures able to specify it. Foremost among the dimensions most frequently taken into consideration are:

- psychological wellbeing and personal satisfaction;
- social relations;
- occupation;
- physical and material wellbeing;
- self-determination, autonomy and opportunity to choose;
- personal competence, community adjustment and the possibility of an independent life;
- community inclusion;

- social acceptance, social status and adjustment;
- personal development and realization;
- quality of residential environment;
- free time;
- normalization;
- some demographic, social and individual aspects;
- responsibility;
- support from services.

Health and social activities must strengthen a range of abilities that can enable individuals with cognitive disability to manage their own lives in community-based settings, to allow them full participation and guarantee them a better quality of life.

Adjustment to community life

Every community inclusion project must come to terms with the analysis of personal and social adjustment levels.

McGrew et al. (1992) state that to favour a good level of community adjustment, social networks, and the inclusion of individuals in leisure and free time activities and competitive employment, their ability to use different support services must be taken into consideration. Bruininks et al. (1992) underline the relationship between community adjustment and the competence and autonomy the individual with disability actually shows. These authors suggest that the following six factors should be considered:

- inclusion in leisure and free time contexts;
- social networks (social support and social relationships);
- community living;
- inclusion in occupational-economic contexts;
- the need for social support services; and
- personal satisfaction with everyday activities, housing, social networks and the leisure activities that they manage to include in their free time.

As regards personal competence, the following abilities would positively characterize community adjustment:

- self-care and ability to carry out the everyday activities necessary for an independent life;
- ability to use community support and services;
- 'housekeeping abilities' concerning the ability to manage and care for one's home;
- behavioural and emotional control;
- family support.

The components identified by Bruininks et al. (1992) strengthen the findings of previous research studies about the importance of some factors (self-care, ability to live in the family, use of community resources, professional abilities and the absence of problem behaviours) by emphasizing that self-management and family interaction management abilities, being able to feel one's way within the community, working, and not showing and coping with problem behaviours, are all skills needed by an individual to be able to integrate into his/her own social context. Ittenbach et al. (1993) have examined the differences between three groups of young and adult individuals with mental disability as regards community adjustment.

The instruments used included an 11-item questionnaire representing 11 aspects of community life adjustment on five macro categories:

* social networks (range and number of friends);
* leisure activities and free time;
* occupation and income;
* housing characteristics and periods of hospitalization;
* extent of need for service support.

Thurlow et al. (1989) reported that the greater the disabilities, the higher the expenses that have to be borne and the lower the likelihood of inclusion.

Community inclusion requires individuals with disability to have considerable financial resources to provide for basic necessities and to allow them to benefit from significant moments of community life (taking part in leisure and free time activities, for instance). Having few disabilities, individuals with mild mental difficulties would benefit from greater opportunities, such as being able to live alone in a fairly independent way, having a job, spending money, and taking part in recreational and social activities (Ittenbach et al., 1993).

What has been presented so far might suggest that the likelihood of successful community inclusion depends only on the characteristics of the individual with disability. On the contrary, however, the importance of environmental characteristics and the quality and extent of support available cannot be neglected.

Only a few intellectually disabled individuals actually show high levels of autonomy; but it is now becoming more widely accepted that most individuals with slight or moderate disability, as well as some of those with more considerable cognitive deficits, can experience some form of adjustment to community life, even if they cannot be totally independent. To this end, careful programming of the activities, adequate support and structured training sessions facilitating the appearance of socially acceptable behaviour are necessary. Obviously, that requires time (teaching individuals with mental disability cannot be done in a hurry), as well as sophisticated professional competence, because community inclusion failures are rarely given a second or third chance and can end up with more greatly restricted life conditions, even if they are not reinstitutionalized.

These programmes have to attribute great importance to learning a new occupation, to self-control, to self-efficacy and to free time, because it is these dimensions that will determine the quality of community living (McDonnel et al., 1993). Individuals with intellectual disability, unlike those with mental disorders, are not generally dangerous, do not become vandals, do not drink alcohol, do not take drugs and are instead often the victims of 'normal' individuals. They dress in a proper way and behave adequately in public, keep themselves clean, and can use public transport. The real problem would not be their negative impact on the community, but rather their isolation from it. Their integration often means simply attending 'special' environments or clubs and doing 'passive' activities in their free time (watching TV or going to the cinema). Only a small minority can actually work in competitive environments, make friends, marry or become parents.

Work inclusion

Employment plays a central role in the social participation of individuals with disability. Impairments or disabilities can restrict participation, especially if performance is not consistent with the ability levels required or if these individuals are not allowed to use the abilities they actually possess.

Among the variables contributing to quality of life, a central role is played by time spent in constructive industriousness and goal-directed mobility, operative actions and cooperation with others (Hoyt, 1985; Rubin and Roessler, 1978; Saxby et al., 1986).

The current risk of unemployment and under-employment is certainly worrying young people more and more, but the situation of individuals with disability is very much worse, as their difficulties entering the world of work can lead to marginalization and reinstitutionalization. Edgar (1987) reports that about 50 per cent to 80 per cent of American adults with disability of working age are in fact without a job, that among students with disability attending high school more than 30 per cent leave school early, and that among those who complete their schooling fewer than 15 per cent manage to find a job that offers more than the national contract minimum salary. As regards the Italian situation, recent data reveal that only 20.8 per cent of individuals with disability and only 11.7 per cent of individuals with mental disability are actually employed (ISTAT, 1999). The job is often carried out in social cooperatives, which in 30 per cent of cases offer employment almost exclusively to individuals with mental disability (Italian Department of Labour). These data, together with the fact that such cooperatives have recently increased dramatically in number, are certainly worrying as they show that social cooperatives might be a 'pocket' of pseudo- or under-employment for individuals with disability and so represent a superficial 'solution' of the work inclusion problem.

The inclusion at work of individuals with disability is a process requiring specific assessment activities and interventions aimed at increasing professional, social and adaptive abilities on the one hand, and at the restructuring of environmental features on the other hand.

First of all, work community employment programmes should be preceded by an analysis of what has actually been accomplished in school in inclusion experiences, activities carried out in rehabilitation services, or in previous occupations, and so on. This should be related to other analyses that are usually necessary to start specific work inclusion processes and intentional and articulate career counselling activities. The latter should aim at:

- analysing the individual's ability to choose, taking into account the limitations associated with his or her impairments and disabilities, and sometimes taking into account prejudices and cultural barriers that may exist in his or her life environment;
- establishing strengths and weaknesses, residual functional abilities, and the cognitive, physical and emotional resources of the individual;
- strengthening the individual's potential in view of possible future learning that could be useful in searching for a job and carrying it out.

For realistic career counselling and, if applicable, for a reassessment of expectations, it is necessary to explore the real possibilities of employment existing in a community (Moon et al., 1990; Browder, 1991). This analysis must be directed toward learning about the local work market in order to obtain important information about what type of abilities should be stimulated in the vocational guidance training, social characteristics of workplaces, sequences of tasks required, expected productivity indices, 'physical' demands of each occupation, barriers, support that is necessary and available, possible reinforcers, and so forth.

To gather this type of information, job analysis is often used, which nowadays represents the basis of most systems of human resource management (Butler and Harvey, 1988; Morgenson and Campion 1997). Job analysis generally refers to processes aimed at the systematic analysis of a job and at the collection of detailed information on it. Especially when the work inclusion of individuals with disability is involved, we think it is appropriate, as McIntire et al. (1995) suggest, to consider the knowledge, skills, abilities and other characteristics (KSAOs) that the worker should have in order to pursue a professional goal successfully. After completing the job analysis, a performance assessment in both simulated and real working contexts should be carried out in order to anticipate possible difficulties that might be encountered in doing a job.

After determining the occupational tasks that may be difficult for the individual in consideration of his or her abilities, it should be ascertained whether there is a need for adjustments and changes to be carried out in the work context. To this end, a number of things could be analysed:

environmental noise, expected productivity level, type and intensity of supervision provided, and quality, type and intensity of relationships with colleagues. The Enhanced Guide for Occupational Exploration (EGOE; Maze and Mayall, 1991) could be useful in this respect. It considers the stress an occupation can involve by specifying:

- amount of emotional control required;
- tolerance of frustrations and repetitiveness;
- amount of bearable responsibilities;
- maintenance of constant and alert attention.

Furthermore, it is necessary to plan for follow-on operations and interventions aiming at helping such individuals

- to show satisfactory ways of adjustment in their work environment;
- to manage possible experiences associated with mobility efficiently;
- at retirement, to deal adequately with the experience of ceasing work.

As regards work adjustment, a series of abilities must be considered, among which are the ability to take on some sort of responsibility toward work (to be punctual, guarantee constant presence, keep a well-groomed appearance, and so on), to show what is called work readiness (for instance, understand work concepts, use work information, show interest in one's work) and the social abilities useful to start and maintain positive social relationships in the workplace (Soresi, 2002).

Work inclusion carried out in this way can actually guarantee professional success to the individual with disability, increase levels of satisfaction of the individuals involved and favour actual participation of individuals with disability. To make work inclusion even more successful it is necessary to continue working particularly on the social context, so that the help and support necessary to carry out the different tasks can be supplied 'naturally' in the employment context. The social and health workers interested in these processes must therefore focus their attention on employers and colleagues. As in the case of school inclusion, meetings with fellow workers can also be useful in order to:

- present the individual who is going to be included, describe impairments, restrictions in activities and difficulties experienced in participation levels;
- underline the importance of work for social participation and for the adjustment processes of individuals;
- describe the specific laws that have been promulgated in this connection and the advantages that society as a whole can receive from the work inclusion of individuals with disability;
- present the specific disabilities of the individual, his or her abilities and the tasks that he or she will have to carry out in the work context;
- describe the specific help that the individual needs to carry out the job,

the responsibilities of the social and health services in this, and the collaboration required from colleagues and fellow workers;
- describe the contribution the individual will give in carrying out the job and the ways in which he or she will be able to collaborate with others;
- describe and present ways in which the possible appearance of maladaptive behaviours can be managed and, above all, to prevent their occurrence;
- describe and present modalities to be implemented to maintain and strengthen the social and working abilities of the individual who is going to be included in that context.

The success of these operations relies on the social and health workers' refined professional abilities, which will be described later, and on precise planning activities that must envisage supervision and monitoring of what is actually going on in the work context.

The Italian law

In Italy, the law governing the social and work inclusion of individuals with disability is the same law 104 that has already been mentioned for school inclusion. Among other things, it states that there is a need to guarantee the timely intervention of the therapeutic and rehabilitative services, which must ensure the recovery allowed by the scientific and technical knowledge currently available, the keeping of the person with disability in the family and social environment, and his or her inclusion and participation in social life. They must also promote, through the help of bodies and associations, permanent initiatives to inform the population and encourage its participation, to prevent and treat handicaps, to rehabilitate affected individuals and include them socially; and to guarantee the right to choose the most suitable services (Article 5). Article 8 addresses social inclusion in the school, in the community and the professional world, through the setting up of services and interventions that might ensure it. Particularly important are the paragraphs that call for:

- adaptation of personnel and equipment of educational, social, sports and leisure services;
- measures favouring full inclusion in the world of work and employment security;
- provisions to ensure enjoyment of public and private transport and the organization of specific transport;
- organization of extramural activities to integrate and extend educational activity consistently with the school's policy.

With regard to work inclusion, Article 18 states that it is the responsibility of the regions to provide whatever is necessary to guarantee competitive employment, to enable individuals with disability to get to their workplace and to carry out autonomous work ventures, and to encourage employers to adapt the workplace to take on individuals with disability (paragraph 6, b).

With regard to the organization and management of the health and social services, law 104:

- explicitly recalls some parameters that are essential for modern health and social services organizations, such as prevention, territoriality and careful planning of interventions by integrated contributions from services (Scortegagna, 1981);
- increases the level of invalidity required to benefit from compulsory employment and introduces much harsher penalties for those enterprises that do not keep to the percentages of compulsory employment;
- sanctions the right to full inclusion in the world of work of all individuals with physical, mental and sensory impairments, meaning the targeted employment of the individual with disability in a manner that is consistent with his or her actual professional abilities and with the production context – so the fears of some entrepreneurs of the 'unruly dumping on enterprises' of individuals unable to produce have been greatly eased;
- envisages assessment tasks and sharing out of the opportunities both to the individual with disability and to the enterprise.

Financial and non-financial incentives are available nowadays to set up a collaboration network between employment offices and employers, especially for those individuals who are more greatly penalized and for whom health services coordinate access to the world of work. Career counselling, sheltered workshops, and training are seen in terms of resources and opportunities that can precede actual employment. In addition to being consistent with the principles that inspired law 104, collaboration between the social and institutional parties, entrepreneurs and unions is necessary to bring about inclusion that takes into due consideration both the individual's disability and the opportunities and production requirements of the world of work. In this way, the kind of productive activity and working environment most suited to the individual with disability can be determined.

More recently, law 68 of 12 March 1999 (and its implementation regulations: DPR of 10 October 2000) gives a ruling on compulsory employment of individuals with disability, be their impairment physical or sensory or mental. Article 2 reiterates the compulsory nature of targeted employment, pointing to the setting up of technical and support instruments to assess the work abilities of individuals with disability and to introduce them to a suitable workplace through the analysis of workplaces, type of support, positive actions and solutions of problems. Interestingly, this law not only makes it compulsory for both public and private enterprises to take on individuals with disability but it also establishes their minimum number. An enterprise with 15 to 35 employees must take on at least one worker with disability, one with 36 to 50 employees must take on at least two, and in an enterprise with more than 50, at least 7 per cent of the employees must be individuals with disability. The law also envisaged the establishment of special employment services that supervise the implementation of work inclusion in collaboration with social, health, educational and training services. Specific committees made up of officers and experts from the social and medico-legal sectors must outline a socio-work profile that specifies the abilities and potential of the worker and, among other things, arranges for specific supports and tutoring actions, carries out career counselling with the individual with disability in order to let him/her pursue training and in-service training activities, and shows employers methodologies that might favour inclusion.

The assessment schema is consistent with what the European Council elaborated in 1995, thanks to the committee for the work inclusion of individuals with disability. It examines the working abilities of the disabled individual and the requirements of performing particular occupations. The following abilities, in particular, are considered: posture (sitting down; standing up; kneeling down; squatting; lying down; changing postures; bending), locomotion (walking; going up; climbing; transportation), limb movement (moving and using arms and legs; handling/lifting weights; handiness; foot control), giving and receiving messages, carrying out complex physical activities, resilience and balance, tolerance of adverse environmental factors (climate; sounds/noises; vibrations; lighting), carrying out cognitive tasks, coping with work stress, working individually or in a group, coping with problem situations, following the working schedule, and travelling to work from home and vice versa.

Scorretti (2002: 14) emphasizes that, in this law, there is the transition from 'percentage evaluations based on impairments or anatomical losses to qualitative definitions of the activities of the individual', the aim of which is to identify the employment or re-employment possibilities of individuals by going beyond the mere quantification of the biological damage.

Article 10 states that 'the workers taken on in accordance with the present law must receive the same financial and normative treatment established by the law and in the national work contracts' (paragraph 1) and that 'the employer cannot ask the employee with disability for a performance incompatible with his/her impairments' (paragraph 2). A series of financial allowances are also envisaged, as is the setting up of a special fund for the financing of regional programmes concerning competitive employment and sanctions for those who do not comply with the provisions of the law.

Another law – i.e. law 328 of 2000, known as the 'General outline law for the realization of the inclusive system of social interventions and services' – sets out the economic treatment of individuals with disabilities: such treatment must aim at fighting poverty, to overcome the personal, family and social limitations of these individuals, enabling them to make the most of their functional abilities and their potential psycho-physical autonomy (Scorretti, 2002). It establishes three types of intervention:

- The first aims to address the loss of income production caused by the impairments of the individual; in other words, it allots what is called an 'inability pension'. This benefit is paid monthly and is granted to 18 to 65 year olds with total and permanent invalidity.
- The second type of intervention provides a minimum income to individuals with partial disability to allow them to attend educational courses, and to be considered for special work contracts and work grants that will be revoked following work inclusion. This sanctions temporary financial help that actually favours work inclusion.
- The third type of intervention defines the financial interventions sanctioned in law 118 of 1980 on the invalidity allowance. For individuals with severe disabilities or multiple impairments the financial benefits aim to favour communication and an independent life and to ensure continuous assistance and supervision that help them to live within the family.

Besides guaranteeing the right to social and work inclusion, this law establishes that assessment carried out in this regard must consider not only the individual's health, but also the judgement of people with different skills, so that a 'life project' can be outlined for these individuals and implemented and supported with precise financial provisions.

Training those who can help social and community inclusion

The implementation of social and community inclusion requires a series of conditions that can be summarized as follows:

- the strengthening of specific abilities in individuals with disabilities as regards management of everyday life, problem solving and decision making, spatio-temporal orientation, social, work and pre-work abilities, and of all those abilities that can be useful to leading a life that is as independent as possible;
- the establishment of a network of financial and social support and, as regards the latter, the establishment of an adequate social network made up of various people (family members, friends, acquaintances, work colleagues, and so forth) and arranging for frequent contact

between its members in order to maintain mutually advantageous relationships (from a social, emotional and financial viewpoint) (Nota and
Soresi, 1997);
- the setting up of environments (family, work, or from the social and
health services) that support the social inclusion, autonomy and self-
determination of individuals with disability and that interact with one
another.

To accomplish the above it is necessary for social and health workers to
be adequately trained and to possess specific skills to intervene in different sectors.

On this basis we set up specific training activities for those providing
services for individuals with disability in some districts of northern and central Italy. As was the case in our work in schools (see Chapter 4), a specific
methodology was used with the aim of ensuring the active participation of
the staff involved, the practicality of what was being proposed, and adher-
ence to principles of teaching and learning that support effective intervention. The training activity was carried out only in those contexts where
it was guaranteed that all the personnel, from the service manager to the
professional nurse, to the rehabilitation operator, to the cloakroom atten-
dant would participate in the project and attend regularly.

In carrying out this training and sensitization activity, particular attention was paid to increasing the habilitation and rehabilitation abilities of
staff members, their ability to carry out specific deficit-centred activities
and to the involvement of specific figures, such as parents, employers, colleagues, in the planning and carrying out of specific inclusive actions. The
training activity was carried out in three phases. The first took place over
20 training units, aiming above all at increasing ability of observation,
setting habilitation and rehabilitation goals, planning interventions necessary to pursue them, and controlling efficacy of interventions carried
out. The issues addressed in the first 15 training units were as follows:

- *First training unit:* habilitation and rehabilitation.
- *Second training unit:* reference principles for the analysis of participa-
tion and activity levels.
- *Third training unit:* systematic observation.
- *Fourth training unit:* observation of activity levels.
- *Fifth training unit:* observation of participation levels.
- *Sixth training unit:* habilitation and rehabilitation objectives.
- *Seventh training unit:* habilitation and rehabilitation objectives for per-
sonal autonomy.
- *Eighth training unit:* techniques to increase abilities.
- *Ninth training unit:* techniques to maintain abilities.
- *Tenth training unit:* planning a training unit.
- *Eleventh training unit:* implementing a training unit.
- *Twelfth training unit:* assessing interventions carried out.

- *Thirteenth training unit:* maladaptive behaviours.
- *Fourteenth training unit:* observing maladaptive behaviours.
- *Fifteenth training unit:* managing maladaptive behaviours.

The first training units aimed to differentiate clearly between caring activities on the one hand, and habilation and rehabilitation activities on the other hand. This was done so that the services could be better able to define the type of proposal they could offer, which users to grant access to, theoretical models to employ, and the assessment criteria to ascertain quality of service and costs incurred. We emphasized that care is associated with severe 'inability' situations and consists mainly in 'serving' those who are not able to autonomously attend to their own needs. Care guarantees survival through regular administration of drugs, feeding, personal hygiene, cleaning clothes, life environments, and so on. In practice it is 'doing for', an 'acting in the place of', without any intention to increase the possibilities of 'doing and acting' of the individual cared for. Its aim is not to improve ability levels, nor to increase active participation; it does not request specific goal setting, it only requires that helpers' tasks be clearly defined (who cares for the individuals with disabilities, who cleans the living places, and so on).

The aim of habilation and rehabilitation interventions is passiveness reduction and ability improvement. Such activities are based on setting goals that describe changes, reduce difficulties and improve ability. Habilitation workers believe that these changes can occur as a result of specific interventions intentionally set up; further, they root their work in firm theoretical assumptions that allow them to recognize those individuals to involve, and choose specific methods of intervention and assessment criteria for their achievements. Habilitation draws on teaching and learning theory and aims to extend the repertory of abilities an individual can perform. It requires the conviction that even individuals with clear difficulties can improve and that in appropriate conditions they can achieve new knowledge and abilities. Habilitation addresses those individuals who have had impairments since birth, and who need to increase their repertory of abilities and so reduce the gap between what they can do and what individuals without impairments can do. It is therefore a type of intervention that should be carried out with developmental age individuals or individuals with impairments, for instance intellectual disability, for whom it is considered appropriate to develop adaptive competencies that could be useful to community living (Soresi and Nota, 2000).

Rehabilitation, on the other hand, concerns the reinstatement of past abilities and should be offered to non-developmental age individuals who, following traumatic events, diseases or damage, show losses, decline or deterioration that prevent activities autonomously carried out in the past from being undertaken. This means individuals who suffered head injuries, elderly individuals, reinstitutionalized individuals. Rehabilitation 'begins when the pathology and symptoms of the acute episode have stabilized. In cardiac rehabilitation for example, the intervention begins after the myocardial infarction and the pain and disorders associated with it have receded' (Anthony and Lieberman, 1997: 68). This is also the case for individuals with mental disabilities who, during their inclusion in school and community contexts, were stimulated to act and interact with others and 'practise', at least now and then, the relational behaviours acquired and their new learning (Moehle et al., 1987). As Wilson (1990) recalls, the aim of rehabilitation must be that of taking patients to the maximum degree of physical, psychological and social adjustment, aiming to reduce the impact of disability and favour optimal inclusion. And so staff must avoid considering caring and recreational practices as habilitation and rehabilitation activities or even as curative or therapeutic (for example, activities that are not specifically tailored to work inclusion or sports and play activities, such as horse riding or swimming). Staff must also be able to avoid pseudo-rehabilitative interventions with individuals needing habilitation therapy or habilitation interventions.

The training continued by examining the World Health Organization's suggestions on classification of impairments, levels of activity and participation (International Classification of Functioning, Disability and Health – ICF), in order to help staff use a common language and determine the areas of intervention to privilege in habilitation and rehabilitation activities.

The third and fourth training units underlined the importance of observing behaviours carefully to make sure that the objectives chosen are actually adequate and to verify the effectiveness of intervention. We suggested that at least the following should be done to promote observation:

- Define the observational field. An observational activity cannot be expected to investigate in an adequately rigorous way either everything that happens or phenomena that have not been previously specified. This first operation concerns what to observe, having clearly in mind the purposes for which observation was required and inserting it in a theoretical framework in which data will be recorded. For instance, if a member of staff interested in the social inclusion of individuals with disability wanted to devise a programme to increase the possibility of community living, he or she should first of all increase his or her knowledge of these issues, choose the approach most appropriate, specify the objectives of the intervention and the behaviours that should be observed in order to have pre-test data, or 'baselines', and post-test data to verify the efficacy of what was proposed and realized.
- Set up and utilize procedures to code and record the collected information (data characterizing intervention recipients, which will determine the choice of objectives and the evaluation of planning efficacy, must be accurately recorded).
- Use techniques to check the reliability and validity of the observation carried out.

Observation should be deliberate and intentional and careful attention must be paid to errors that may be made.

The staff involved were trained to carry out specific direct or indirect observation activities centred on the collection of data about cognitive performances, judgements and evaluations supplied by users, and also by other individuals such as parents, staff and family members, about areas such as social and professional abilities.

The sixth and seventh training units aimed, in particular, to strengthen staff abilities to define habilitation and rehabilitation objectives accurately by focusing primarily on personal autonomy. Staff were trained to use an operational language and to describe performances to be improved in the presence of certain conditions, and about the mastery criteria considered adequate.

Training units eight and nine particularly aimed to enable staff to choose the intervention techniques that best fitted the given goals. In particular, it was proposed to distinguish between situations in which abilities not in the individual's repertory had to be taught and situations in which the frequency of performance had to be increased. The techniques referred to in the first case were shaping, chaining, giving suggestions and fading.

Shaping requires the specification of a series of 'steps' (objectives) that can gradually lead an individual to implement what has been taught. In presenting this fairly simple technique the need to follow some guidelines was emphasized:

- After choosing the target behaviour, it is necessary to ascertain what the individual can actually do, so as to establish a satisfactory starting point for the intervention.
- Subsequently, only the behaviour that is most similar to the behaviour specified in the specific goal must be strengthened. The individual must be adequately reinforced – not too much and not too little – to avoid the extinction of the behaviour itself on the one hand, and to favour the transition to the next on the other hand (Meazzini and Battagliese, 1995). This can be used to teach a variety of abilities, such as motor, cognitive, linguistic and social abilities.

Chaining is appropriate for teaching actions with a fairly invariant sequence. For instance, the act of putting one's socks on implies a chain of behaviours: take the sock, roll it up between the fingers to reach the tip, rest the sock on the tip of the toes, pull the sock about a bit to get the foot inside, and so on. What is interesting in this technique is that each action supplies a discriminant stimulus for the next behaviour and at the same time is a reinforcer of the previous action.

Both anterograde and retrograde chaining was proposed: in the former case, the first ability of a sequence is taught first, then the second, then the third, and so on, whereas in the latter, the last ability of a sequence is taught first, helping the individual to do the previous ones, then the last but one, and so on. The student must analyse and establish the behaviours that allow the completion of an activity as a whole (brushing one's teeth, taking a shirt off, combing one's hair, settling the bill at the restaurant, and so forth) and verify which abilities are present and which show a deficit. The operator must improve the abilities that show a deficit and decide the order in which the behaviours must be carried out and what reinforcers to give (Kozloff, 1974).

Finally, prompts and fading were introduced, as they allow the use of additional external stimuli that facilitate the desired behaviours, whose attenuation in time, however, is expected.

In proposing the use of reinforcement to favour the frequency of some performances we recommended the following 'rules':

- reinforcers must be chosen not on the basis of subjective preferences, but on the basis of the actual effects they can produce on individuals' behaviours;
- although, given the different individual characteristics and difficulties, it would be possible to make use of many reinforcers (primary and secondary, dynamic, symbolic and tangible), social reinforcers (praising, showing agreement, affection, respect, and so forth) are to be privileged given that the aim of habilitation and rehabilitation interventions is inclusion.

In the final training units the aim was to enable staff to deal with maladaptive behaviours, which can interfere greatly with the effectiveness of habilitation interventions and with the start of inclusion experiences.

The last five training units aimed at strengthening the social and assertive abilities of the staff. This intervention seemed particularly important as they need to collaborate in order to plan and set up specific habilitation and/or rehabilitation projects, as well as to create a stimulating environment that can supply adequate models of positive social interactions.

The second phase of the training planned another seven modules concerning the following issues:

- *First training unit:* deficit-centred training.
- *Second training unit:* increasing personal autonomy abilities.
- *Third training unit:* increasing school reading and writing abilities.
- *Fourth training unit:* increasing logical-mathematical abilities.
- *Fifth training unit:* increasing social abilities.
- *Sixth training unit:* increasing self-determination abilities.
- *Seventh training unit:* increasing work abilities.

After staff had acquired the basic skills needed for habilitation and rehabilitation interventions, the second phase of the training was devoted to issues concerning their professional interests. The concept of deficit-centred training was examined with reference to the principles and theories of neuropsychological rehabilitation.

Programmes were presented that could be used to strengthen a number of abilities, such as feeding and washing oneself, using the bathroom, looking after one's appearance, moving about in the environment and handling the most common objects, socializing, communicating needs, and to stimulate a series of more strictly 'school abilities', such as reading, writing and arithmetic.

In choosing intervention programmes, particular attention was paid to the needs of individuals with mental disability. As regards *personal hygiene*, it was pointed out that useful information could be found in Azrin and Foxx (1971); for *feeding autonomy*, information could be found in Bensberg et al. (1965) and in O'Brien and Azrin (1972); and for the development of *motor abilities*, Sherman (1971) has described an intervention essentially based on motor modelling to teach the initiation of both simple and complex movements.

Community inclusion also implies the introduction of individuals with disability into the world of work and access to career counselling and professional training, both of which must be started as early as possible. Relevant works are those of Screven et al. (1971), Hunt and Zimmerman (1969), Zimmerman et al. (1969) and, more recently, Mithaug et al. (1987), Brolin (1988), and Anderson and Hohenshil (1990). The development of *language*, as underlined by Rondal in this volume, requires attention from the very first years of life. All disability classifications include lists of difficulties that concern communication, yet being able to understand and use language is an essential prerequisite to independence and to social adjustment. To strengthen *school abilities* (reading, writing, arithmetic) many programmes are available that have been used for some time with children with severe cognitive disability: Gray et al. (1969) proposed one for reading called Performance Determined Instruction, and Resnick et al. (1973) proposed one for learning mathematical abilities. More recently, useful information has also been available in a number of Italian publications such as Perini (1992, 1997), Perini and Bijou (1993), Soresi (1991), Meazzini (1981, 1997), Moderato (1988), Cammà (1988), Larcan (1984) and Vianello (1990, 1999). Specific suggestions were also given on social abilities.

The third phase of training involved another five modules:

- *First training unit:* inclusion and integration.
- *Second training unit:* social inclusion and involvement procedures.
- *Third training unit:* school inclusion and involvement procedures.
- *Fourth training unit:* work inclusion and involvement procedures.
- *Fifth training unit:* community inclusion and involvement procedures.

Meetings and specific supervision activities aimed to enable staff to differentiate between the concept of integration and that of inclusion and to ensure that they facilitate inclusion. We also suggested that they show family members, employers, colleagues, and other community members (the priest, the basketball coach, the bus driver, neighbours, and so forth) which behaviours promote autonomy, gratify adaptive performances, facilitate reduction of maladaptive behaviours, and stimulate decision-making abilities and independent management of difficulties. Consequently, in the meetings staff were also asked to carry out specific observational activities looking at the inclusive characteristics of various environments, to conduct specific interviews to gather information and make evaluations, to select specific abilities in need of strengthening and to hold individual meetings with the other people in the disabled person's environment. In the meetings the staff were asked to use teaching techniques, such as instructions, modelling, and role-play. They were also asked to supervise and stimulate the action of individuals with disability, so that it would be possible to say that those individuals also had frequent, diversified and satisfactory opportunities to socialize and carry out a job in an environment that was adapted to some of their characteristics to take full advantage of their efforts and possibilities.

Checking the effectiveness of the training activity

Criterion verification of the achievement of specified goals allowed us to see that about 90 per cent of participants reached the mastery criteria in almost all the units and that the amount of learning observed at the end of each unit could be considered satisfactory.

Furthermore, about two months after the end of the course, questionnaires were distributed in which, among other things, participants were asked to evaluate the training activity and comment on how what was learned applied to their specific professional context. We think that the results show that the experience, on the whole, was evaluated rather positively (Soresi and Nota, 2000).

Social abilities

In dealing with inclusion and the enjoyment of environments that are as little restrictive as possible, the issues of adjustment and increasing social skills should be addressed to reduce the risk of rejection and marginalization. Today, unlike three decades ago, there are many programmes available ranging from those reducing maladaptive behaviours that 'hinder development', such as Bijou (1963, 1966), to those aiming at improving the interpersonal skills necessary to establish significant positive relationships with others.

The first examples of these types of interventions can be found especially in the North American literature; for example, Hopkins (1968) taught two youths with severe cognitive deficits to smile; Dinkmeyer (1970) aimed at teaching preschoolers to understand themselves and others; and Stephens et al. (1982) focused their attention above all on the increment of those social abilities necessary to good adjustment to the school environment.

Only since the early 1990s have social abilities finally been granted a central role in the analysis and treatment of individuals with impairments, with learning difficulty, and with mental disability, thanks especially to research on the issue of inclusion (Greenspan and Granfield, 1992; Soresi, 1998; Soresi and Nota, 2000). Several studies have shown that, throughout their entire developmental life and in adulthood, individuals with cognitive disability, for instance, show scarce or inadequate social interactions with others, and that, when they are compared with their peers in their early years of life, they are seen to develop fewer social contacts and group-play activities and to give fewer positive answers to the social invitations they receive (Guralnick and Groom, 1987; Kopp et al., 1992).

At school age these same children are at risk of inadequately adjusting to the requests of the school and in general they show difficulties in receiving satisfactory levels of social acceptance (Elliott, 1988; Walker et al., 1992). Kavale and Forness (1996) emphasize that about 75 per cent of individuals with learning difficulties show social ability deficits. In particular, their deficits show up in two large classes of behaviours that are critical to school adjustment: relational behaviours with teachers and relational behaviours with peers. The former concern the ability to adequately respond to teachers' requests and expectations in the school context, the latter the ability to participate in complex group dynamics through negotiation and the start of positive relationships with peers (Walker et al., 1985). Koegel et al. (2001) highlighted the fact that autistic children initiated fewer social interactions with their peers and responded less frequently to the initiatives of their peers toward them, spending more time on their own. The authors maintained that, although these children are not totally devoid of a certain level of social ability, specific support and systematic intervention are needed to make them better able to act appropriately in social situations and develop more satisfactory friendships and relationships.

In adolescence, individuals with mental disability often show difficulty in establishing and maintaining interactions with peers and people in authority and this certainly reduces the extent and quality of their experiences, anticipating a negative effect on the processes of adjustment to adult life and difficulties in social inclusion (Margalit, 1993; Soresi and Nota, 1995). As adult life approaches, deficits can also be seen in those abilities that facilitate work in competitive settings, such as following requests and instructions, completing tasks, cooperation and positive interaction with supervisors. Non-task-centred social skills, which are important to start friendships, set up a social support network and increase work satisfaction, are often absent – skills such as joking with colleagues, conversing about various topics, and asking about family members (Chadsey-Rusch and Gonzales, 1988; Williams et al., 1989;

Chadsey-Rusch, 1990; Soresi and Trionfi, 1995; Cristiano and Nota, 1998).

Alongside rehabilitation and teaching programmes aiming to reduce learning difficulties, it is also necessary to hold specific training activities on social abilities in order to achieve:

• the development of positive relationships between individuals with and without disability;
• effective reaction to requests and expectations that might exist in the different social settings that individuals with disability happen to frequent;
• an improvement in the skills necessary to communicate one's needs, wishes and objectives to others in order to make it easier to obtain assistance (Walker et al., 1994; Nota and Soresi, 1997).

These interventions are particularly important as they allow the maximum benefit to be drawn from educational processes, they facilitate inclusion, contribute to increased acceptance by peers and teachers and can increase the likelihood of finding a successful job. They increase too the individual's potential to lead an independent life and to develop an adequate social support network (Williams et al., 1989; Rusch et al., 1995; Nota and Soresi, 1997).

It must, however, be remembered that this is possible only if these interventions occur over time so as to allow each individual to modify and adjust his or her own social competencies according to the task, the context and the different people with whom he or she is interacting. Along with other teaching 'subjects', and within a psychoeducational perspective, these objectives should be included in curricula with a horizontal structure, as they increase abilities from the same conceptual area, but also in curricula with a vertical structure, as they aim to develop more and more complex abilities belonging to different fields (Nota, 1997). Educational services are then required to plan 'intentional' educational activities that take into consideration that what is required of a preschool child is not the same as what is required of an elementary school child, and that the social abilities an adolescent should possess are not the same as those required of an adult or an elderly individual.

This needs concerted action and shared programming between the educational services and the territorial structures that deal with disability and inclusion/integration processes so as to handle the issue of maintenance and generalization of results in an adequate and coordinated way. On that basis, the programme 'Staying with others: No Problem!' has been devised. It draws on a number of experimental works present in the literature (Stephens et al., 1982; Thorkildsen, 1986; Walker et al., 1988) and its methodological and educational choices draw on the theories of learning and the contributions of those who underline the importance of setting up conditions facilitating learning and its generalization (Hughes and Sullivan, 1988; Christopher et al., 1993).

We have paid particular attention to the latter two components, as research on evaluation of efficacy of intervention and the meta-analyses conducted on them have yielded conflicting results, with effect sizes from 0.20 to 0.87 (Mathur et al., 1998; Forness and Kavale, 1999; Gresham et al., 2001). Changes in individuals' behaviour following social ability training are not, in fact, always significant, and even if they appear immediately after the training, often they are not sustained over time. One of the factors that can affect lack of success is the severity of the individual's difficulties: the more severe they are, the longer the programme should be (Gresham et al., 2001).

In accordance with the difficulties shown by individuals with mental disability, we have planned a substantial number of training sessions, or training units as we prefer to call them. To be applied fully they require systematic teaching activities to be carried out over a number of years and the use of precise observation procedures that can allow staff to choose the most fitting training units – as can be seen in the experiments we present here. The programme aims to improve the following:

- *Basic skills:* to strengthen those social skills that are usually considered as indispensable for the development of more complex relational competencies.
- *Social skills to start social relations with peers in a school context:* school inclusion often creates rejection and isolation because of the absence of competencies that can elicit positive reactions and acceptance from peers.
- *Social skills to start social relations with peers in a recreational context and in free-time activities:* these are important training units because the possession of skills in this field facilitates the development of important social networks and offers opportunities for integration in extramural contexts.
- *Social skills to start social relations with superiors (teachers and social and health operators) in a school and rehabilitation context:* evaluation of inclusion and its success are often mediated by school staff attitudes and depend on the quality of relationships between teachers and schoolchildren with disability; teaching the latter to activate positive behaviour toward teachers is, in our opinion, particularly important.
- *Social skills to start social relations with colleagues and employers:* they are relational abilities that, when adequate, can facilitate employment and job maintenance.
- *Social skills to start social relations in the family context:* quality of life of individuals with disability often correlates with that of their family members, who are considerably affected by the type of behaviours the former have toward them.
- *Social skills to start social relations in the community context: results and importance of school inclusion* could be considered really 'valid'

if they actually manage to prepare and facilitate social inclusion of individuals with disability; besides favourable environmental conditions, community living requires individuals with disability to possess social abilities, which a curriculum aiming at increasing the likelihood of inclusion cannot possibly overlook.

Programming interventions and verifying what has been accomplished requires a variety of observational measures and instruments to determine the difficulties shown by the individuals involved. Among them there is direct observation for the analysis of frequency of positive and negative social behaviours in the school context and indirect observation for the analysis of social competence (McFall, 1982; Gresham and Elliott, 1984; Schlundt and McFall, 1985; Mathias, 1990). Use of specific observational procedures should also show whether individuals have the so-called 'acquisition deficits', that is to say whether they lack the knowledge necessary to behave in an adequately social way or are unable to recognize the objectives necessary for a given interaction; or whether they have 'production deficits' associated with lack of practice and exercise in the field of interpersonal relations and that produce little acceptable social behaviour; or the so-called 'fluidity deficits', which are also due to inadequate practice and/or lack of adequate models in their lives, in such a way as to manifest insecure, clumsy and 'faked' social repertories that often induce others to make negative judgements, or to become perplexed and even suspicious (Elliott and Gresham, 1993; Gresham et al., 2001). Taking this into consideration can help in the choice of more suitable intervention objectives and more adequate teaching techniques; if individuals with acquisition deficits must be taught new abilities, it is necessary to devise situations in which participants have access to adequate models and opportunities for practice, full of reinforcements and suggestions. The use of direct and indirect observational procedures can actually determine which are the 'critical' behaviours within a given environment. Examining the most significant social behaviours in a particular environment and at a particular time (for example, conversations at the school canteen), and singling out the behaviours that characterize them and the levels (intensity, frequency, duration) at which they are considered adequate (for instance, via role-play and specific evaluations of participants) can be helpful in promoting socially valid training interventions, to save precious time, and to teach individuals with mental disability skills that will very probably increase social acceptance (Hughes et al., 1995; Hughes, 1999).

A number of experiments have been carried out with participants with different levels of cognitive disability, with children, adolescents and adults either living in shared accommodation or resident in rehabilitation institutions. The participants with slight cognitive disability underwent the following intervention, which took place over 10 two-hour training units taking place once a week:

- *First training unit:* interpersonal communication.
- *Second training unit:* aggressive behaviours.
- *Third training unit:* passive behaviours.
- *Fourth training unit:* assertive behaviours.
- *Fifth training unit:* how to speak to others.
- *Sixth training unit:* how to express wishes.
- *Seventh training unit:* how to get others to become your friends.
- *Eighth training unit:* how to get teachers to become your friends.
- *Ninth training unit:* how to defend oneself from others.
- *Tenth training unit:* recall and summary.

The promotion of two types of skill was regarded as an important objective: ability to differentiate and recognize different typologies of communication situations, and ability to activate social skills that are appropriate for the purposes, contexts and characteristics of the interacting individuals. The intervention produced a significant increase in positive social task-centred and non-task-centred behaviours toward both schoolmates and teachers (Soresi and Nota, 1995).

For participants with more severe cognitive difficulties the following ten training units were used:

- *First training unit:* greet schoolmates.
- *Second training unit:* greet teachers.
- *Third training unit:* introduce oneself to a new schoolmate.
- *Fourth training unit:* introduce oneself to a new teacher.
- *Fifth training unit:* pay attention in class.
- *Sixth training unit:* start a brief conversation with schoolmates.
- *Seventh training unit:* start a brief conversation with teachers.
- *Eighth training unit:* maintain a brief conversation with schoolmates.
- *Ninth training unit:* maintain a brief conversation with teachers.
- *Tenth training unit:* recall and summary.

Unlike in the training described above, teaching techniques were drawn from behaviouristic approaches rather than from cognitive models (self-observation, 'cognitive' anticipation of the different situations, and so forth) as they seem more effective when dealing with individuals with moderate to severe disabilities (Schumaker et al., 1988). Each unit teaching a new ability took place once a week, lasted one-and-a-half hours and was followed by a generalization unit. The latter was meant to encourage the use of teaching behaviours not only in a training situation, but also in others (Fox and McEvoy, 1993). Here the analyses carried out clearly showed differences concerning positive task-centred and non-task-centred behaviours toward teachers and non-task-centred behaviours toward schoolmates (Soresi and Nota, 2000).

As an example, the objective of training unit 3 and that related to the generalization activity are reported in Table 5.1.

Table 5.1 Example of an objective

Objective of the third training unit

Conditions:
A role-play situation, where the participant is invited to simulate the meeting with a new schoolmate.

Performance:
The participant approaches the newcomer, smiles, looks him/her in the eye, greets him/her by saying 'Hi', introduces him/herself by saying 'My name is . . .' and asks 'What's your name?'.

Mastery criterion:
The objective is considered achieved when the participant manages to do that described above; he/she may also not smile.

Objective:
Conditions:
In presence of a boy/girl who has come to visit the school;

Performance:
The participant approaches the newcomer, smiles, looks at him/her in the eye, greets him/her by saying 'Hi', introduces him/herself by saying 'My name is . . .' and asks 'What's your name?'.

Mastery criterion:
The objective is considered achieved when the participant manages to do what described above; he/she may also not smile.

With regard to increasing social skills in residential environments, two phases of intervention were considered necessary:

First phase
1. Acknowledge staff greetings.
2. Greet members of staff.
3. Acknowledge other guests' greetings.
4. Greet other guests.
5. Be polite with the staff.
6. Be polite with other guests.
7. Begin a brief conversation with a member of staff.

Second phase
1. Recognize the anger expressed by a member of staff.
2. Recognize the happiness expressed by a member of staff.
3. Recognize the sadness expressed by a member of staff.

4. Recognize the fear expressed by a member of staff.
5. List reasons for which one can feel anger.
6. List reasons for which one can feel happiness.
7. List reasons for which one can feel sadness.
8. List reasons for which one can feel fear.
9. Recognize the moments when one experiences anger.
10. Recognize the moments when one experiences happiness.
11. Recognize the moments when one experiences sadness.
12. Recognize the moments when one experiences fear.
13. Describe one's own anger.
14. Describe one's own happiness.
15. Describe one's own sadness.
16. Describe one's own fear.

Again, behavioural techniques were heavily used. For each training unit, two units of generalization were employed and individualized maintenance intervention was carried out during normal everyday activities. The intervention allowed participants to achieve the mastery criterion in 80 per cent of the training units and produced significant changes in social behaviour toward the institution's staff (Cristiano et al., 1997).

The results emphasize that programmes such as those presented here, which can be defined in terms of behavioural social skills training (SST) (Frederickson et al., 1989), can actually produce changes in the quality and frequency of the social behaviours shown by the individuals who participate in the training. However, this requires considerable involvement from significant others from the life environment to create the conditions that Maag (1990) calls 'entrapment'. The interventions described took place in environments where specific activities in favour of inclusion had been carried out, where school and non-school participants were able to implement specific operations in favour of generalization (resorting to reinforcement in natural contexts, use of 'natural' situations in order to stimulate and support the use of social abilities, setting up of training units concerning the maintenance, generalization and supervision of situations that participants found hard to manage, analysis of the social abilities that could be used, assignment of 'exercises' and 'homework', analysis of specific recordings and diaries, and involvement of significant others in reinforcement activities) (Gresham et al., 2001; Vaughn et al., 2001; Soresi and Nota, 2001).

References

Anderson WT, Hohenshil TH (1990) Vocational assessment in the USA. School Psychology International 11: 91–7.
Anthony WA, Lieberman RP (1997) Principi della riabilitazióne psichiàtrica. In RP Lieberman (ed.) La riabilitazióne psichiàtrica [Psychiatric Rehabilitation]. Milan: Raffaello Cortina Editore, pp. 63–103.

Azrin NH, Foxx RM (1971) A rapid method of toilet-training the institutionalized retarded. Journal of Applied Behavior Analysis 4: 89–99.

Bandura A (1977) Social Learning Theory. Englewood Cliffs NJ: Prentice-Hall.

Bensberg GJ, Colwell CN, Cassel RH, (1965) Teaching the profoundly retarded self-help activities by behavior shaping techniques. American Journal of Mental Deficiency 69: 674–79.

Bijou SW (1963) Theory and research in mental (developmental) retardation. Psychological Record 13: 95–110.

Bijou SW (1966) A functional analysis of retarded development. In NR Ellis (ed.) International Review of Research in Mental Retardation 1: 1–19. Orlando FL: Academic Press.

Borthwick-Duffy SA (1992) Quality of life and quality of care in mental retardation. In L Rowitz (ed.) Mental Retardation in the Year 2000. Berlin: Springer-Verlag, pp. 52–66.

Brolin DE (1988) Are we denying special education students a proper education? The Career Educator 3: 1 (Newsletter of the Career Development Projects, Department of Education and Counseling Psychology, University of Missouri – Columbia).

Browder D (1991) Assessment of Individuals with Severe Disabilities: An Applied Behavior Approach to Life Skills Assessment (2nd edn). Baltimore MD: Brookes.

Bruininks RH, Tsuey Hwa Chen, Lakin KC, McGrew KS (1992) Components of personal competence and community integration for persons with mental retardation in small residential programs. Research in Developmental Disabilities 13: 463–79.

Butler SK, Harvey RJ (1988) A comparison of holistic versus decomposed rating of position analysis questionnaire work dimensions. Personnel Psychology 41: 761–71.

Cammà M (1988) La didàttica della lettura a bambini insufficiènti mentali: anàlisi di una propósta curriculare per l'insegnaménto. In E Caracciolo, F Rovetto, Handicap. Nuove Metodologie per il Ritardo Mentali [Handicap. New Methodologies for Mental Retardation]. Milan: Franco Angeli, pp. 152–79.

Chadsey-Rusch J (1990) Teaching social skills on the job. In FR Rusch (ed.) Supported Employment. Models, Methods and Issues. Sycamore IL: Sycamore, pp. 161–80.

Chadsey-Rusch J, Gonzales P (1988) Social ecology of the workplace: employers' perception versus direct observation. Research in Development Disabilities 9: 229–45.

Christopher JS, Nangle DW, Hansen DJ (1993) Social-skills intervention with adolescents. Behavior Modification 17: 314–38.

Cohen H, Conroy J, Frazer D, Snelbecker G, Spreat S (1977) Behavioral effects of interinstitutional relocation of mentally retarded residents. American Journal of Mental Deficiency 82: 12–18.

Cowen EL (1994) Community psychology and routes to psychological wellness. In JR Rappaport, E Seidman (eds) Handbook of Community Psychology. New York: Wiley.

Cristiano G, Nota L (1998) Abilità sociali e lavoro: osservazióne a margine di una ricérca. Abilitazione e Riabilitazione 1: 16–34.

Cristiano G, Rocco M, Fiabane D (1997) Training di abilità sociali. In Foresti G, Mazzella G, Schiavon S, Cristiano G (eds) L'Adulto con Ritardo Mentale.

Assessment, Cura e Riabilitazióne [Adults with Mental Retardation: Assessment, Intervention and Rehabilitation]. Milan: Edizioni Fatebenefratelli.

Dinkmeyer D (1970) Developing Understanding of Self and Others. Circle Pines MN: American Guidance Service.

Edgar E (1987) Secondary programs in special education: are many of them justifiable? Exceptional Children 53: 555–61.

Edgerton R (1990) Quality of life from a longitudinal research perspective. In R Schalock (ed.) Quality of Life: Perspectives and Issues. Washington DC: American Association of Mental Retardation, pp. 149–60.

Elliott SN (1988) Children's social skills deficits. Paper presented at the annual convention of the American Educational Research Association, New Orleans.

Elliott SN, Gresham FM (1993) Social skills interventions for children. Behavior Modification 17: 287–313.

Emener WG (1993) Empowerment in rehabilitation: an empowerment philosophy for rehabilitation in the 20th century. In M Nagler (ed.) Perspective on Disability. Palo Alto CA: Health Markets Research, pp. 295–305.

Felce D, Perry J (1995) Quality of life: its definition and measurement. Research in Development Disabilities 16: 51–74.

Fine MA, Tangeman PJ, Woodard J (1990) Changes in adaptive behavior of older adults with mental retardation following deinstitutionalization. American Journal on Mental Retardation 94: 661–8.

Forness SR, Kavale KA (1999) Teaching social skills in children with learning disabilities: a meta-analysis of the research. Learning Disability Quarterly 19: 2–13.

Fox JJ, McEvoy MA (1993) Assessing and enhancing generalization and social validity of social-skills interventions with children and adolescents. Behavior Modification 17: 339–66.

Frederickson N, Simms L, Simms J (1989) Teaching social skills to children: towards an integrated approach. Educational and Child Psychology 1: 5–17.

Gray BB, Baker RD, Stancyk SE (1969) Performance determined instruction for the teaching of remedial reading. Journal of Applied Behavior Analysis 2: 255–63.

Greenspan S, Granfield JM (1992) Reconsidering the construct of mental retardation: implications of a model of social competence. American Journal on Mental Retardation 96: 442–53.

Gresham FM, Elliott SN (1984) Assessment and classification of children's social skills: a review of methods and issues. School Psychology Review 13: 292–301.

Gresham FM, Sugai G, Horner RH (2001) Interpreting outcomes of social skills training for students with high-incidence disabilities. Exceptional Children 3: 331–44.

Guralnick MJ, Groom JM (1987) The peer relations of mildly delayed and non-handicapped preschool children in mainstreamed playgroups. Child Development 58: 1556–72.

Hemming H, Lavender T, Pill R (1981) Quality of life of mentally retarded adults transferred from large institutions to new small units. American Journal of Mental Deficiency 86: 157–69.

Hopkins BL (1968) Effects of candy and social reinforcement, instructions, and reinforcement schedule leading on the modification and maintenance of smiling. Journal of Applied Behavior Analysis 1: 121.

Hoyt KB (1985) Career guidance, educational reform and career education. Vocational Guidance Quarterly 34: 6–14.

Hughes C (1999) Identifying critical social interaction behaviors among high school students with and without disabilities. Behavior Modification 23: 41–60.

Hughes C, Harmer ML, Killian DJ, Niarhos F (1995) The effects of multiple – exemplar self – instructional training on high school students' generalized conversational interactions. Journal of Applied Behavior Analysis 28: 201–18.

Hughes C, Hwang B, Kim J, Eisenman LT, Killian DJ (1995) Quality of life in applied research: a review and analysis of empirical measure. American Journal on Mental Retardation 6: 623–41.

Hughes JN, Sullivan KA (1988) Outcome assessment in social skills training with children. Journal of School Psychology 26: 167–83.

Hunt JG, Zimmerman J (1969) Stimulating productivity in a sheltered workshop setting. American Journal of Mental Deficiency 74: 43–9.

ISTAT (1999) La revisióne delle sèrie storiche delle forze lavoro. Ottobre 1992–aprile 1999. Rome: Istituto Nazionale di Statistica.

Ittenbach RF, Bruininks RH, Thurlow ML, McGrew KS (1993) Community integration of young adults with mental retardation: a multivariate analysis of adjustment. Research in Developmental Disabilities 14: 275–90.

Kavale KA, Forness SR (1996) Social skills deficits and learning disabilities: a meta-analysis. Journal of Learning Disabilities 29: 226–37.

Kleinberg J, Galligan B (1983) Effects of deinstitutionalization on adaptive behavior of mentally retarded adults. American Journal of Mental Deficiency 88: 21–7.

Koegel LK, Koegel RL, Frea WD, Fredeen RM (2001) Identifying early intervention targets for children with autism in inclusive school settings. Behavior Modification 25: 745–61.

Kopp CB, Baker BL, Brown KW (1992) Social skills and their correlates: preschoolers with developmental delays. American Journal on Mental Retardation 96: 357–66.

Kozloff AM (1974) Educating Children with Learning and Behavior Problems. Wiley: New York.

Landesman S (1986) Quality of life and presonal life satisfaction. Definition and measurement issues. Mental Retardation 24: 141–3.

Larcan R (1984) Il reversal shift: sperimentazióni e applicazióni [The Reversal Shift: Research and Application]. Messina: Carbone.

Lipsky DK, Gartner A (1989) Building the future. In DK Lipsky, A Gartner (eds) Beyond Separate Education: Quality Education for All. Baltimore MD: Paul H Brooks.

Maag JW (1990) Social skills training in schools. Special Services in the Schools 6: 1–19.

McDonnell J, Hardman ML, Hightower J, O'Donnell RK, Clifford D (1993) Impact of community-based instruction on the development of adaptive behavior of secondary-level students with mental retardation. American Journal on Mental Retardation 97: 575–84.

McFall RM (1982) A review and reformulation of the concept of social skills. Behavioral Assessment 4: 1–33.

McGrew KS, Bruininks RH, Thurlow ML (1992) Relationship between measures of adaptive functioning and community adjustment for adults with mental retardation. Exceptional Children 58: 517–29.

McIntire SA, Buckland MA, Scott DR (1995) Job Analysis Kit. Odessa, FL: Psychological Assessment Resources.

Margalit M (1993) Social skills and classroom behavior with mild mental retardation. American Journal on Mental Retardation 97: 685–91.

Maze M, Mayall D (1991) The Enhanced Guide for Occupational Exploration. Indianapolis IN: Jist Works.

Mathias J (1990) Social intelligence, social competence, and interpersonal competence. International Review of Research in Mental Retardation 16: 125–60.

Mathur SR, Kavale KA, Quinn MM, Forness SR, Rutherford RB (1998) Social skills interventions with students with emotional and behavioral problems: a quantitative synthesis of single-subject research. Behavioral Disorders 23: 193–201.

Meazzini P (1981) La lettura e i suoi prerequisiti [Reading and its Prerequisites]. Udine: CAMPP.

Meazzini P (1997) Psicopatologia dell'handicap. In P Meazzini (ed.) Handicap, passi verso l'autonomia [Handicap and Autonomy]. Florence: Giunti, pp. 461–91.

Meazzini P, Battagliese G (1995) Psicopatologìa dell'handicap [Psychopathology of Handicap]. Milan: Masson.

Mithaug D (1998) Your right, my obligation? Journal of Association for Persons with Severe Disabilities 23: 41–3.

Mithaug D, Martin JE, Agran M (1987) Adaptability instruction: the goal of transitional programming. Exceptional Children 53: 500–5.

Moderato P (1988) La valutazióne cognitivo-comportamentale del ritardo mentale: presupposti, metodologie, strumenti. In E Caracciolo, F Rovetto (eds) Handicap. Nuove metodologie per il ritardo mentale [Handicap. New Methodologies for Mental Retardation]. Milan: Franco Angeli, pp. 101–50.

Moehle KA, Rasmussen JL, Fitzhugh-Bell A (1987) Neuropsychological theories and cognitive rehabilitation. In JM Williams, CJ Long. The Rehabilitation of Cognitive Disabilities. New York: Plenum Press.

Moon M, Inge K, Wehman P, Brooke V, Barcus J (1990) Helping Persons with Severe Mental Retardation Get and Keep Employment: Supported Employment Issues and Strategies. Baltimore MD: Brookes.

Morgenson FP, Campion MA (1997) Social and cognitive sources of potential inaccuracy in job analysis. Journal of Applied Psychology 82: 627–55.

Nihira K, Foster R, Shellhaas M, Leland H (1974) AAMD Adaptive Behavior Scale. Washington DC: American Association on Mental Deficiency.

Nota L (1997) Stare con gli altri: no problem! In R Vianello, C Cornoldi (eds) Metacognizióne e sviluppo della personalità: ricerche e propóste di intervènto [Metacognition and Personality Development: Research and Treatment]. Bergamo: Edizioni Junior, pp. 182–200.

Nota L, Rondal J, Soresi S (2002) La valutazióne delle disabilità [The Evaluation of Disabilities]. Vol. 1. Pordenone: ERIP Editrice.

Nota L, Soresi S (1997) I comportamenti sociali: dall'anàlisi all'intervènto [Social Abilities: From Assessment to Treatment]. Pordenone: ERIP Editrice.

Nota L, Soresi S (2002) L'anàlisi della qualità della vita di persone adulte con ritardo mentale: propósta di uno struménto di eterovalutazióne. Giornale Italiano delle Disabilità 2: 10–26.

O'Brien F and Azrin NH (1972) Developing proper mealtime behaviors of the institutionalized retarded. Journal of Applied Behavior Analysis 5: 389–99.

Pellegri A (2003) L'educazióne al movimento nelle paralisi cerebrali infantili. In S Soresi (ed.) Disabilità, Trattaménto, Integrazióne [Disability, Treatment, Inclusion]. Pordenone: ERIP Editrice.

Perini S (1992) Controllo degli stimoli e soluzióne di problemi lògico-formali. Acta Comportamentalia 4: 85–106.

Perini S (1997) Psicologìa dell'educazióne [Psychology of Education]. Bologna: Il Mulino.

Perini S, Bijou WS (1993) Lo sviluppo del bambino ritardato [The Development of Mentally Retarded Child]. Milan: Franco Angeli.

Resnick TR, Wang MC, Kaplan J (1973) Task analysis in curriculum design: a hierarchically sequenced introductory mathematics curriculum. Journal of Applied Behavior Analysis 6: 679–710.

Rubin SE, Roessler RT (1978) Guidelines for successful vocational rehabilitation of the psychiatrically disabled. Rehabilitation Literature 39: 70–7.

Rusch FR, Wilson PG, Hughes C, Heal LW (1995) Interaction of persons with severe mental retardation and their nondisabled co-workers in integrated work settings. Behavior Modification 19: 59–77.

Saxby H, Thomas M, Felce D, Kock V (1986) The use of shops, cafés and public houses by severely and profoundly mentally handicapped adults. British Journal of Mental Subnormality 32: 69–81.

Shedler J, Mayman M, Manis M (1993) The illusion of mental health. American Psychologist 48: 1117–31.

Schlundt DG, McFall RM (1985) New directions in the assessment of social competence and social skills. In L Abate, MA Milan (eds) Handbook of Social Skills Training and Research. New York: Wiley, pp. 22–49.

Schumaker J, Hazel JE, Pederson C (1988) Social Skills for Daily Living: Program Basics. Circle Pines MN: American Guidance Service.

Scorretti C (2002) Valutazióne delle disabilità sociali e reinseriménto lavorativo sociale. Giornale Italiano delle Disabilità 1: 3–23.

Scortegagna R (1981) L'inseriménto degli handicappati e l'organizzazióne dei servizi nel território. In S Soresi (ed.) Problemi ed Esperiènze di Integrazióne Scolàstica e Sociale degli Handicappati [Problems and Experiences in School and Social Inclusion of Handicapped People]. Pordenone: ERIP Editrice.

Screven CG, Straka JA, La Fond R (1971) Applied behavior technology in a vocational rehabilitation setting. In Gardner (ed.) Behavior Modification in Mental Retardation. Chicago: Aldine.

Sherman Y (1971) Operant therapy for excessive checking. Canadian Journal of Behavioral Sciences 3: 194–7.

Skinner BF (1973) Oltre la Libertà e la Dignità [Beyond Freedom and Dignity]. Milan: Mondadori; originally published: New York: Knopf, 1971.

Soresi S (1991) Le difficoltà nell'apprendiménto della matemàtica. In C Cornoldi (ed.) I Disturbi dell'Apprendiménto [Learning Difficulties]. Bologna: Il Mulino, pp. 372–434.

Soresi S (1998) Psicologìa dell'Handicap e della Riabilitazióne [Psychology of Handicap and Rehabilitation]. Bologna: Il Mulino, pp. 63–89.

Soresi S (2001) Riflessióni a margine della seconda edizióne della Classificazióne Internazionale delle Menomazióni, delle Disabilità e degli Handicap [International Classification of Impairments, Disability and Handicap: Second Edition]. Giornale Italiano delle Disabilità 1: 5–22.

Soresi S (2001) La facilitazióne dell'integrazióne scolàstica [The Facilitation of School Inclusion]. Pordenone: ERIP Editrice.

Soresi S, Nota L (1995) Ritardo mentale e abilità sociali: una propósta di intervènto [Mental retardation and social abilities: training]. Psicoterapia, Cognitiva e Comportamentale 1: 13–28.

Soresi S, Nota L (2000) A social skill training for persons with Down's syndrome. European Psychologist 5: 34–43.

Soresi S (2002) Autodeterminazióne e inseriménto lavorativo [Self-determination and work]. Paper presented at the 2nd National Congress 'Disabilità, trattamento e integrazione' [Disability, Treatment and Inclusion], Maggio, Padua.

Soresi S, Trionfi C (1995) Abilità sociali ed integrazióne lavorativa di persone con ritardo mentale [Social abilities and work inclusion of persons with mental retardation]. Abilitazióne e Riabilitazióne 4(1): 14–28.

Soresi S, Nota L, Sgaramella T (2003) La valutazióne delle disabilità. [The Evaluation of Disability]. Vol. 2. Pordenone: ERIP Editrice.

Stancliffe R (1997) Community living-unit size, staff presence, and residents' choice-making. Mental Retardation 35: 1–9.

Stancliffe R, Abery B, Smith J (2000) Personal control and the ecology of community living settings: beyond living-unit size and type. Mental Retardation 105: 431–54.

Stancliffe R, Wehmeyer ML (1995) Variability in the availability of choice to adults with mental retardation. Journal of Vocational Rehabilitation 5: 319–28.

Stephens TM, Hartman AC, Lucas VH (1982) Teaching Children Basic Skills: A Curriculum Handbook. Columbus OH: Merril.

Thompson T, Carey A (1980) Structured normalization: intellectual and adaptive behavior changes in a residential setting. Mental Retardation 18: 193–7.

Thorkildsen RJ (1986) Training di abilità sociali, istruzióne diretta e tecnologìa videodisk [Social abilities, training and instructions]. Psicologìa e Scuola 27: 57–61.

Thurlow M, Bruininks R, Lange C (1989) Assessing Post-school Outcomes for Students with Moderate to Severe Mental Retardation (Project Report No. 89-1). Minneapolis MN: University of Minnesota, Department of Educational Psychology.

Thurlow M, Bruininks R, Wolman C, Steffens K (1989) Occupational and Social Status of Persons with Moderate, Severe and Profound Mental Retardation after Leaving School (Project Report No. 98-3). Minneapolis MN: University of Minnesota, Institute on Community Integration.

Tossebro J (1995) Impact of size revisited: relation of number of residents to self-determination and deprivatization. American Journal on Mental Retardation 100: 59–67.

Vaughn S, Elbaum B, Boardman A (2001) The social functioning of students with learning disabilities: implications for inclusion. Exceptionality 9: 47–65.

Vianello R (1990) L'adolescènte con handicap mentale e la sua integrazióne scolastica [The Adolescent with Mental Retardation and School Inclusion]. Padua: Liviana.

Vianello R (1999) Difficoltà di apprendiménto, situazióni di handicap, integrazióne [Learning Disability, Handicap and Inclusion]. Bergamo: Edizioni Junior.

Walker HM, Irvin LK, Noell J, Singer GH (1992) A construct score approach to the assessment of social competence. Behavior Modification 16: 448–74.

Walker HM, McConnell SR, Clarke JY (1985) Social skills training in school settings: a model for the social integration of handicapped children into less
restrictive settings. In RJ McMahon and RD Peters (eds) Childhood Disorders:
Behavioral Development Approaches. New York: Brunner/Mazel, pp. 140–68.

Walker HM, Schwarz IE, Nippold MA, Irvin LK, Noell JW (1994) Social skills in
school-age children and youth: issues and best practices in assessment and
intervention. Topics in Language Disorders 14: 70–82.

Walker HM, Todis B, McConnell SR, Walker J, Holmes D, Golden N (1988) The
Walker Social Skills Curriculum: The ACCEPTS Program. Austin TX: Pro-Ed.

Wehmeyer ML, Bolding N (2001) Enhanced self-determination of adults with
intellectual disability as an outcome of moving to community-based work or
living environments. Journal of Intellectual Disability Research 45: 371–83.

Wehmeyer ML, Kelchner K, Richards S (1995) Individual and environmental factors related to the self-determination of adults with mental retardation. Journal
of Vocational Rehabilitation 5: 291–305.

Wehmeyer ML, Schwartz M (1998) The relationship between self-determination
and quality of life for adults with mental retardation. Education and Training
in Mental Retardation and Developmental Disabilities 33: 3–12.

Williams S, Walker HM, Holmes D, Todis B, Fabre T (1989) Social validation of
adolescent social skills by teachers and students. Remedial and Special
Education 10: 18–27.

Wilson B (1990) Mètodi innovativi di riabilitazióne della memòria [Rehabilitation
methods for memory]. In L Caldana (ed.) Atti del corso di aggiornamento
teorico – pratico. Rome: Editore Marrapese.

World Health Organization (2001) New Guidelines to Measure Health. Geneva:
WHO.

Zimmerman J, Stuckey T, Garleck BJ, Miller M (1969) Effects of token reinforcement on productivity in multiply handicapped clients in a sheltered workshop.
Rehabilitation Literature 30: 34–41.

Perspectives

In the years ahead, the real potential of the knowledge generated by the biobehavioural sciences will be evaluated in terms of its ability to optimize the developmental and inclusion outcomes for individuals with developmental disabilities, and what has concerned us particularly throughout this book, namely individuals with intellectual disabilities.

Although intensive research efforts in recent years have helped us to start defining more precisely the major developmental shortcomings in a limited series of genetic syndromes of ID (witness the empirical review and theoretical prospects offered in this book), it is obvious that the work ahead of us is tremendous and will pose conceptual and practical difficulties, if only because of the sheer number of genetic syndromes associated with ID. And yet there is no way we could honestly dispense with this work, for reliably defining the partial specificity of the behavioural phenotypes in each syndrome is necessary to assess the intervention targets and strategies best suited to meeting the particular needs of the people with each condition. It is debatable whether inclusion strategies should be completely reformulated according to aetiologically based principles. At the present time, as this book has shown, and despite important theoretical and practical progress in recent years, they are not. Whereas it would certainly seem desirable to take into account the partially differing abilities existing in various genetic syndromes of ID, it is understandable that schools and social communities cannot, and probably should not (for fear of possible discrimination in the latter case), base curricular programming and recruiting policies entirely on systematic indicators of intrasyndromic variability. These pertain to basic biobehavioural science and only minimally, it would seem, to the domains of school and social inclusion.

Yet, it is worth repeating that genetic factors alone typically account for only a fraction of the variance in human behaviour. The remaining variance cannot be accounted for without taking into consideration the functional interaction between biological and environmental factors. In this respect, sound school and social policies will always be of the utmost importance in order to prepare ID individuals to function in the best possible ways in open societies.

Index

Page numbers in *italics* refer to tables